Thanksgiving 101

Thanksgiving 101

Celebrate America's Favorite Holiday with America's Thanksgiving Expert

Rick Rodgers

Photographs by Ben Fink

WILLIAM MORROW
An Imprint of HarperCollins*Publishers*

This book was originally published in 1998 by Broadway Books.

HarperCollins books may be purchased for educational, business, or sales promotional use. For information please write: Special Markets Department, HarperCollins Publishers, 10 East 53rd Street, New York, NY 10022.

FIRST WILLIAM MORROW EDITION

Designed by rlf design

Library of Congress Cataloging-in-Publication Data

Rodgers, Rick, 1953–
Thanksgiving 101: celebrate America's favorite holiday with America's Thanksgiving expert / Rick Rodgers.
p. cm.
ISBN: 978-0-06-122731-8
ISBN-10: 0-06-122731-5
1. Thanksgiving cookery. I. Title. II. Title: Thanksgiving one hundred one.

TX739.2.T45R63 2007
641.5'68—dc22 2006050414

---

07 08 09 10 11 WBC/QWF 10 9 8 7 6 5 4 3 2 1

Contents

Acknowledgments

This book was born from my Thanksgiving cooking class, which I have taught from Washington to Florida every autumn for over fifteen years. When the book was first published, new methods of roasting turkeys, such as brining, high-temperature roasting, and deep-frying, were being introduced. A lot can change in ten years, both in the public's taste and the way that an author might approach a recipe. Organic turkeys were not commonly available, and heritage turkeys were hardly sold at all. This new edition reflects these changes, and the reader will find some tweaks, adjustments, and new approaches along the way, all developed from continued testing, tasting, and observation. You'll also see some recipes that have become new favorites. On the other hand, other well-established Thanksgiving recipes and traditions have been left alone, and I hope that they serve to bring back happy memories of great holiday meals.

In order to keep up with creating new recipes for my cooking classes, I have to work well ahead of my annual tour. I have prepared many a Thanksgiving meal in July—often in other people's kitchens. Harriet Bell tops this list of people who have happily lent me their kitchens and taste buds. She was the editor of many of my books, and she's been a great friend over many years, too. And we shared the fun of deep-frying a turkey together—a bonding experience if ever there was one. Steven and Cynthia Stahl and Ron Dier were always generous with their kitchens, friendships, and dishwashing talents during the many years of wonderful Thanksgivings we've shared. And, of course, my parents, Dick and Eleanor Rodgers, who produce a flawless Thanksgiving year after year, and showed me how fun and easy it can be.

Many cooking schools throughout the country allowed me to hone my Thanksgiving dinner-making skills. Thanks to Adventures in Cooking (Wayne, New Jersey, with a special hug to owner Arlene Ward and my long-standing assistants, Maria and Paul Lee), The Silo (New Milford, Connecticut, and "The Rickettes," Barbara, Caryl, Cynthia, Lauren, and Ann), Draegers' Markets (San Mateo and Menlo Park, California), Let's Get Cookin' (Westlake Village, California, with extra appreciation to owner Phyllis Vacarelli and my sous-chef there, JoAnn Hecht), Sur La Table (many locations nationwide), Dierberg's School of Cooking (St. Louis, Missouri), Kroger's Markets (various locations in Georgia and Florida), Cook 'n Tell (Colt's Neck, New Jersey), Classic Recipes (Westfield, New Jersey), King's Markets (Short Hills, New Jersey), A Southern Season (Chapel Hill, North Carolina), Cook's of Crocus Hill (Edina, Minneapolis), In Good Taste (Portland, Oregon, owned by the ever-loyal Barb Dawson), Ramekins (Sonoma, California, with an extra helping of thanks to Bob Nemerovski and Lisa Lavagetto, and Central Market (various locations in Texas). And while I certainly can't list all of my students by name, there are special ones who always show up, year after year, to taste and collect the current recipes, and I am especially thankful for their loyalty and appetite.

Susan Wyler, cookbook editor and friend, encouraged my affection for turkey and stuffing by providing projects on those subjects that helped establish me as the expert on Things Thanksgiving. The first edition of this book was vastly improved by the input of my friend and colleague Judith Sutton.

For researching assistance and permission to use their companies' products and recipes, I am grateful to: Linda Compton (Ocean Spray Cranberries), Ann Marie Murray (Campbell Soup Company), Roz O'Hearn (Nestlé USA/ Libby's Pumpkin), and Cynthia Giorgio (General Foods/ Jell-O and Kraft Philadelphia cream cheese). Thanks to Valerie Tully of the National Turkey Federation for the turkey industry statistics and information. For the history of American food companies and eating habits, two books proved invaluable: James Trager's *The Food Chronology* (Henry Holt, 1995) and Jean Anderson's *The American Century Cookbook* (Clarkson Potter, 1997).

Thanks to Sonia Greenbaum, copy editor, and Ann Cahn, production editor. At HarperCollins, my longtime publishing home, thanks for the continued support of Michael Morrison, David Sweeney, Gail Winston, and Sarah Whitman-Salkin.

In my life, very little would get done if it weren't for Diane Kniss. Her helpfulness and diligence are combined with a sense of humor that makes her the kind of co-worker that makes you want to get to work so you can try to top yesterday's laughs. As you know, Thanksgiving makes for a lot of dishwashing, but Diane never complains. Thanks, as always, to my agent and dear friend of many years, Susan Ginsburg, and her lovely and diligent assistant, Emily Scardino. Finally, Thanksgiving dinner is never better than when I share the table with my partner, Patrick Fisher, who has eaten almost as many turkeys as I have.

Introduction

Talking Turkey

Over the last fifteen years, I have prepared scores of Thanksgiving dinners for thousands of people. Turkey addict? Pumpkin pie groupie? A victim of gravy obsession syndrome? Yes, but there is a better reason. I travel all over the country teaching a cooking class called Thanksgiving 101. Now everything I teach in my classes is in this book, with my favorite recipes, Make ahead tips, anecdotes, organization secrets, and insights into what makes this holiday so special.

How did I become a Thanksgiving guru? In 1985, I created a catering company, Cuisine Américaine, and specialized in cooking regional American foods. And what is more American than Thanksgiving dinner? My customers loved my holiday spreads. In 1990, when one of the East Coast's largest poultry producers was looking for a media spokesperson to represent their turkey products, they came to me. I learned everything there was to know about turkey, spending lots of time on turkey farms and in the kitchen, and wrote my first cookbook on the subject.

Since then, I have traveled all over the country teaching Thanksgiving cooking classes and making television and radio appearances on how to have the perfect Thanksgiving meal. Everyone, from friends to television producers, now calls me "Mr. Thanksgiving" or "The Turkey Meister."

One of the best things about my work as a cooking teacher is that I get personal contact with our country's home cooks—I am not a restaurant chef who is out of touch with how people actually cook. No matter where I go, from Seattle to Miami, I ask my students about their personal Thanksgiving dishes and customs. First, *Thanksgiving 101* is a collection of these favorite recipes—even if some of them start with a can of soup or a box of Jell-O. Some of Thanksgiving's most cherished recipes are brand-name specific. I call these "Classic Recipes," and they include some background on how they rose to the top to become holiday icons.

We all know the generic recipes that form the backbone of the quintessential Thanksgiving dinner. Mashed potatoes, gravy, piecrust, and stuffing all fit into this category. With practice, these dishes become simple, but they can intimidate novices and elude practiced cooks looking for the perfect version. These recipes are labeled "101," and if they seem long, it's because I have included extra details that even old hands can learn from.

Certain Thanksgiving foods have achieved almost religious significance, and must be served at that meal on the fourth Thursday of every November. While researching recipes for my classes, I became fascinated with how these particular foods became so important. These are discussed in the sections titled, "It Isn't Thanksgiving Without . . ." You'll find information on classics like cranberries, pumpkin, gelatin salads, and, of course, turkey.

What I hear most from my students is that they are desperate for help in *organizing* the meal. So, in addition to a host of tips, I've provided suggestions for complete menus with preparation and cooking timetables. (I can just hear all of you worried cooks going "Whew! Thank you!!")

My students also tell me that these recipes are too good to reserve for just one day of the year, and I agree. Thanksgiving isn't the only time when turkey makes an appearance—it's perfect for a Sunday supper, creating leftovers to use for other meals, and many families serve the bird with fixings for Christmas and Easter, too. You'll savor many of the other dishes year-round also, especially the side dishes and desserts. For example, I rarely serve grilled pork chops without a cranberry chutney (I keep a stash of frozen cranberries to use when they're out of season). Because most of my Thanksgiving first course soups and salads feature seasonal ingredients, I use them often during cool months. No matter what the season, hardly a party goes by without one of the appetizers from this book. And it certainly doesn't have to be Thanksgiving to make apple pie!

I have been gathering these recipes for this book for years, listening to countless American home cooks tell me about the fun (and fear) they experience while getting the big meal on the table. I promised them I would write a *practical* guide on this beloved holiday. Many of these recipes are downright simple, but that doesn't make them any less delicious. *Thanksgiving 101* is a culinary insurance policy to having the best Turkey Day ever.

Happy Thanksgiving!

Getting It Together

Everyone loves Thanksgiving. But even experienced cooks look at making Thanksgiving dinner with a mixture of trepidation and nostalgia. After all, it has probably been 364 days since the last time they were asked to make such a huge meal. Some of those dishes are made on Thanksgiving and Thanksgiving only, so it is like starting from scratch. Someone once asked a famous Wagnerian soprano how she performed her long, grueling roles night after night. "No problem," she modestly replied. "All you need is a good pair of shoes." When people ask me how I pull off my Thanksgiving dinners, I know how that singer felt. I want to say, "All you need is a good pair of shoes . . . and a plan!"

The happiest Thanksgiving cook is the most organized. No one ever sees the pile of lists that guides me through the organization and preparation of the meal. It's not enough just to want to serve a delicious holiday dinner—you'd better think about how to get all of that food on the table at the same time. Plot it out on paper, and you'll be one giant step closer to serving a perfect meal. A written plan is reassuring—you can look it over as many times as you want to check and double-check, or make the changes that will inevitably occur.

Lists, Lists, and More Lists

Thanksgiving Rule Number One

There are never too many lists. And nothing feels better than seeing every item checked off. You will need the following lists:

- **Guest List:** Invite your guests, by mail or by phone, at least three weeks ahead. As soon as possible, try to get your friends to notify you if they are bringing guests. I always plan on one last-minute phone call from someone saying, "I just found out that so-and-so at the office has nowhere to go.

Can I bring him along?" Especially for large gatherings, keep track of RSVPs. Unfortunately, a confirmed RSVP doesn't mean much these days, and you may want to call the night before to confirm your guest's attendance, and how many will be in the party. When necessary, include directions to your house with the invitation.

- **Grocery Lists:** You should have at least three grocery lists and a beverage list. Spread out the shopping over a couple of weeks so you're not one more person standing in line at the supermarket with an overflowing cart. Buy as many nonperishables as possible before that final Tuesday or Wednesday. That way, you'll only need a quick trip to the market to pick up the fresh items. My dream is to be able to stand in the Express lane on Thanksgiving Eve, and I have accomplished this more than once.

  The first grocery list should be nonperishables that can be purchased two or three weeks ahead of the dinner. You may not know exactly how many people are coming yet, but you can get candles, coffee filters, guest towels, cocktail napkins, camera film or fresh digital camera batteries, paper towels, guest soap, aluminum foil, plastic wrap, bathroom tissue, and other incidentals. Play it safe and buy staples like flour, sugar, salt, and such. Buy coffee and put it in the freezer. If you are barbecuing your turkey, put charcoal or propane gas on this list.

  The second grocery list is for the week before the meal. By now (hopefully) your guest list is confirmed. You know what your menu is, and what groceries you'll need. Buy all the produce that will keep for a week (onions, garlic, potatoes, yams, carrots, lemons, and limes), dairy items (cheese, eggs, milk, cream, and butter), canned goods, and spices. When you write down the groceries you need, try to organize them by category (or, if you are really familiar with your market, by aisle), so you don't have to run all over the store. If necessary, order your turkey and other meat or seafood items.

  The last grocery list is for Tuesday or Wednesday's shopping, which will include only fresh turkey, vegetables, and fruit, and maybe a couple of extra bags of ice. If you can, purchase your produce at a greengrocer—the line will be shorter and the produce better than at most supermarkets.

  In some states that sell alcohol at grocery stores, your beverage list can be part of the regular shopping list. Otherwise, make a separate list for the liquor store. Don't forget mixers and nonalcoholic beverages and any garnishes like celery for the Bloody Marys.

- **Prep Lists:** There are a lot of cooking chores that can be done well ahead of time. Look at your menu for potential freezable items. I am not a big freezer person, mainly because I don't have a large freezer, but I do freeze a few quarts of homemade turkey stock, and maybe some piecrusts.

  Be realistic about how much time it will take for you to make each dish. Only you know how fast you can chop. Also, schedule in cleaning time. It is much easier to clean as you go along than to wait until the piles of utensils are so high you can't stand it anymore.

- **Utensil List:** French chefs call this a *batterie de cuisine*. It means all the pots, pans, basters, spoons, roasting racks, coffeemakers, measuring cups, rolling pins, pie pans, and other things that you'll need to get the dinner on the table. Check all of the recipes and be sure that you have everything you need. If a recipe calls for a 9 × 13-inch baking dish and yours is a different size, you can either buy the right pan or throw caution to the wind and hope that the recipe turns out all right in your pan. I vote for buying the new dish. I have made every effort to use pots and pans that can be found in the average home. Where necessary, unusual equipment is listed after the ingredients in a recipe.

Be sure to have plenty of large self-sealing plastic bags on hand. Whenever possible, store prepared food in the plastic bags instead of bowls. You'll save lots of refrigerator space that way.

- **Tableware List:** Check to see that you have all of the serving dishes and utensils you need. Many items may be stored away; take them out and wash them. To keep all of those bowls and platters straight, list what food goes in what dish, and identify the utensils with sticky notes. This way, in the heat of the battle, when a helper asks, "What dish do the mashed potatoes go into?" you can reply, "The blue one with the 'mashed potatoes' sticker," not "I don't remember!" If there is silver to be polished or linens to be washed and pressed, schedule those jobs well ahead of time.

  If you don't have enough china and silver, try to avoid paper plates and plastic utensils. Inexpensive dishes and silverware can be found at wholesale clubs, or borrow them from friends and family. You may not have a matching set, but at least no one's gravy will seep through his plate. Along the same lines, try to use real napkins, not paper ones—it's a festive holiday.

  Everything has its place, but even more so at Thanksgiving. Draw a "map" of the table that includes the serving dishes and centerpiece to be sure everything will fit. If it doesn't, figure out where you will put the excess. If you don't have enough chairs, borrow them from a friend or rent them. If you need to move any furniture to make room, take note and add it to another "To Do" list.

  If you plan to have a buffet, you may want to put the plates and eating utensils on a separate sideboard or table. If you have a large crowd, pull the table away from the wall, if necessary. Make two stacks of plates and place them on opposite sides of the table. Now there can be two lines, as guests can serve themselves from both sides. Put two serving utensils in each bowl so guests can serve themselves faster. To save space, roll the eating utensils in napkins and tie with ribbons, then stack them in a basket. Place the basket at the opposite end of the buffet, so guests don't have to juggle the utensils while they are trying to fill their plates.

- **The Bill of Fare:** It may sound compulsive, but I always tape the complete menu, including beverages and appetizers, on the refrigerator door to double-check that everything makes it out to the table. More than once, after the meal, I have found a bowl of cranberry sauce hidden in the refrigerator (and my guests were too polite to say, "How chic! No cranberry sauce!" to remind me).

Your Menu and You

There are many variables that make a menu the right one. Sure, personal taste comes into play, but more important are the logistics. Do you have enough refrigerator space? Do you have only one oven? How big is it? How many people can you really seat, even with the card table? Brutally assess your cooking skills. Some people are entranced by what they see on television cooking shows (or read in cookbooks), and overdo it. Instead of enjoying your guests, you see a lot of your kitchen.

Most of the recipes in this book are for eight to twelve servings. A serving is an average-sized portion. I can't say "Serves Eight," because if your eight guests have big appetites, and take big spoonfuls, the eight servings become four. With the exception of the desserts, all the recipes can be multiplied or divided to fit your guest count. Desserts have to be prepared by the unit—you wouldn't bake half a pie to get four extra servings.

If you are new to the Thanksgiving routine, concentrate on one or two dishes (like turkey and gravy) and learn to do them well. Let someone else bring side dishes and desserts or pick them up at a takeout place. Next year, expand your repertoire to cranberry sauce and pumpkin pie. Pretty soon, you'll be able to execute the entire menu.

Being a slave to fashion is bad enough, but being a slave to the traditional Thanksgiving menu is worse. You don't have to serve the exact same meal that Mom made. Design a balanced meal with different colors, textures, and flavors. If you think there are too many sweet things or starches on the menu, scratch one off and replace it with something else. In my opinion, most people just serve too much food at this meal. Thanksgiving should be about visiting with loved ones over a special feast, not about how much turkey you can eat in twenty minutes because the football game is about to come on.

And speaking of football, my heart goes out to you cooks whose meal has to vie for attention with the game. When people come to my house for Thanksgiving, they come for a great meal and company, and the television never gets turned on except, when necessary, to keep the kids occupied. Perhaps you should try my friend Monica's tactic. She decided that she wasn't going to let the football schedule call the shots. So, she roasted a turkey, but only served it with fixings for fresh sliced turkey sandwiches. This tactic went over so well, it has become her family's annual Thanksgiving meal.

Help!

Another Thanksgiving Rule

Let your friends help you . . . kinda.

There are times when being a control freak can come in handy . . . like on the fourth Thursday of November. The first few times I made Thanksgiving, people asked if they could bring something, and I was glad to let them pitch in. But I couldn't help noticing a few recurring trends. One friend always brought something different than he said he would. If he said he'd bring cranberry sauce, he'd bring a green bean bake . . . but only when I already had four other vegetable side dishes, and didn't make cranberry sauce. Another friend considered it a crime to follow a recipe, and always got "creative" with her contribution. The problem was that her experiments rarely turned out as expected. (Like the year she substituted honey for sugar in the pumpkin pie and the filling wouldn't set.) I considered having a sampler made saying "No More Potlucks . . . Ever!" to hang in the kitchen. It's much better to be in complete charge of the menu.

It's not that I'm ungrateful, it's just that there are other ways my friends can help. My favorite friend is the one who comes over on Wednesday night to keep me company while I prep. Even if he isn't a good cook, he can run to the store if I left something off the list, clean up the dirty dishes, pour us a glass of wine, order pizza (Who has time to make dinner?), set the dining room for the big dinner. . . . Of course, on Thanksgiving Day, anyone who wants to wash dishes is my friend for life.

If you must have a potluck, here's a strategy that has worked for me. I designed my menu from clipped newspaper, magazine, and cookbook recipes, and assigned them according to the person's cooking skills, along with instructions for multiplying the recipe for a certain number of servings. I knew exactly what everyone was going to bring, and that it was all going to fit together. My friends were relieved because they didn't have to fret about what they were going to bring.

When the going gets rough, remember that at the first Thanksgiving, only six women prepared all the food for ninety-one Native Americans and fifty-six settlers, and that the party lasted three days.

The Kids' Table

When kids are a part of your Thanksgiving guest list, be sure you have activities that don't just keep them busy but let them contribute to the festivities.

My young friends love helping in the kitchen. Sometimes I let them do easy chores like peeling vegetables or whipping cream. But they really love it when they can create something to share with the whole group. The day before the dinner, bake turkey-shaped cookies. Set up a corner in the kitchen with icing and colored sugar, and let the kids decorate the cookies to serve with coffee for dessert.

If there is just too much activity in the kitchen for small bodies to be around, I provide crayons, construction paper, paste, and scissors in another area for them to create place cards. I'll get them going by making turkey-shaped cutouts—it's their job to cut out and paste colorful paper feathers onto the tails and write the guests' names on the bodies. (Some craft stores also sell inexpensive small, real feathers that can be used.)

When you've set up a kids' table, make it something special. Don't make them feel like they're in Siberia. Once, when up in the country, we sent the youngsters out to collect the best-looking autumn leaves. When they returned, they washed and dried the gathered leaves well. I covered the kids' table with a piece of white butcher paper, and they glued the leaves all over the paper as a tablecloth. It looked so great that the adults were envious. Another time, we simply stenciled outlines of turkeys all over the butcher paper, and put out crayons to color the turkeys during dinner.

Of course, there's the time-honored tradition of the touch football game to help the kids let off steam. But I wonder if it's really to keep the kids occupied or to help the adults burn off calories?

Setting the Scene

I know caterer types that seem to have hot-glue guns at the ready. Not me. I prefer to spend my creative time in the kitchen. When it comes time to decorate, I subscribe to the philosophy "less is more."

You can do very simple things that say "Thanksgiving." Roll up napkins with an autumn leaf around the center, and tie with a piece of raffia straw. Put a foil-wrapped chocolate turkey at each place setting. One of my favorite settings wasn't especially elegant, but it was fun. Each setting had a lighted kitschy candle (Pilgrims, Indians, and turkeys) that I had collected from different candle stores. They looked great, all grinning and blazing away. And everyone took his candle home.

Remember that centerpieces for a dining table must be low enough for people to see over. Pumpkins are a great start. Large, hollowed-out ones can serve as vases. Mini-pumpkins or apples can hold candles (remove the stem and carve a hole in the center). Another simple centerpiece is a floating candle in a glass bowl, with cranberries added to the water. Sometimes I do nothing more complicated than a basket filled with autumn foods (persimmons, grapes, apples, and nuts), entwined with a length of French wired ribbon. The food can be eaten at the end of the dinner, so it doesn't go to waste. If you wish, substitute brightly colored gourds and dried corn for the fruit. I often steal items from this centerpiece to decorate the turkey platter.

At formal table settings, place cards are appropriate, and they look great taped to the side of a mini-pumpkin at each plate. I have also baked large turkey- or leaf-shaped cookies and decorated them with my guests' names inscribed in icing. They rarely get eaten that evening because people like to take them home as a memento. (To each his own. I eat *mine*.) If you want to try this, just use your favorite rolled sugar or gingerbread cookie recipe.

Pilgrim's Progress

The Thanksgiving Story

In the middle of all the planning and festivities, keep in mind what Thanksgiving is about. It's not about football, or pumpkin pie, or even turkey. The Pilgrims (aka Puritans) used the feast as a celebration to give thanks for the good in their lives, in spite of the fact that it had been a very difficult year. But it was no solemn occasion. One professor of American history said that Thanksgiving "was a party, and a three-day party, at that!"

The Puritans wanted to purify the Church of England of rituals that had their roots in Catholicism. They were driven from England by James I, and fled to Holland in 1608. Twelve years later, tiring of Dutch customs and language, they made the difficult decision to immigrate to the New World,

where they could practice their own customs and language. One hundred and two passengers made the sixty-six-day journey on the *Mayflower,* landing in Provincetown Harbor (not Plimouth Rock), on Cape Cod, on November 21, 1620. Exactly one month later, after exploring the area, they chose Plimouth as the settling spot.

By harvesttime the next year, forty-six of the original group had succumbed to scurvy or pneumonia. However, the autumn crop had been good, mainly due to the help of one Pawtuxet Indian, Squanto, who taught the settlers much about farming in their new home. Squanto, who had been a slave in Spain and escaped to England, spoke English. He had returned to his native village only six months before the Puritans arrived.

The Puritans were familiar with harvest festivals, which were common in England. So, it was a natural turn of events for Governor William Bradford to declare a thanksgiving feast. The exact date has never been established. According to Bradford's own history, *Of Plimouth Plantation*, on September 18, he sent men to trade with the Indians. The harvest was gathered after they returned. The first written mention of the party was in a letter dated December 11. But with all of the outdoor activities described by the original sources, the event probably happened while the weather was still reasonably warm.

As for the menu, we know that Bradford sent "four men fowling" to gather wild poultry for the feast. They returned with ducks and geese and a "great store of wild Turkies." However, to the Puritans, turkey meant any kind of guinea fowl, which also roamed the wilds of the Atlantic coast, and we can't be sure that our familiar turkey was served. Venison was surely on the menu (the Indian chief Massasoit sent braves into the woods who "killed five Deere which they brought to our Governour"), along with lobsters, clams, sea bass, corn, boiled pumpkin, watercress, leeks, and dried fruit. Corn cakes, fried in venison fat, were served as the bread, as there was no wheat. It is assumed that cranberries, an Indian favorite, would have been included, probably cooked in maple syrup. As there were no cows, there could be no dairy products like butter, milk, or cheese. Contrary to popular belief, the Puritans did drink alcohol, although they did not tolerate drunkenness, and quaffed a strong beverage that probably resembled brandy.

After the meal, a little exercise was in order. Of course, football hadn't been invented yet, but the Indians and Puritan soldiers played other games. Marksmanship was exhibited with both the bow and arrow and the musket, and athletic prowess with footraces and jumping matches.

The Thanksgiving feast did not become an annual event. The only other Thanksgiving occurred in 1623, to celebrate the end of a drought. Harvest festivals continued throughout the colonial period, but actual "thanksgivings" were saved for major events, like the one in 1789 proclaimed by George Washington to commemorate the new Constitution. It was around this time that the

term "Pilgrim" came into use. The Puritans referred to themselves as "First Settlers," or "First Comers." They eventually became known as the "Forefathers," but during the American revolution, "Pilgrim" became an alternative.

We have our modern holiday thanks to the dogged efforts of one woman, Sarah Josepha Hale, the influential editor of the popular woman's magazine *Godey's Lady's Book*. With over 150,000 subscribers, Hale used her editorials to promote a national day of Thanksgiving, and wrote letters to presidents, governors, and other high-profile people. She espoused a day to "offer to God our tribute of joy and gratitude for the blessings of the year." The magazine did much to romanticize the Pilgrim as a steadfast, hardworking, religious model of American perseverance. After years of grandstanding, she finally got the support of President Abraham Lincoln, who declared Thursday, November 23, 1863, a national holiday. Over the years, Thanksgiving was always an excuse for unabashed feasting and fun. Staid New Englanders considered Christmas a religious holiday, and hardly "celebrated" it at all. It wasn't until German immigrants brought their customs to America in the late 1880s that Christmas got a makeover.

Until 1941, it was up to each president to declare the holiday each year, which usually took place on the last Thursday of November. In 1939, President Franklin D. Roosevelt, who felt Thanksgiving was too close to Christmas and diluted the effect of the later holiday, moved the date to the third Thursday of that year. The country responded bitterly, and a lot of people took off the fourth Thursday anyway. The next year, emotions were even higher. The only people who liked the change were the merchants, who saw a longer Christmas buying season. Finally, in December 1941, a joint resolution of Congress specified the fourth Thursday in November (which is sometimes, but not always, the last Thursday) as Thanksgiving.

The first Thanksgiving Day parade was held in Philadelphia in 1923. It was sponsored by Gimbels department store. Macy's first parade occurred the next year, in New York City. The first professional football game on Thanksgiving was played by the Detroit Lions and the Chicago Bears in 1934.

Thanksgiving doesn't enjoy the same literary attention as Christmas. Few Thanksgiving songs, movies, or books have established themselves like the Christmas classics "Jingle Bells," *It's a Wonderful Life*, and *A Visit from St. Nicholas*. My favorite Thanksgiving story is "A Thanksgiving Visitor" by Truman Capote, and I don't like to let the holiday go by without playing my old LP of Arlo Guthrie's "Alice's Restaurant." "Over the River and Through the Woods" just doesn't stand up to Arlo. Also, the turkey-cooking scenes in the films *Home for the Holidays* and *Pieces of April* are hilarious, but don't expect these movies to make you feel like phoning your family.

Appetizers and Beverages

Just a Little Something to Keep the Edge Off . . .

The concept of "Make Ahead cuisine" is of paramount importance at Thanksgiving, but even more so when planning your appetizer and beverage strategy. Serve tasty goodies that will keep the edge off everyone's hunger, but nothing that needs last-minute preparation or warming up. Little individual hors d'oeuvres that need to be baked are definitely out, if for no other reason than the ovens will probably all be in use, cooking the main event. The best tactic is to set out foods that need no attention other than an occasional refill. Spiced nuts, hot or cold dips, cheese balls and cheese boards, savory cookies—all of these can be prepared well ahead of time.

Some foods, such as cheese balls and pâtés, *must* be prepared ahead for their flavors to mellow; they are among my favorites because they allow me to scratch an item off my preparation list days in advance. The only time of year I serve a relish tray is at Thanksgiving. (When I was growing up, all of us kids would stick pitted black olives on our little fingers and eat them off, one by one.) If I have home-preserved goodies from my summer canning, they get place of honor. Otherwise I buy high-quality goods like pickled okra, Italian giardiniera, and stuffed olives from a specialty food market. And at least two kinds of pickles, one sweet and one sour.

The visual appeal of your appetizer platters is really important. Here are a few ideas I learned from my days as a Manhattan caterer:

- Choose crackers for their shape as well as their flavor.
- Pick crudité vegetables for a variety of colors and textures. Place contrasting vegetables next to each other, i.e., broccoli next to

carrots, next to cauliflower, next to green beans, next to cherry tomatoes. Don't put the green broccoli next to the green beans.

- Line serving baskets with colorful napkins. Tie bunches of dried berries around the handles with raffia to give a harvest look.
- Garnish platters with bunches of tiny Indian corn or small gourds or line them with leaves of curly kale or collard greens.
- Serve dips in hollowed-out cabbages (look for curly varieties with the outer leaves attached) or winter squash (the larger and more exotically colored, the better).

Don't forget incidental details. Put cocktail napkins on your shopping list. If you are serving a warm dip in an electric mini–slow cooker, be sure you have a long enough extension cord and that it can be plugged in where no one will trip over it. If you are using a fondue pot or a chafing dish to keep the dip warm, purchase a supply of the appropriate liquid fuel.

When it comes to beverages, remember that you are under no obligation to provide a fully stocked bar. And, just like becoming an excellent cook, it takes practice and a bit of skill to be a fine bartender with an extensive cocktail repertoire. If you have narrowed down your menu choices to make an intelligent, balanced meal, you can do the same with the drinks. Remember your obligation to your guests' well-being, and don't encourage overdrinking, especially from drivers. If you offer homemade nonalcoholic beverages, it doesn't make abstainers feel as if they are cursed to an evening of club soda. Always offer one beverage that is just as tasty spiked as it is without alcohol, such as Bloody (Virgin) Marys or Autumn Glow Punch (pages 22 and 23). If someone isn't driving and wants to add a splash of vodka or rum, he can go ahead. Sparkling apple cider is a great choice—I like to serve it in champagne flutes to make the drinkers feel that their drinks are just as important as the alcoholic ones. Set up the bar outside of the kitchen, in such a way that everyone can help themselves.

Glittering Spiced Walnuts

It makes no difference how many of these addictive nibbles I make, they are always gone by the end of the evening. They have many irresistible qualities. The unusual deep-frying procedure gives them a delectably thin glaze, and the seasoning mixture is so much better and fresher than any Asian five-spice powder you can buy in a bottle. I've changed the recipe a bit over the years, increasing the spice mixture to reflect our collective palate's growing appreciation of bold seasonings. Walnut halves, not pieces, give the best results, as the smaller pieces tend to burn. They can be found at most supermarkets, or look for them at specialty food stores or online.

Makes about 4 cups, 8 to 12 appetizer servings

Make Ahead: The walnuts can be prepared up to 2 weeks ahead.

ASIAN SPICES

1 whole star anise (use 6 or 7 "points" if pod is broken)
¾ teaspoon ground cinnamon
¾ teaspoon coriander seed
¾ teaspoon whole Sichuan peppercorns
¾ teaspoon fennel seeds
6 whole cloves
⅛ teaspoon cayenne pepper or more to taste
Vegetable oil, for deep-frying
1 pound walnut halves
½ cup sugar
Salt, for sprinkling (use fine sea, plain, or iodized salt)

SPECIAL EQUIPMENT

A deep-frying thermometer
A large wire skimmer

1. To make the spice mixture, finely grind the spices in a spice or electric coffee grinder. Set aside.

2. Place a rimmed baking sheet next to the stove. Line a second baking sheet with paper towels. In a deep Dutch oven, add enough vegetable oil over high heat to come halfway up the sides, and heat to 365°F.

3. Meanwhile, bring a medium saucepan of water to a boil over high heat. Add the walnuts and cook for 1 minute. The water does not have to return to a boil. (This heats the walnuts and removes excess bitterness.) Drain in a large colander. Do not rinse. Immediately, toss the walnuts in the colander with the sugar until the hot water clinging to the walnuts melts the sugar to form a thin glaze.

4. In two batches, carefully add the nuts to the oil and deep-fry them until they are golden brown, about 3 minutes. Using a large wire mesh skimmer, transfer the walnuts to the unlined baking sheet (the hot walnuts would stick to paper towels) and cool completely. When cooled, transfer the walnuts to the paper towels to drain excess oil.

5. Place the walnuts in a bowl. While tossing the nuts, sift the spice mixture through a fine-meshed wire sieve over them. Discard the hulls in the sieve. Season with the salt. (The walnuts can be prepared up to 2 weeks ahead, stored in an airtight container at room temperature.)

Note: If you want to make more than one batch, have extra oil on hand. The sugar on the nuts "caramelizes" the oil after deep-frying a pound or two, and makes it necessary to use fresh oil.

Buttered Cajun Pecans

Even when it isn't a holiday, these have become my stand-by snack to make for cocktails, because they are so easy to toss together from pantry staples. The secret is making your own Cajun seasoning. There are many Cajun/Creole spice mixtures on the market, but they can be salty, and it's easy to make a batch from the spices in your kitchen cabinet. Use any left over to season grilled poultry, fish, or pork, or sprinkle on popcorn.

Makes about 4 cups, 8 to 12 appetizer servings

Make Ahead: The pecans can be prepared 1 day ahead.

3 tablespoons unsalted butter
1 pound pecan halves
1 tablespoon Cajun Seasoning (recipe follows)
2 teaspoons sugar

In a very large nonstick skillet, melt the butter over medium heat. Add the pecans and cook, stirring often, until heated through, about 2 minutes. Sprinkle with the Cajun Seasoning and sugar, and stir until the sugar melts, about 1 more minute. (While they are best freshly made, the pecans can be prepared 1 day ahead of serving, stored in an airtight container at room temperature.) Serve warm or at room temperature.

Cajun Seasoning: In a small bowl, combine 2 tablespoons sweet paprika (preferably Hungarian), 1 tablespoon each dried thyme and dried basil, 1 teaspoon each garlic powder and onion powder, ½ teaspoon freshly ground black pepper, and ⅛ teaspoon cayenne pepper.

Spicy Cheddar and Pecan Balls

Most of us who grew up in the fifties and sixties remember those party animals, nut-covered cheese balls. Here's an updated, zesty cheese ball for today's tastes, chunky with roasted red pepper, green olives, capers, and pickled jalapeños. It's a great recipe for large gatherings. The mixture can be rolled into one large ball, but two smaller balls make for easier serving, as they can be placed in different spots within reach of more people.

Makes 2 medium cheese balls, 8 to 12 servings each

Make Ahead: The cheese balls can be prepared up to 3 days before serving.

Two 8-ounce packages cream cheese, at room temperature
1 pound extra-sharp Cheddar cheese, shredded
1 medium red bell pepper, roasted (see Note) and cut into ¼-inch dice
½ cup pitted and chopped Mediterranean green olives
2 tablespoons bottled nonpareil capers, rinsed
2 tablespoons chopped pickled or fresh, seeded jalapeños
1 to 2 teaspoons chili powder
2 teaspoons Worcestershire sauce
2 garlic cloves, crushed through a press
¼ teaspoon hot red pepper sauce
1 cup coarsely chopped pecans
Assorted crackers, for serving

1. At least 4 hours before serving, in a large bowl, using a rubber spatula, mash the cream and Cheddar cheeses together until combined. Using the spatula, work in the remaining ingredients except the pecans.

2. Transfer half of the cheese mixture to an 18-inch long piece of plastic wrap. Bring up the edges of the plastic wrap and twist them to form the cheese mixture into a ball. Repeat with the remaining cheese. Refrigerate until chilled and firm, at least 4 hours. (The cheese balls can be prepared up to 3 days ahead.)

3. Before serving, roll the cheese balls in the pecans to cover completely. Let stand at room temperature for 1 hour. Serve with the crackers.

Note: It is easiest to roast bell peppers in the broiler. Position a broiler rack about 4 inches from the source of heat and preheat the broiler. Cut the top and bottom from a red bell pepper, discarding the green stem (it pops out from the cut top). Slice each bell pepper vertically, and open it up into a long strip. Cut out and discard the ribs and seeds. Place the bell pepper pieces, including the top and bottom, skin sides up, on the broiler rack. Broil until the skin is blackened and blistered, about 5 minutes. Transfer to a plate and let stand until cooled. Scrape off the blackened skin. If you need to rinse the pepper, do so briefly under cold water. Bell peppers can be roasted up to 2 days ahead, covered, and refrigerated.

The Famous Disappearing Spinach Dip

A colorful selection of crudités with a tasty dip is just enough to hold some folks over until the big meal. It's always hard to decide which dip to serve, but this creamy, green-flecked mixture often makes my final cut. It makes a huge bowl, but on the rare occasion when some is left over, I turn it into a great salad dressing by blending the dip with buttermilk and a dash of vinegar. This recipe is from the collection of my dear friend Diane Kniss, who insists that its secret lies in store-bought ingredients.

Makes about 5½ cups, enough for 20 appetizer servings

Make Ahead: The crudités can be prepared 1 day ahead. The dip can be prepared up to 5 days ahead.

One 10-ounce box chopped frozen spinach
One 15-ounce container sour cream
2 cups mayonnaise
½ cup finely chopped fresh scallions
½ cup finely chopped fresh parsley
½ cup finely chopped fresh dill
One 1.8-ounce package leek-vegetable soup, such as Knorr's
1 tablespoon cheese-based salad seasoning, such as Salad Supreme
Assorted crudités, for serving

1. Put the spinach in a wire sieve and run under lukewarm water until thawed. A handful at a time, squeeze the moisture out of the spinach and transfer the spinach to a large bowl.

2. Add the sour cream, mayonnaise, scallions, parsley, dill, leek soup, and salad seasoning, and mix well. Cover and refrigerate until ready to serve. (The dip can be prepared up to 5 days ahead.) Serve with crudités.

The Crudité Garden

Crudités (the French word for raw vegetables) are always a welcome addition to the appetizer spread. Crudités should be thought of as an appetite-teasing, color-filled, crunchy, delicious cornucopia, not just a few carrot sticks in a bowl. Of course, the vegetables should be fresh and appealing, but choose them with an eye to contrasting colors, shapes, and textures to make the selection interesting to the eye and the palate. To set them off, place the crudités in a basket lined with curly kale leaves.

Some vegetables are fine raw, but others benefit from a quick parboiling to set their color or make them less crunchy. Vegetables that are best parboiled include asparagus, broccoli, carrots, green beans, and cauliflower. Cherry tomatoes, cucumbers, celery sticks, mushroom caps, bell pepper (green, yellow, red and/orange) strips, and zucchini should be served raw.

To parboil crudités, cut the vegetables in the desired shape—florets, spears, or sticks. Bring a large pot of lightly salted water to a boil over high heat. In separate batches, cook the vegetables just until crisp-tender, 1 to 2 minutes, no longer. Drain the vegetables and rinse well under cold running water to stop the cooking and set the color. Some cooks plunge the crudités into bowls of ice water, but that is a huge bother, and you can easily run out of ice—something to be avoided during a holiday. If you are cooking a number of vegetables, start with the most mild-tasting vegetable first, as the vegetables will leach some flavor into the cooking water. Using a large wire skimmer, transfer them from the water to the colander, and keep the water boiling to cook subsequent batches.

Drain the vegetables well. Pat them completely dry with paper towels, or your crisp vegetables could become soggy. As added insurance against waterlogging, wrap them in paper towels before storing in self-sealing plastic bags. Refrigerate the crudités for up to 1 day.

Shrimp Cocktail Dip

For years, my family's Thanksgiving dinner began with a little glass of shrimp cocktail. Even though it was the supermarket variety, my brothers and I understood that shrimp cocktail was reserved for very classy occasions, and that serious eating was ahead. Now the shrimp cocktail is back, reestablishing itself on the menus of tony restaurants from coast to coast. This is shrimp cocktail for a crowd.

Makes 8 to 12 appetizer servings

Make Ahead: The cocktail sauce can be prepared up to 2 days ahead.

1 cup ketchup-style chili sauce, such as Heinz 57
1 medium celery rib with leaves, finely chopped
1 scallion, white and green parts, finely chopped
1 tablespoon chopped fresh parsley
1 tablespoon fresh lemon juice
1 tablespoon bottled horseradish
Hot red pepper sauce, to taste
8 ounces cooked, deveined, finely chopped shrimp
One 8-ounce package cream cheese, at room temperature
Crackers, baguette slices, or celery sticks, for serving

1. In a medium bowl, mix the chili sauce, celery, scallion, parsley, lemon juice, horseradish, and hot pepper sauce. Cover and refrigerate for 2 hours to allow the flavors to blend. (The cocktail sauce can be prepared up to 2 days ahead, covered, and refrigerated.)

2. Reserve about ½ cup of the chopped shrimp. Stir the remaining shrimp into the cocktail sauce. Place the cream cheese on a serving platter, and pour the shrimp mixture over the top. Top with the reserved shrimp, and serve immediately with the crackers.

Hot Crab Salsa Dip

Here's another update of an old favorite that my guests can't get enough of. This recipe makes a large amount, but it always disappears. If your appetizer menu is long, the recipe is easily halved. It's a natural for tortilla chips, but try it with fresh crudités like broccoli, cauliflower, sweet red pepper strips, and cherry tomatoes. There are a number of options to keep the dip warm. I use a mini–slow cooker, but fondue pots or electric warming plates also work. For the best flavor, use fresh crabmeat, not canned.

Makes about 12 appetizer servings

Make Ahead: The dip can be prepared up to 8 hours ahead.

1 cup chunky tomato salsa
Two 8-ounce packages cream cheese
½ cup mayonnaise
1 teaspoon Worcestershire sauce
1 pound fresh lump crabmeat, picked over to remove shells and cartilage, and flaked
Hot red pepper sauce to taste
⅓ cup fresh bread crumbs, preferably from day-old French or Italian bread
Tortilla chips and assorted fresh vegetables, for serving

1. Position a rack in the center of the oven and preheat the oven to 350°F.

2. Drain the salsa in a wire sieve to remove excess liquid. Place the drained salsa in a bowl and add the cream cheese, mayonnaise, and Worcestershire sauce. Using a rubber spatula, work the ingredients until combined. Stir in the crabmeat. Season with the hot pepper sauce. Transfer to a round 1-quart baking dish. (The dip can be prepared up to 8 hours ahead, covered tightly with plastic wrap, and refrigerated.)

3. Sprinkle the bread crumbs over the dip. Bake until the dip is bubbling, about 30 minutes. Serve hot, with the tortilla chips and vegetables.

Savory Cheddar and Jalapeño Jelly Cookies

My friend Ruth Henderson owns The Silo, a kitchen shop, art gallery, and cooking school nestled in the gorgeous Litchfield Hills in Connecticut. (In fact, many of these recipes debuted at my annual Thanksgiving classes there.) Ruth often serves these delectable appetizer cookies at their gallery opening parties. The dough should be made in a food processor, but the butter and cheese mixture could be creamed by hand, if necessary, if you shred the cheese as finely as possible (use the smallest holes on a box grater, not the usual large holes). If you don't have jalapeño jelly, use apple butter or your favorite chutney instead.

Makes about 4½ dozen

Make Ahead: The cookies can be baked up to 2 days ahead.

8 ounces (about 2½ cups) shredded extra-sharp Cheddar cheese
6 tablespoons (¾ stick) unsalted butter, at room temperature
1 cup all-purpose flour
⅓ cup jalapeño jelly, apple butter, or chopped chutney

1. Place the cheese and butter in a food processor and pulse a few times to combine. Add the flour and process until the mixture forms a soft dough. Gather up the dough and divide into two flat disks. Wrap in wax paper and freeze until chilled, about 45 minutes.

2. Position two racks in the center and top third of the oven and preheat the oven to 400°F. Line baking sheets with parchment paper or silicone baking pads. Place the jelly in a small plastic bag and force it into one corner. Snip off the corner of the bag to make a small hole. Set the bag of jelly aside.

3. Using 1 teaspoon of dough for each, roll the dough into small balls. Place the balls 1 inch apart on the prepared baking sheets. Bake for 5 minutes. Remove from the oven. Using the end of a wooden spoon or a ½-inch-wide dowel, poke an indentation in each cookie. Pipe the jelly from the bag into the indentations.

4. Return to the oven and bake, switching the positions of the sheets from top to bottom halfway through baking, until the tops are very lightly browned, about 10 minutes (the cookies will continue to crisp as they cool). Transfer to wire cake racks and cool completely. (The cookies can be baked up to 2 days ahead. Place the cookies in an airtight container, separating the layers with wax paper, and store at room temperature.)

Potato Tortilla with Smoked Salmon

In America, tortilla means one thing, and it is made from corn and used in Mexican cooking. In Spain, however, a tortilla is a thick egg omelet that resembles the Italian frittata. Cut into golden squares, a tortilla can be the beginning of a perfect Thanksgiving bite, topped with sour cream and smoked salmon. When guests are arriving in the late morning, these give a brunchlike feel to the appetizer menu. The tortillas could also be garnished with black or red caviar, whatever type fits into the budget.

Makes about 48 squares, 8 to 12 appetizer servings

Make Ahead: The tortilla can be prepared up to 4 hours ahead. Top with the sour cream and salmon just before serving.

2 tablespoons olive oil
½ teaspoon salt
⅛ teaspoon freshly ground black pepper
1 pound (3 small) Russet or Idaho potatoes, peeled and sliced into ⅛-inch-thick rounds
5 large eggs, at room temperature
Hot red pepper sauce, to taste
Approximately ½ cup sour cream
6 ounces smoked salmon, cut into 1- by ¼-inch strips
Minced chives or green tops of scallions, for garnish

1. In a 9-inch nonstick skillet, heat the oil over medium-low heat. In a small bowl, combine ¼ teaspoon of the salt and the pepper. In four batches, add the potatoes to the skillet, seasoning each layer with some of the salt and pepper mixture. Stir each addition well to coat with the oil and prevent sticking. Cook, stirring often, until the potatoes begin to soften, about 3 minutes. Cover and cook, stirring often, to keep the potatoes from sticking to each other, until the potatoes are just tender, 20 to 25 minutes.

2. In a large bowl, beat the eggs with the remaining ¼ teaspoon salt and the hot pepper sauce. Using a slotted spoon, stir the potato slices into the eggs, leaving any oil in the pan.

3. Position the broiler rack 6 inches from the source of heat, and preheat the broiler. Reheat the skillet over medium-low heat. Pour in the egg mixture and spread out the potatoes to make an evenly thick cake. Using a rubber spatula, lift up the cooked part of the tortilla, and tilt the skillet so the uncooked eggs run underneath. Continue cooking, occasionally lifting the tortilla and tilting the skillet as described, until the top is almost set, 4 to 5 minutes.

4. Broil the frittata until the top is puffed and lightly browned, about 1 minute. Place a round plate over the top of the skillet and invert the frittata onto the plate. Cool completely. (The frittata can be prepared up to 4 hours ahead, covered, and refrigerated. Return to room temperature before serving.)

5. Cut the frittata into 1-inch squares (you will have a few odd-shaped trimmings that you may serve if you wish, or eat as the cook's treat). Top each square with a small dab of sour cream, then a strip of salmon, curled into a decorative shape. Sprinkle with chives and serve.

Pork and Veal Pâté with Dried Cranberries

Pâté is the kind of indulgence that only seems to appear at special occasions. This is a favorite, scented with brandy and studded with sweet-sour cranberries. A pâté is a boon to the busy cook—it's as easy to make as a meat loaf, homey and sophisticated at the same time. And, because it must be made a day or two ahead for the flavors to mellow, it allows one more thing to be checked off the prep list well ahead of time. Serve it with thin baguette slices or crackers, a crock of grainy mustard, and maybe some tiny pickles (cornichons) or pickled onions.

Makes 8 to 12 servings

Make Ahead: The pâté must be prepared at least 1 day ahead of serving; it can be refrigerated for up to 5 days.

½ cup dried cranberries
⅓ cup Cognac or brandy
1 tablespoon unsalted butter
½ cup finely chopped shallots
2 garlic cloves, minced
½ cup fresh bread crumbs, prepared from crusty bread
⅓ cup heavy cream
2 large eggs
¼ cup chopped fresh parsley
2 teaspoons salt
½ teaspoon dried thyme
½ teaspoon dried rosemary
¼ teaspoon ground allspice
¼ teaspoon freshly ground black pepper
1 pound ground veal
1 pound ground pork
4 ounces smoked or boiled ham, sliced ¼ inch thick and cut into ¼-inch cubes

1. Start the pâté at least 1 day before serving. In a small bowl, plump the cranberries in the Cognac for about 1 hour. (Or place in a small microwave-safe bowl, cover with plastic wrap, and microwave on High for 30 seconds. Stir and let stand for 10 minutes.)

2. Position a rack in the center of the oven and preheat the oven to 350°F. Lightly oil an 8½ × 4½ × 2½-inch loaf pan.

3. In a medium skillet, melt the butter over medium heat. Add the shallots and garlic and cook, stirring often, until softened, about 2 minutes. Set aside.

4. In a large bowl, mix the bread crumbs, heavy cream, eggs, parsley, salt, thyme, rosemary, allspice, and pepper. Let stand for 5 minutes. Add the ground veal and ground pork, and mix well (your hands work best). Stir in the ham, shallot mixture, and the cranberries with the Cognac. Pack into the prepared loaf pan and cover tightly with a double thickness of aluminum foil.

5. Place the loaf pan into a roasting pan. Transfer to the oven. Pull out the oven rack slightly and pour enough hot water into the roasting pan to come ½ inch up the sides. Slide the rack back into the oven. Bake until an instant-read thermometer inserted in the center of the pâté (right through the foil) reads 160°F, about 1¼ hours.

6. Remove the loaf pan from the water and place on a wire cake rack. Cool to room temperature.

7. Run a knife around the inside of the pan. Invert to unmold the pâté, wiping away any congealed juices with paper towels. Wrap tightly in plastic wrap. Refrigerate overnight before serving. (The pâté can be prepared up to 5 days ahead.) Serve the pâté chilled or at room temperature.

Mini-Meatballs in Wild Mushroom Sauce

I have a fondness for retro dishes—they're comforting, familiar, and make guests feel at home. But that doesn't mean that they have to be one of your mom's recipes. Take these updated Swedish meatballs, which definitely do not include canned soup. I often make a double batch to be sure to have leftovers to serve the day after the party over noodles. Polish up the chafing dish to serve these creamy morsels.

Makes 48 meatballs, 6 to 8 servings

Make Ahead: The meatballs can be made up to 2 days ahead; the sauce can be made 1 day ahead.

1 cup (1 ounce) dried porcini mushrooms
1 cup boiling water

MEATBALLS

⅓ cup plain dried bread crumbs
1 large egg plus 1 large egg yolk
2 tablespoons finely chopped fresh parsley
1¼ teaspoons salt
½ teaspoon freshly ground black pepper
12 ounces ground beef round
12 ounces ground veal
12 ounces ground pork
2 cups beef broth, preferably homemade, heated

SAUCE

10 ounces cremini (baby portobello) mushrooms
4 tablespoons unsalted butter
3 tablespoons finely chopped shallots
⅓ cup all-purpose flour
⅓ cup heavy cream
Salt and freshly ground black pepper to taste

Chopped fresh parsley, for garnish

Tossing Crumbs

Few kitchens are without a box of dried bread crumbs stashed in a cabinet corner. These have their place (to bind some meat loaves and meatballs), but I use fresh bread crumbs more often. The lighter texture and superior flavor of freshly prepared bread crumbs make them much more versatile than the sandy, store-bought kind. Whenever I have leftover bread, I make bread crumbs and freeze them to have ready when needed.

For the best results, use firm, day-old bread, such as crusty French or Italian bread or a high-quality sandwich loaf. English muffins or sandwich rolls also work well, as long as they aren't sweetened. Don't bother to trim off the crusts—they'll add color and texture. In a food processor, with the machine running, drop the bread through the feed tube and process until finely ground and fluffy. (The crumbs can also be prepared in a blender in small batches.) The crumbs can be frozen in a self-sealing plastic bag for up to 2 months. There's no need to defrost the crumbs before using.

1. Quickly rinse the dried mushrooms in a wire sieve under cold water to remove grit. Combine the mushrooms and boiling water in a small bowl until the mushrooms soften, about 25 minutes. Strain the mushrooms in a wire sieve lined with a single layer of moistened paper towels set over a bowl; reserve the soaking liquid. Chop the soaked mushrooms and set aside.

2. To make the meatballs, position two racks in the center and top third of the oven and preheat the oven to 375°F. Lightly oil two large rimmed baking sheets.

3. Mix the bread crumbs, egg, yolk, parsley, salt, and pepper in a large bowl. Add the beef, veal, and pork, and mix with your clean hands until the mixture is combined. Using about 2 teaspoons for each, roll into 48 balls. Place on the baking sheets. Bake the meatballs until lightly browned and cooked through, about 20 minutes.

4. Transfer the meatballs to a bowl. Pour off the fat from the baking sheets. Pour 1 cup of the hot broth into each baking sheet and scrape with wooden spatula to loosen the browned bits. Pour the liquid into a 1-quart glass measuring cup. Add the mushroom soaking liquid and enough hot water to make 3 cups. Set aside. (The meatballs can be made up to 2 days ahead, cooled, covered, and refrigerated.)

5. To make the sauce, in batches, pulse the cremini mushrooms in a food processor fitted with the metal chopping blade until they are finely chopped. Melt 2 tablespoons of the butter in a large skillet over medium-high heat. Add the chopped mushrooms and cook until the juices evaporate, about 8 minutes. Add the shallots and cook until the mushrooms are lightly browned, about 2 minutes longer.

6. Add the remaining 2 tablespoons butter to the skillet and melt. Sprinkle in the flour and stir well. Stir in the beef-mushroom liquid and heavy cream. Boil until reduced by about one-fourth, about 5 minutes. Season with salt and pepper. (The sauce can be made 1 day ahead, cooled, covered, and refrigerated. Reheat gently in a large skillet until simmering.)

7. Add the meatballs to the sauce and cover. Cook over medium heat until the meatballs are heated through, about 5 minutes. Transfer to a chafing dish, sprinkle with parsley, and serve hot with toothpicks for spearing the meatballs.

A Pitcher of Bloody Marys

I've been using this blue-ribbon recipe for perfectly seasoned Bloody Marys for many years, having learned it at one of my first restaurant jobs. So that guests can have Virgin Marys, too, leave the vodka out of the pitcher and serve it on the side. For a Bloody Mary, allow 1 jigger (3 tablespoons) vodka for every ¾ cup of the spicy tomato juice mixture.

Makes 8 servings

Make Ahead: The tomato juice mixture can be prepared up to 1 day ahead.

One 48-ounce can tomato-and-vegetable-juice cocktail, such as V-8
⅓ cup bottled horseradish
⅓ cup fresh lime juice
2 tablespoons Worcestershire sauce
1½ teaspoons ground celery seed
1 teaspoon hot red pepper sauce, or more to taste
Vodka, as needed
Celery sticks, for garnish

1. In a large pitcher, stir the tomato juice, horseradish, lime juice, Worcestershire sauce, celery seed, and hot pepper sauce. (The tomato juice mix can be prepared up to 1 day ahead, covered, and refrigerated.)

2. To serve, pour ¾ cup of the tomato mix into each ice-filled glass. Add vodka and stir. Garnish with celery sticks.

A Blender of Ramos Fizzes

This is my extended family's Thanksgiving cocktail of choice. Most of us are from San Francisco, where Ramos Fizzes are the ne plus ultra of brunch drinks, and we drink them every year as a toast to our beloved hometown. (New Orleans, the birthplace of the Fizz, is the only other city where it is commonly served at bars and restaurants. I suspect that San Francisco's Fairmont Hotel may have gotten the recipe from the Crescent City's Fairmont Hotel, and popularized the Fizz on the West Coast.) The most important thing to know about these potent drinks is that they may taste like grown-up milk shakes, but they aren't as innocent as they look.

Makes 4 servings

Make Ahead: The fizzes are best prepared just before serving.

1 cup gin
½ cup half-and-half
½ cup fresh lime juice
¼ cup superfine sugar
1½ teaspoons orange blossom water (available at specialty food stores and many liquor stores and supermarkets)
4 large ice cubes
4 egg whites or 2 large eggs or ½ cup liquid egg substitute
Approximately ½ cup club soda

1. In a blender, combine the gin, half-and-half, lime juice, sugar, orange blossom water, ice cubes, and egg whites. Blend at high speed until well mixed.

2. Pour into individual serving glasses and top off with approximately 2 tablespoons club soda to provide the "fizz." Serve immediately.

Autumn Glow Punch

There are two kitchen aromas guaranteed to make your guests feel all warm and fuzzy. One belongs to a roasting turkey, and the other comes from a simmering pot of mulled cider. So your friends don't get *too* warm and fuzzy, make the punch without any alcohol, but have a bottle of dark rum available for those who wish to spike their cup.

Makes 3 quarts, 12 to 16 servings

Make Ahead: The punch can be prepared up to 4 hours ahead of serving.

1 teaspoon allspice berries
½ teaspoon whole cloves
Two 3- to 4-inch cinnamon sticks, broken
2 quarts apple juice
One 32-ounce bottle cranberry juice cocktail
2 large oranges, sliced into rounds
Dark rum, optional

1. Tie the allspice, cloves, and cinnamon sticks into a bundle with rinsed cheesecloth and kitchen string. In a large saucepan over medium-low heat, heat the apple juice, cranberry juice, orange slices, and spices just until simmering. (The punch can be prepared up to 4 hours ahead of serving and kept at room temperature. Reheat gently before serving.)

2. To keep the punch warm, transfer to a slow cooker or place the saucepan on a hot plate. Serve hot, allowing each guest to add dark rum as desired.

Soups and Salads

Who's on First?

You can be sure that there will be a lot of last-minute activity when it's time to put the main course on the Thanksgiving table. So, I want a first course that is as carefree as possible. Again, Make Ahead is the order of the day. Soups that just need a quick reheating or a marinated salad that only needs to be spooned onto a plate are my two standbys, and they have never done me wrong. To decide whether I serve soup or salad this year, I usually toss a coin. No matter which one wins, these first courses celebrate the season's bounty with winter squash, sweet potatoes, fennel, celery root, pears, and other ingredients that say "autumn."

More important, a first course acts as a diversion while the side dishes are cooking. Here's the game plan. When the turkey is roasted, remove it from the oven. It needs to stand for at least twenty minutes before carving, anyway, and will stay piping hot for an hour or more. Place the side dishes that need baking in the oven. Finish the first course (reheat the soup or spoon out the salad) and serve. It will take about fifteen minutes to enjoy the first course, and you have started your dinner on a leisurely, relaxed note.

Soup is always best prepared with homemade stock. If necessary, a good canned reduced-sodium broth is fine, but a homemade version can be prepared with very little effort, and frozen for weeks or months before using. If you only want to make one big batch of all-purpose stock, make it with turkey instead of chicken. Its deeper flavor will heighten the taste of most of these soups. I know chefs who use turkey stock instead of veal stock at their restaurants because it's lighter, yet more flavorful and versatile, and you can follow suit.

There is a tradition of shellfish soup at many

Thanksgiving tables, especially in New England. But overcooked shellfish is tough and rubbery. Always heat up the soup without the shellfish and add it at the last minute, just to heat through.

To serve the soup at its piping-hot point of perfection, serve it from a warmed soup tureen. If an empty oven is available, place the tureen in a 200°F oven for a few minutes. Otherwise, fill the tureen with very hot water and let stand until warmed. Then pour out the water and dry the tureen. Try to warm the soup bowls, too. (I know you're not a restaurant, but who wants lukewarm soup?) Garnishes that are usually chilled, such as sour cream, should be at room temperature so they don't cool down the soup.

At my parents' Thanksgiving dinner, as it is in millions of other households, a fruity gelatin salad is always the first course of choice. I generally serve savory salads, and relegate the gelatin mold to the side-dish category. The components to my Thanksgiving salads are all made in advance. When greens are called for, they have been washed early in the day (or even the night before), and are waiting in the refrigerator to be dressed with the (made-ahead) vinaigrette. The salads all feature a mixture of ingredients that are as delicious as they are eye-catching. If possible, serve the salads on large dinner plates—they'll look more attractive and dramatic. Chilled plates are really an affectation, and aren't as necessary as warmed soup bowls.

New England Oyster Stew

In New England, oyster stew is a Thanksgiving must-have. Oysters are at their best during cold weather, and are a fine example of how autumn's bounty can be celebrated. Simplicity is the name of the game here—use the finest, freshest oysters, the best cream (go to a natural food store for full-flavored cream that hasn't been ultrapasteurized), and a gentle hand with seasoning.

Makes 8 servings

Make Ahead: The oyster stew should be prepared just before serving.

2 tablespoons unsalted butter
1 scallion, white and green parts, finely chopped
2½ cups milk
2 cups heavy cream, preferably not ultrapasteurized
3 dozen large oysters, shucked, with their juices
Salt
⅛ teaspoon freshly ground white pepper
Sweet paprika, preferably Hungarian or Spanish, for garnish (see Note)

1. In a Dutch oven or soup pot, melt the butter over medium heat. Add the scallion and cook, stirring constantly, until wilted, about 1 minute. Add the milk, heavy cream, and oyster juices. Cook, stirring often, just until small bubbles appear around the edges of the liquid, about 5 minutes.

2. Add the oysters and cook just until they curl at the edges, about 2 minutes. Season with the salt and pepper. (The oysters are already briny, so season with caution.) Transfer to a warmed soup tureen and serve immediately in warm soup bowls, sprinkling each serving with a dash of paprika.

Note: Hungarian and Spanish paprika have more flavor than domestic varieties, so they act like more than a colorful garnish. If you like spicy seasonings, use hot paprika. Pimentón de La Vera, a smoked Spanish paprika, will add another flavor that you may or may not find welcome in the stew.

Aw, Shucks

Large to medium-sized oysters make the best stew, as they give off more delicious, briny juices than smaller specimens. There are many varieties on the East Coast, usually named for the place they were raised, such as Malpeque (Prince Edward Island) or Pemmaquid (Maine). Pacific (also called Japanese) or European flat oysters, both of which have distinctly different flavor characteristics than eastern oysters, can also be used. Small oysters, such as Kumamoto and Olympia, are too tiny to give off enough juice to make a proper stew.

Freshly shucked oysters have better flavor and texture than prepacked, shucked ones. Unfortunately, oyster shucking is one of the most challenging jobs in the home kitchen. New Englanders and folks who live in the Pacific Northwest might know someone who prides themselves as a master oyster shucker, and if you can enlist that person, you're home free. Otherwise, place an order with the fish store for freshly shucked oysters (instructing them to save the juices) to be picked up on Wednesday afternoon. They'll charge extra for opening the oysters, but it's worth it.

Sometimes, you'll have no choice but to open the oysters yourself. There are two methods. Use the first technique when serving oysters that must remain raw and uncooked, such as those on the half shell. The second method can be used if the oysters are going to be cooked in stuffings or stews.

To shuck raw oysters, try Julia Child's technique, taught to her by an oyster fisherman. Instead of an oyster knife (with its sturdy blade and pointed, somewhat blunt tip), use an old-fashioned can opener, the kind some people call a church key. Scrub the oysters well with a stiff brush under cold running water. Place an oyster, curved side down, on a folded kitchen towel. Oysters are usually teardrop shaped. Locate the spot where the top shell meets the bottom shell at the pointed tip of the "teardrop." With the pointed end up, wedge the tip of the can opener into the crack about ¼ inch below the pointed tip of the shell. Push the end of the can opener downward, and the shell should pop open from the leverage. If the shell crumbles, you'll have to use an oyster knife to wedge open the crack further down the shell. Holding the oyster over a wire sieve, placed over a bowl to catch and strain bits of shell from the juices, run a small, sharp knife around the top shell to release it. Slip the knife under the flat top shell to cut the oyster free, and discard the top shell.

Run the knife underneath the oyster to loosen it from the curved bottom shell. If you are serving the oysters on the half shell, leave the oyster in the shell, place the shell on a bed of ice, and loosely cover with plastic wrap until ready to serve, within 2 hours. If you are going to cook the oysters, place the oyster meat in a small bowl, add the strained oyster juices, and cover tightly. Refrigerate until ready to use, up to 24 hours.

If the oysters are going to be cooked in a soup or stuffing, they can be baked in a very hot oven until the shells open. The oysters will be slightly cooked, but not enough to overcook them in the finished dish. This is the method I use most often, as I rarely serve raw oysters at my Thanksgiving table, while oyster stew and oyster stuffing sometimes show up.

Preheat the oven to 500°F. Choose a roasting pan or baking dish large enough to hold the oysters in a single layer, and fill the pan with a thick layer of rock or coarse (kosher) salt or crumpled aluminum foil. Place the pan in the oven to heat for 10 minutes. Remove the pan from the oven, and nestle the oysters, curved sides down, in the salt or foil to keep them from rocking. Bake until the oyster shells gap open, 7 to 20 minutes, depending on the size of the oysters (they never open all at once). Discard any oysters that do not open after 20 minutes of baking. (The oysters can also be opened in a microwave oven. Microwave 6 oysters at a time on High until opened, 1 to 2 minutes.) When all of the oysters are open, and cool enough to handle, remove the oyster meat from the shells and place in a small bowl. Strain the oyster juices over the oysters, cover, and refrigerate. Use the partially cooked oysters within 2 hours.

Celery Root and Oyster Chowder

This is my gussied-up version of standard oyster stew, bolstered with celery root and red bell pepper. If you aren't familiar with celery root (also called celeriac or knob celery), give it a try. This gnarly tuber isn't related to celery at all, but has a delicious, mild celery flavor that makes it a superior addition to cold-weather soups and chowders. Its tough brown skin is often coated with dirt, so do rinse it before trimming or the dirt will turn to mud. Just give the peeled celery-root cubes a good rinse before using.

Makes 8 servings

Make Ahead: The chowder vegetables can be prepared up to 4 hours ahead.

1 pound celery root (2 medium or 1 large)
2 tablespoons unsalted butter
1 medium red bell pepper, cored, seeded, and chopped into ¼-inch dice
½ cup chopped leeks, white and pale green parts only
4 cups half-and-half
2 dozen oysters, shucked, with their juices
½ teaspoon salt
⅛ teaspoon freshly ground white pepper
Chopped fresh parsley, for garnish

1. Cut off the gnarly parts of the celery root (it is too much trouble to pare the nooks and crannies). Using a sharp knife, peel the celery root. Cut in half, and remove any soft, spongy center parts. Remove any skin still in the crevices with the tip of the knife. Cut into ½-inch cubes and place in a bowl of cold water.

2. Bring a large pot of lightly salted water to a boil over high heat. Drain the celery root and add it to the boiling water. Return to the boil and reduce the heat to medium. Cook the celery root until tender when pierced with the tip of a knife, about 7 minutes. Drain and rinse under cold running water. Transfer to a bowl, cover, and set aside. (The celery root can be prepared up to 4 hours ahead, stored at room temperature.)

3. In a Dutch oven or soup pot, melt the butter over medium-low heat. Add the red bell pepper and leeks, and cover. Cook, stirring occasionally, until the red bell pepper softens, 5 to 7 minutes. (The leek–red pepper mixture can be prepared up to 4 hours ahead, kept at room temperature. Reheat over low heat before proceeding.)

4. Pour the half-and-half and oyster juices into the Dutch oven, and increase the heat to high. Cook just until small bubbles appear around the edges, about 5 minutes. Add the oysters and celery root, and cook just until the oysters curl around the edges and are heated through, about 2 minutes. Season with the salt and pepper. Transfer to a warmed soup tureen, and serve immediately in warmed soup bowls, garnished with the parsley.

Leeking Information

Leeks are grown in sandy soil and need to be cleaned carefully. Leeks are best cleaned after chopping, as the sand often hides between the layers of the leek. To clean leeks, trim off the roots. Chop the leeks, using only the white part and about 1 inch of the pale green top, discarding the tops. (Some cooks use the dark green leek tops in stock, but I find they make the stock too dark.) Place the chopped leeks in a wire sieve and place under cold running water, mixing them with your hand to be sure that all the surfaces are rinsed well. You will be able to tell by touch if the leeks are still sandy. Drain completely.

Clam and Mushroom Soup

This recipe is based on one that I first enjoyed years ago at the Stanford Court Hotel in San Francisco. While it is an excellent Thanksgiving soup, you'll want to keep it in mind for other occasions, too. It is at its best with deeply flavored mushrooms, such as cremini or stemmed shiitakes, although regular mushrooms will work, too.

Makes 8 servings

Make Ahead: The clams can be prepared up to 6 hours ahead and the mushroom soup base up to 8 hours ahead.

3 dozen littleneck clams, well scrubbed
½ cup dry white wine
3 tablespoons unsalted butter
1½ pounds thinly sliced fresh mushrooms, preferably brown cremini, or white button mushrooms
½ cup finely chopped shallots
3 tablespoons all-purpose flour
3½ cups Homemade Turkey Stock 101 or Homemade Chicken Stock (pages 34 and 35), or canned reduced-sodium broth
1 teaspoon dried marjoram or thyme
¾ cup heavy cream
¼ teaspoon salt
¼ teaspoon freshly ground black pepper
½ cup crème fraîche or sour cream, at room temperature, for garnish
Chopped fresh parsley, for garnish

1. Place the clams and wine in a Dutch oven or soup pot. Cover tightly and bring the wine to a boil over high heat. Cook, occasionally checking the progress of the clams, until the clams open, about 5 minutes. As the clams open, use kitchen tongs to transfer them to a large bowl. When the clams are cool, working over the bowl, remove the clam meat. Transfer the meat to a small bowl. Cover tightly and refrigerate until ready to use. (The clams can be prepared up to 6 hours ahead.)

2. Line a wire sieve with rinsed and wrung-out cheesecloth or paper towels. Strain the clam juices into a small bowl and refrigerate until ready to use.

3. Rinse and wipe out the Dutch oven and return to the stove. Add the butter and melt over medium heat. Add the mushrooms, cover, and cook, stirring occasionally, until the mushrooms give off their juices, about 3 minutes. Uncover and cook until the juices evaporate and the mushrooms are beginning to brown, about 3 minutes more. Add the shallots and stir until the shallots soften, about 2 minutes. Sprinkle with the flour and stir until the mushrooms are well coated with the flour, about 1 minute.

4. Add the stock, strained clam juice, and marjoram. Reduce the heat to low and simmer for 10 minutes. (The soup can be prepared up to this point 8 hours before serving, cooled, covered, and refrigerated. Reheat to simmering before proceeding.)

5. Add the heavy cream and clams, and heat until very hot but not boiling. Season with the salt (be careful, as the clams could have added enough salt of their own) and pepper.

6. Transfer to a warmed soup tureen. Ladle the soup into warmed soup bowls, topping each serving with a dollop of crème fraîche and a sprinkle of parsley. Serve immediately.

Pumpkin Tortellini in Chicken Broth

Pumpkin tortellini are very popular in northern Italy, although the authentic filling recipe can be on the sweet side, flavored with amaretti cookie crumbs and an unusual fruit relish called *mostarda*. This version, with Parmesan cheese in the filling and made with round wonton wrappers, gets no points for authenticity, but it is delicious. Enlist another pair or two of hands when making the tortellini, and they'll be stuffed in no time. When serving tortellini *in brodo* (in broth), it is very important to use the very best homemade broth.

Makes 8 to 10 servings

Make Ahead: The broth can be made up to 3 days ahead or frozen for up to 2 months. The tortellini can be prepared up to 1 day ahead.

PUMPKIN TORTELLINI

1 cup pumpkin puree, canned or freshly prepared (see page 153)
1/3 cup freshly grated Parmesan cheese
3 tablespoons dried bread crumbs
1 large egg, separated
A few gratings of fresh nutmeg
1/8 teaspoon salt
1/8 teaspoon freshly ground black pepper
40 round wonton (gyoza) wrappers
8 cups Homemade Chicken Stock (page 35)
Finely chopped fresh rosemary, for garnish
1/2 cup freshly grated Parmesan cheese, for serving

1. To make the tortellini, line a baking sheet with wax paper and dust it with cornstarch. In a medium bowl, mix the pumpkin, Parmesan cheese, bread crumbs, the egg yolk, nutmeg, salt, and pepper. Place the egg white in a small bowl and beat until foamy. Using a small pastry brush, lightly brush the edges of one wonton wrapper with egg white. Place a teaspoon of the pumpkin filling in the center of the wrapper. Fold the wrapper so the edges meet and enclose the filling, and firmly press the edges to seal, making a half moon–shaped dumpling. Place a dab of egg white on one corner of the tortellini. Curve the tortellini around your index finger so the two corners meet, and press them together. Place the tortellini on the prepared baking sheet and cover with a large sheet of plastic wrap. Repeat the procedure with the remaining filling and wrappers. (The tortellini can be prepared up to 1 day ahead, covered tightly with plastic wrap, and refrigerated.)

2. In a large Dutch oven or soup pot, bring the broth to a boil over high heat. Reduce the heat to very low and keep hot. Fill a large pot with lightly salted water and bring to a boil over high heat. One at a time, quickly drop the tortellini into the boiling water (don't dump the tortellini into the water all at once or you'll get too much cornstarch into the cooking water). Reduce the heat to medium and gently cook the tortellini until the pasta is tender and the filling is heated through, 3 to 5 minutes. Using a slotted spoon, transfer the tortellini to a warmed soup tureen. Pour the hot broth into the tureen.

3. Ladle the tortellini and broth into warmed soup bowls, and sprinkle with rosemary. Serve hot, passing the Parmesan at the table.

Winter Squash Soup with Prosciutto and Sage

This bright orange soup seems rich and creamy without a drop of cream in sight. You have many choices of squash, from sugar or cheese pumpkin to butternut, Hubbard, or calabaza. Because each squash has a different moisture content, you may find that you need to adjust the consistency of the finished soup. If it is too thick, just thin it with more broth. If it is too thin, dissolve 2 tablespoons cornstarch in ⅓ cup cold water. Bring the soup to a boil, and stir in enough of the cornstarch mixture to thicken to your taste. (Remember, though, that the soup must be boiling for the cornstarch thickening to work.)

Makes 8 servings

Make Ahead: The soup can be made up to 2 days ahead.

2 pounds winter squash (see above)
2 tablespoons unsalted butter
1 medium onion, chopped
1 medium carrot, chopped
1 medium celery rib, chopped
2 garlic cloves, minced
3 cups Homemade Chicken Stock (page 35) or canned reduced-sodium chicken broth
3 ounces (¼-inch-thick) prosciutto, chopped (about ½ cup; see Note)
1 tablespoon finely chopped fresh sage or 1½ teaspoons dried sage
¼ teaspoon salt
¼ teaspoon freshly ground white pepper

1. Using a large, sharp knife, cut the squash into large pieces. Using a large spoon, scrape away and discard any fibers and seeds. Cut the squash into 1-inch pieces. Using a small, sharp paring knife, pare away the thick skin. Set the squash aside.

2. In a Dutch oven or soup pot, melt the butter over medium heat. Add the onion, carrot, and celery, cover, and cook, stirring often, until the vegetables soften, about 5 minutes. Add the garlic and cook for 1 minute. Add the squash and the stock. Bring to a boil. Reduce the heat to medium-low and simmer, covered, until the squash is tender when pierced with the tip of a knife, 15 to 20 minutes.

3. In batches, transfer the soup to a blender and puree, being sure to leave the lid slightly ajar so the steam can escape. Return the pureed soup to the Dutch oven and add the prosciutto and sage. Cook over low heat for 5 minutes to blend the flavors. Season with the salt and pepper. (The soup can be prepared up to 2 days ahead, cooled, covered, and refrigerated. The soup will thicken when chilled. Reheat over medium-low heat, stirring often and thinning the soup as needed with additional chicken stock, until hot, about 10 minutes.)

4. Transfer the soup to a warmed soup tureen. Ladle into warmed soup bowls and serve immediately.

Note: When you order prosciutto from the delicatessen counter or this soup, be sure to ask that it be sliced about ¼ inch thick, not paper thin. Any leftover prosciutto can be double-wrapped in aluminum foil and frozen for up to 2 months.

Sweet Potato and Peanut Soup

Two Southern favorites, sweet potatoes (also called yams) and peanuts, blend beautifully in this elegant soup made with humble ingredients. With just a few seasoning vegetables (and a little zip from jalapeño pepper and garlic), this soup has a depth of flavor that belies its simplicity. Use a smooth, traditional-style peanut butter, as the natural-style ones tend to separate.

Makes 8 to 10 servings

Make Ahead: The soup can be made up to 2 days ahead.

2 tablespoons unsalted butter
½ cup chopped shallots
1 medium carrot, chopped
1 medium celery rib, chopped
1 jalapeño, seeded and minced
2 garlic cloves, crushed under a knife
2 pounds sweet potatoes (yams), peeled and cut into 1-inch cubes
3½ cups Homemade Turkey Stock 101 or Homemade Chicken Stock (pages 34 and 35) or canned reduced-sodium chicken broth
½ cup smooth peanut butter (not natural)
1 tablespoon fresh lime juice
¾ teaspoon salt
¼ teaspoon freshly ground white pepper
Approximately 2 tablespoons heavy cream, for garnish
Chopped fresh cilantro, for garnish (optional)

1. In a Dutch oven or soup pot, melt the butter over medium heat. Add the shallots, carrot, celery, jalapeño, and garlic. Cover and cook, stirring often, until the vegetables soften, about 5 minutes. Add the sweet potatoes, stock, and 1½ cups water. Bring to a boil. Reduce the heat to medium-low and simmer, covered, until the sweet potatoes are tender when pierced with the tip of a knife, about 15 minutes.

2. In batches, transfer the soup to a blender and puree. Return the pureed soup to the Dutch oven and whisk in the peanut butter and lime juice. Cook over low heat, whisking often, until very hot but not simmering. Season with the salt and pepper. (The soup can be prepared up to 2 days ahead, cooled, covered, and refrigerated. Reheat over very low heat, stirring often, adding stock or water if the soup seems too thick.)

3. Transfer to a warmed soup tureen. To serve, spoon the soup into individual warmed soup bowls. Drizzle each serving with heavy cream and sprinkle with the cilantro if desired.

Two-Tone Root Vegetable Soups

This wonderful first course has to win the "simple sophistication" prize. Root vegetables are harbingers of autumn cooking, and certainly have pride of place at the Thanksgiving table. The idea here is to make two easy soups with complementary flavors but opposite colors, then serve them next to each other in the same bowl for a dramatic presentation. You will need at least one 2½- to 3-inch-wide open-ended charlotte ring or leaf-shaped cookie cutter for each serving. You can assemble the soups with one ring, but the more rings, the quicker the assembly. I have provided two more presentations for serving, side by side and swirl, following the recipe.

Makes about 12 servings

Make Ahead: The soups can be made 1 day ahead.

CELERY ROOT SOUP

2 tablespoons unsalted butter
1 medium celery rib, chopped
½ cup coarsely chopped shallots
1 pound celery root (celeriac), pared, woody portions trimmed out, cut into 1-inch chunks
1 medium baking potato, peeled and cut into 1-inch chunks
3½ cups Homemade Chicken Stock (page 35) or canned reduced-sodium chicken broth, as needed
½ teaspoon dried thyme
Salt and freshly ground black pepper to taste

CARROT SOUP

2 tablespoons unsalted butter
1 medium celery rib, chopped
½ cup coarsely chopped shallots
1 pound carrots, peeled and cut into ½-inch rounds
1 medium (5 ounces) baking potato, peeled and cut into 1-inch chunks
4 cups Homemade Chicken Stock (page 35) or canned reduced-sodium chicken broth, as needed
1½ teaspoons dried rosemary
Salt and freshly ground black pepper to taste

1. For the celery root soup: Melt the butter in a large saucepan over medium heat. Add the celery and cover. Cook until the celery softens, about 3 minutes. Add the shallots and cook until they soften, about 3 minutes. Stir in the celery root and potato, and cook for a minute or so. Add the stock and thyme, and bring to a boil over high heat. Reduce the heat to medium-low. Cover partially and simmer until the vegetables are tender, about 30 minutes. In batches, puree in a blender, being sure the lid is slightly ajar to allow the steam to escape. Adjust the thickness with additional stock, if needed. In order for the pattern to stay distinct, the soup should be on the thick side, with a consistency between heavy cream and yogurt. Season with salt and pepper. (The soup can be made 1 day ahead, cooled, covered, and refrigerated, although it will thicken. Reheat over low heat, adding additional broth as needed.)

2. For the carrot soup: Melt the butter in a large saucepan over medium heat. Add the celery and cover. Cook until the celery softens, about 3 minutes. Add the shallots and cook until they soften, about 3 minutes. Stir in the carrots and potato, and cook for a minute or so. Add the stock and rosemary, and bring to a boil over high heat. Reduce the heat to medium-low. Cover partially and simmer until the vegetables are tender, about 30 minutes. In batches, puree in a blender, being sure the lid is slightly ajar to allow the steam to escape. Adjust the thickness with additional stock, if needed. In order for the pattern to stay distinct, the soup should be on the thick side, with a consistency between heavy cream and yogurt. Season with the salt and pepper. (The soup can be made 1 day ahead, cooled, covered, and refrigerated, although it will thicken. Reheat over low heat, adding additional broth as needed.)

3. To serve, place a 2½- to 3-inch cookie cutter in the center of each soup bowl. Ladle the celery soup into the center of the bowl—the cookie cutter will keep the soup from spreading. Immediately ladle the carrot soup into the soup around the cutter. Lift up and remove the cutter—the soups will remain in place and create a two-tone bull's-eye effect. Serve immediately.

Side-by-Side Presentation: You won't use a cookie cutter for this method. In each bowl, create a "wall" from aluminum foil, pressing the foil to make a dam that separates the bowl into two equal portions in the center. Pour each soup into the bowl on either side of the dam. Lift up and remove the foil. The soups will remain in place, creating a side-by-side effect.

Swirl Presentation: Ladle enough carrot soup into each soup bowl to fill by about half. Ladle dollops of the celery root soup into each bowl. Using a knife, swirl the soups together.

Homemade Turkey Stock 101

Every Thanksgiving, I prepare a big pot of stock to use all Thanksgiving Day long. This luscious stock is one of the secrets to a moist, beautifully colored roast bird with wonderful gravy, as shown in Perfect Roast Turkey with Best-Ever Gravy on page 56. Some of the stock also goes into the stuffing, some usually gets turned into soup, and I often use it in side dishes as well. The recipe is easily doubled or even tripled, assuming you have a stockpot big enough to hold the ingredients. If you want a smaller amount of stock, make the Small-Batch Turkey Stock variation on page 35. But don't worry about having too much stock. Any leftovers can be frozen or used the next day to make a terrific soup.

- **Turkey parts with lots of bone, like wings and backs, make the best stock. Use the turkey neck, heart, and gizzard from a whole turkey in the stock, but not the liver. (Liver makes the stock bitter.) When the stock is strained, you can retrieve the neck and giblets to use in giblet gravy. If you want to use liver in the gravy, add it to the stock during the last 15 minutes of simmering, and poach it just until cooked through.**
- **Browning the turkey parts first gives the stock a rich color that will make a dark gravy. Cooking the vegetables brings out their flavor. Too many cooks throw the giblets in a pot with some water to boil up a weak, pale stock that doesn't have much flavor.**
- **Never let stock come to a rolling boil or it will become cloudy and have a less refined flavor. Cook the stock uncovered.**
- **Add the herbs to the stock after you've skimmed it. If you add them at the beginning, they will rise to the surface and be skimmed off with the foam. By the way, the foam isn't anything unwholesome—it's just the coagulating proteins in the bones. They are removed to make the stock clearer.**
- **The longer a stock simmers, the better, up to 12 hours. Replace the water as needed, as it evaporates. While I trust my stove to simmer the stock at a safe temperature overnight, some of my students have been shocked at the idea. A great alternative is to make the stock in a 5½-quart slow cooker. Transfer the browned turkey and vegetable mixture to the stockpot, add the herbs, and pour in enough cold water to cover well. Cover and cook on Low, and the stock will barely simmer all night long to create a clear, delicious stock.**
- **If time is a factor, just simmer the stock for an hour or two—it will still be better than using canned chicken broth to make your gravy. Or make a pot of stock well ahead of Thanksgiving and freeze it.**
- **Don't add salt to your stock. The stock is often used in recipes where it must reduced, and the finished dish could end up too salty. To check the stock's flavor, ladle some into a cup and season lightly with salt before tasting. Without the salt, it may taste deceptively weak.**

Makes about 2½ quarts

Make Ahead: Turkey stock can be made up to 3 days ahead or frozen for up to 3 months.

3 pounds turkey wings
2 tablespoons vegetable oil
Turkey neck and giblets (liver reserved, if desired; see headnote)
1 medium onion, chopped
1 medium carrot, chopped
1 medium celery rib with leaves, chopped
6 parsley sprigs
½ teaspoon dried thyme
¼ teaspoon whole black peppercorns
1 dried bay leaf

1. Using a heavy cleaver, chop the wings and neck into 2-inch pieces. (If necessary, ask the butcher to do this for you.) Using a sharp knife, trim away any membranes from the giblets.

2. In a large pot, heat the oil over medium-high heat. In batches, add the turkey wings, neck, and giblets, and cook, turning occasionally, until browned on all sides, 8 to 10 minutes. Transfer the turkey to a plate. Add the onion, carrot, and celery to the pot, and cook, stirring often, until softened, about 6 minutes.

3. Return the turkey to the pot. Add enough cold water to cover the turkey by 2 inches. Bring to a boil, skimming off the foam that rises to the surface. Add the parsley, thyme, peppercorns, and bay leaf. Reduce the heat to low. Cook at a bare simmer for at least 2 and up to 12 hours. As needed, add more water to the pot to keep the bones covered.

4. Strain the stock through a colander into a large bowl. Let stand for 5 minutes and skim off the clear yellow fat that rises to the surface. If desired, remove the giblets, cool, finely chop, and refrigerate for use in gravy. The neck meat can be removed in strips, chopped, and reserved as well. Cool the stock completely before refrigerating or freezing. (Turkey stock can be prepared up to 3 days ahead, cooled completely, covered, and refrigerated. It can also be frozen in airtight containers for up to 3 months.)

Small-Batch Turkey Stock: A smaller amount of stock can be prepared with just the turkey neck and giblets. As this relatively small amount of turkey won't give a very full-flavored stock, use chicken broth (homemade or canned) as a booster. Following the instructions above, brown the neck and giblets from 1 turkey in 1 tablespoon oil. Add 1 small onion, 1 small carrot, and 1 small celery rib with leaves, all chopped, and cook until softened. Add 1 quart water, and one 13¾-ounce can reduced-sodium chicken broth and bring to a simmer. Add 3 parsley sprigs, ¼ teaspoon dried thyme, 6 peppercorns, and 1 small bay leaf. Simmer for 2½ to 3 hours (the smaller amount of liquid would evaporate away if cooked longer). Makes about 1 quart.

Homemade Chicken Stock: Substitute 3 pounds chicken wings, cut into 2-inch pieces, for the turkey wings. Delete the turkey neck and giblets.

Cranberry Waldorf Salad

This magenta-colored mold can be served as a side dish, but it really shines when served as a special first-course salad. I love it just as is, but if you like, serve it the way my grandma would: Mix equal portions of mayonnaise and sour cream, and place a dollop alongside each serving. The recipe is easily doubled to fit a 9-cup mold.

Makes 16 to 20 first-course salad servings

Make Ahead: The salad must be made at least 8 hours ahead; it can be refrigerated for up to 2 days.

1 tablespoon (about 1½ envelopes) unflavored gelatin
2 cups bottled apple juice, divided
One 12-ounce bag fresh cranberries, rinsed and picked over
⅔ cup sugar
1 Granny Smith apple, peeled, cored, and chopped into ½-inch pieces
1 medium celery rib, chopped
⅓ cup coarsely chopped walnuts

1. In a small bowl, sprinkle the gelatin over ½ cup of the apple juice; set aside. In a large saucepan, mix the cranberries, the remaining 1½ cups apple juice, and sugar. Bring to a boil over medium-high heat, stirring often to dissolve the sugar. Cook until all the cranberries have popped, about 5 minutes. Reduce the heat to very low. Stir in the gelatin mixture and continue stirring until the gelatin is completely dissolved, 1 to 2 minutes. Transfer the cranberry mixture to a large bowl. Refrigerate until cool and partially thickened (a spoon drawn through the mixture will leave a definite impression), about 2 hours. Or place the bowl in a larger bowl filled with ice water. Let stand, stirring the mixture often and adding more ice to the water as it melts, until the mixture is cool and partially thickened, about 45 minutes.

2. Lightly oil a 5-cup mold. Stir the apple, celery, and walnuts into the cranberry mixture. Pour into the prepared mold and cover with plastic wrap. Refrigerate until the mixture is completely set, at least 8 hours or overnight. (The salad can be prepared up to 2 days ahead.)

3. To unmold, fill a sink or large bowl with hot tap water. Dip the mold, just to the top edge, into the water and hold for 5 seconds. Remove from the water and dry the outside of the mold. Remove the plastic wrap. Invert the mold onto a serving platter. Holding the mold and the platter firmly together, shake them until the salad releases from the mold. Cut the salad into wedges and serve chilled.

Baby Spinach and Fuyu Persimmon Salad with Ginger Vinaigrette

This unusual but absolutely mouthwatering salad will generate a conversation on the merits of persimmons. Be sure to use Fuyu (sometimes called Sharon) persimmons, which can be eaten while crisp-ripe. Other varieties, such as Hachiya, need to be ripened until very soft or they will be inedibly tannic, and they don't make the best salads. Also buy fresh, plump ginger with smooth, unwrinkled skin, as it will yield the most juice.

Makes 8 servings

Make Ahead: The ginger dressing and spinach can be prepared up to 1 day ahead; the persimmons can be prepared up to 4 hours ahead.

GINGER VINAIGRETTE
6 ounces firm, fresh ginger
⅓ cup cider vinegar
1 tablespoon sugar
¾ teaspoon salt
½ teaspoon freshly ground black pepper
1 cup vegetable oil
1 tablespoon dark Asian sesame oil
2 tablespoons finely chopped shallots

18 ounces baby spinach
3 firm Fuyu persimmons
1 tablespoon plus 1 teaspoon sesame seeds, for garnish

1. To make the dressing, shred the unpeeled ginger on the large holes of a box grater. Wrap half of the shredded ginger in the corner of a clean kitchen towel. Wring the ginger over a small bowl to extract the juice. Discard the juiced ginger. Repeat with the remaining ginger. You should have about 1/4 cup of juice.

2. In a medium bowl, whisk the vinegar, ginger juice, sugar, salt, and pepper. Gradually whisk in the oil. Stir in the shallots. Cover tightly and refrigerate until ready to serve; whisk the dressing well before using. (The dressing can be prepared up to 1 day ahead.)

3. Rinse the spinach and spin-dry in a salad spinner. Wrap the spinach loosely in paper towels and place in a large plastic bag (a grocery bag is perfect). Refrigerate until ready to serve. (The spinach can be prepared up to 1 day ahead.)

4. Using a small, sharp knife, cut out the green calyx from the top of each persimmon. Using a vegetable peeler, peel the persimmons, moving the peeler vertically around the outside of each persimmon to remove the peel in a long strip. Cut the peeled persimmons into 1/4-inch-wide wedges. Place in a small bowl, cover tightly, and refrigerate until ready to serve. (The persimmons can be prepared up to 4 hours ahead.)

5. To serve, toss the persimmons with 2 tablespoons of the ginger dressing. In a large bowl, toss the spinach with as much of the remaining dressing as desired; refrigerate the leftover dressing for another use. Divide the spinach equally among chilled salad plates. Top with the persimmon wedges. Sprinkle with the sesame seeds and serve immediately.

Roasted Beet, Endive, and Blue Cheese Salad with Walnuts

I'm not suggesting that this salad will be a hit at the kids' table. But it will be welcome at an "adults only" Thanksgiving, especially one with other European-inspired dishes on the menu. Roasting works wonders with beets, bringing out their sweetness and maintaining their color better than boiling or steaming. Use a high-quality, but not artisanal, balsamic vinegar, which is less acidic than inexpensive versions. If the dressing is too sharp, balance it with a little brown sugar.

Makes 8 servings

Make Ahead: The beets can be prepared up to 1 day ahead. Chop the endive and toss the salad just before serving.

9 medium beets (about 2 1/4 pounds)
3 heads Belgian endive, wiped with a moist paper towel (do not rinse)
1/3 cup balsamic vinegar
1/2 teaspoon salt
1/4 teaspoon freshly ground black pepper
1/3 cup walnut oil (see Note)
4 ounces crumbled blue cheese, such as Roquefort
1/2 cup (2 ounces) toasted, coarsely chopped walnuts

1. To roast the beets, preheat the oven to 400°F. If the beets have their greens attached, trim the greens, leaving about 1 inch of the stems attached to the beets. Scrub the beets under cold running water. Wrap each beet in aluminum foil and place on a baking sheet. Bake until the beets are tender when pierced

with the tip of a long, sharp knife, about 1 hour, depending on the size of the beets. Unwrap the beets and cool.

2. Slip the skins off the beets. Cut the beets into ½-inch cubes. Place in self-sealing plastic bags and refrigerate until chilled, at least 2 hours. (The beets can be prepared up to 1 day ahead.)

3. Using a sharp knife, cut the endive crosswise into ½-inch-wide pieces. Separate the endive pieces into rings, discarding any tough, solid center pieces. Set the endive aside.

4. In a large bowl, whisk the vinegar with the salt and pepper. Gradually whisk in the oil. Add the beets, endive, blue cheese, and walnuts, and toss well. Spoon onto chilled salad plates and serve immediately.

Note: Walnut oil can be found in specialty food stores, many supermarkets, and some natural food stores. Imported French walnut oil has the richest flavor. If you can't find it, you can make an excellent substitute. In a blender, blend ½ cup toasted, coarsely chopped walnuts with ½ cup vegetable oil until the walnuts are very finely chopped. Let stand for a few minutes, then strain through a fine-mesh wire sieve.

Fennel, Pear, and Hazelnut Salad in Radicchio Cups

Fennel is another one of those winter vegetables that deserve to be better known by American cooks. European cooks love it for its crisp texture and mild anise flavor. The interplay of the crunchy fennel and hazelnuts with sweet and tender pears makes this an exceptional salad. It's also lightly dressed—a perfect choice when the menu requires a first course that isn't filling.

Toasting Nuts

I always try to find the time to toast nuts for cooking, especially for use in salads and desserts. The difference is dramatic and well worth the trouble. In the case of hazelnuts, they must be toasted in order to loosen and remove their skins. Toasted nuts can be prepared up to 2 days ahead, stored airtight at room temperature.

To toast almonds, pecans, walnuts, and hazelnuts, place the nuts in a single layer on a baking sheet. Bake them in a preheated 350°F oven, stirring the nuts occasionally (the ones on the edges toast more quickly and need to be incorporated into the center so they don't burn), until the nuts are lightly browned and fragrant, 8 to 10 minutes. Let the nuts cool completely before chopping them.

To skin hazelnuts, wrap the warm toasted hazelnuts in a clean kitchen towel and let them stand for about 10 minutes. Using the towel, rub off as much of the skins as possible. You can rarely get all of the skin off, so don't try. Besides, a little skin will add flavor.

Makes 8 servings

Make Ahead: The salad can be prepared up to 6 hours ahead, covered, and refrigerated.

1 large head fennel (about 1¼ pounds)
3 tablespoons fresh lemon juice
3 ripe Red Bartlett or Comice pears, or a combination
3 tablespoons extra virgin olive oil
⅛ teaspoon salt
¼ teaspoon freshly ground black pepper
1 large or 2 medium heads radicchio
¾ cup (3 ounces) toasted, skinned, and coarsely chopped hazelnuts

1. Using a large, sharp knife, trim the fennel of any bruises. If the feathery green fronds are still attached, trim them off, too. (If you want the salad to have a more pronounced anise flavor, chop the fronds and stir into the salad to taste.) Cut the fennel in half lengthwise. Locate the tough, solid "heart" that grows up from the bottom of each half, and remove by cutting it out in a wedge. Place the fennel, cut side down, on the work surface, and cut crosswise into ½-inch-thick strips. Transfer the fennel to a large bowl and toss with 2 tablespoons of the lemon juice.

2. Rinse the pears well, but do not peel. Cut each pear lengthwise into quarters and trim away the core. Cut the pear into ½-inch-wide wedges. Add to the bowl and toss with the remaining 1 tablespoon lemon juice. While tossing gently, drizzle with the olive oil and season with the salt and pepper. (The salad can be prepared 6 hours ahead, covered tightly, and refrigerated.)

3. To serve, separate the radicchio leaves into separate "cups." (Save any leftover radicchio for another use.) Mix the hazelnuts into the salad. Using a slotted spoon, place equal amounts of the salad into the radicchio cups. Place the radicchio cups on individual plates. Drizzle the radicchio cups and the area on the plate around it with the juices in the bowl, and serve immediately.

Shrimp Salad on Mesclun with Saffron Vinaigrette

Mesclun, the colorful combination of baby greens that can be found in just about every supermarket these days, is the foundation of many a fine salad. With firm, pink shrimp in a bright yellow saffron dressing, this combination of flavors really piques the appetite. The problem is, it's so delicious that guests could easily fill up on it, so this recipe makes modest servings.

Makes 6 to 8 servings

Make Ahead: The shrimp salad and dressing can prepared up to 1 day ahead, covered, and refrigerated. Toss the dressing with the mesclun just before serving.

SAFFRON VINAIGRETTE
1 tablespoon boiling water
½ teaspoon crumbled saffron threads
⅓ cup fresh lemon juice
1 tablespoon honey
2 garlic cloves, crushed through a press
½ teaspoon salt
¼ teaspoon freshly ground black pepper
1 cup olive oil (not extra virgin, which is too strong for this recipe)
2 pounds medium shrimp
1 large red bell pepper, cored, seeded, and finely chopped
2 tablespoons chopped fresh parsley
12 ounces mesclun or other mixed salad greens

1. To make the vinaigrette, combine the boiling water and saffron in a medium bowl and let stand for 5 minutes. Add the lemon juice, honey, garlic, salt, and pepper. Gradually whisk in the olive oil. Set the vinaigrette aside.

2. Bring a large pot of lightly salted water to a boil over high heat. Add the shrimp and cook until the shrimp turn opaque and firm, about 3 minutes (the water does not have to return to a boil). Drain and rinse under cold running water until easy to handle. Peel and devein the shrimp.

3. Transfer the shrimp to a medium bowl. Add ½ cup of the saffron vinaigrette, the red bell pepper, and the parsley, and toss well. Cover tightly with plastic wrap and refrigerate for at least 2 hours and up to 1 day. Cover and refrigerate the remaining vinaigrette.

4. When ready to serve, in a large bowl, toss the mesclun with the remaining dressing. On one side of each chilled dinner plate, spoon equal amounts of the shrimp salad. Heap the mesclun on the other side. Serve immediately.

Turkey and Friends

The Main Event

Everyone wants a perfect, moist, golden-brown bird on the Thanksgiving table. Over the years, I have listened to friends and students relate their special, secret, ultimate, best-ever ways to roast the bird. I have tried them all, and just when I thought I was finished, along came even more techniques. In the last few years alone, these included roasting in a very hot oven, deep-frying outside in a huge pot of fat, and soaking overnight in a big pot of brine. Each absolutely guaranteed the best turkey ever. While I have my favorite method (Perfect Roast Turkey with Best-Ever Gravy on page 56), there are reasons to consider the other recipes. For example, you may be cooking against the clock, so the high-temperature method will save valuable time (if you don't factor in the cleaning of the oven before and after roasting). Or maybe this year you have an itch to smoke the bird outside on the grill, and need to know how to pull it off. So I offer the other recipes, but with my frank evaluations and detailed instructions based on my experience.

Turkey is not always the only game in town on Thanksgiving Day. Ham often makes a guest appearance. For my many friends of Italian heritage, it isn't Thanksgiving if there isn't lasagna on the table, so I give a classic version of that beloved dish. There's also a special squash and rice dish for vegetarian guests.

But regardless of how you plan to cook your turkey, there are general questions that have to be answered first.

Types of Turkey

Other than gender, are there any differences between hen and tom turkeys? Is one more tender than the other?

Hens are female turkeys, weighing 8 to 16 pounds. Male toms, bred to yield a high proportion of the white breast meat that most Americans prefer, weigh 14 to 26 pounds. The size of the bird relates to its age. Turkeys are often labeled "young," because no commercial turkey is much older than twenty-six weeks. Thanks to modern animal-husbandry methods, there is no difference in flavor or tenderness between toms and hens. In the old days, a younger bird meant a more tender one, and while an old tom had plenty of flavor, it was also tougher. Unlike beef, turkeys are hormone- and steroid-free.

What are the differences between fresh and frozen turkeys?

There are actually three designations for fresh and frozen turkeys:

- "Frozen" turkeys have been deep-chilled at 0°F and below. They are at their best if defrosted and cooked within one year of purchase. (If you've ever wondered how your supermarket can give away free frozen turkeys as premiums at Thanksgiving time, it's probably because they are using up last year's surplus.)
- "Fresh" birds have never been chilled below 26°F, and have a correspondingly short shelf life. Since poultry freezes at 8°F lower than water does, turkeys with partially frozen flesh can still be considered fresh, though this discrepancy may seem odd. This partial freezing greatly extends the turkey's shelf life, so we have to cut the industry a little slack in this department. Fresh turkeys are easily available at supermarkets or butchers. You rarely have to special-order them anymore unless your butcher requires you to do so or you are concerned about getting a certain size. Buy fresh turkey no earlier than two days before roasting, even if a weekend purchase would be more convenient. Keep in mind that home refrigerators are warmer than the commercial walk-ins, and that the sell-by date is more useful for the retailer than the consumer. I always buy a fresh turkey.
- A turkey kept at temperatures between 0° and 26°F is considered "hard-chilled." You won't see turkeys labeled hard-chilled, though, as each turkey producer is allowed to create their own name for this designation, as long as it isn't misleading. In 2005, about 40 million turkeys were consumed over Thanksgiving. In order to get that many holiday turkeys to market and sold within a reasonable time, the hard-chilled method is necessary. Sometimes flash-chilled turkeys feel soft on the outside, but the giblets are frozen inside. If that happens, just run cold water in the water cavity until the bird thaws.

What about frozen turkeys?

Frozen turkeys are the least expensive, but freezing dries out the turkey meat, and more moisture is lost down the drain during defrosting. Good turkey producers always inject the birds with a moistening solution to replace the lost liquid. The best frozen turkeys have been injected with only wholesome ingredients like broth, vegetable oil, and seasonings. I don't like birds that have been pumped with artificial flavorings and preservatives. (On the other hand, it's not a good idea to freeze a fresh bird that hasn't been injected with any moisteners.) Also, frozen birds require advance planning to defrost. I hardly have enough room in my refrigerator at holiday time as it is, without a huge turkey taking up space for three to five days while it thaws. Considering the minor difference in price between the average frozen and fresh turkeys, why not get the best you can afford?

I have to get a frozen bird because I can only shop on weekends. How do I defrost it?

First and foremost, never defrost a turkey at room temperature.

Allow enough time for the turkey to thaw. *It takes a full 24 hours to defrost each 5 pounds of turkey in the refrigerator.* So, if you want a 25-pound turkey to be thoroughly defrosted by Thanksgiving morning, you must buy it by the preceding Sunday at the latest. (I'd buy it on Saturday, just to be sure.)

If you are in a hurry, a second-best option is to defrost the bird in a large sink of cold water, allowing 30 minutes per pound, changing the water and turning the turkey often. Do *not* add warm water to hasten the process.

Don't defrost a turkey in the microwave oven. The turkey is irregularly shaped, and some parts of the bird will cook while others are still defrosting. Besides, most microwave ovens won't hold a bird larger than 12 pounds.

What do you think about self-basting birds?

Self-basting birds, available fresh and frozen, have been "enhanced" (in the eyes of the producer) with flavorings, some natural and some artificial. They purport to make the turkey moist—I say they make the turkey soggy and wet, and predisposed to fall apart when being lifted from the pan. They say the basting liquid makes the turkey taste better—I believe a turkey tastes good enough without fake flavorings. I want to promote turkeys that taste like turkey, not canned soup. And, I *like* to baste the bird, so the concept of "self-basting" leaves me cold. Not only does opening the oven and basting give the cook an idea of the turkey's progress, but the hot basting liquid helps burnish the skin with tasty browned juices.

My farmers' market has organic, free-range birds. Are they worth the price?

While the terms "organic" and "free-range" may seem clear-cut to the consumer, conjuring up visions of turkeys on pastoral farms, contentedly pecking away in outdoor pens under a cloudless sky, the actual USDA definitions are somewhat loose. Generally, "organic poultry" has been raised on organically grown, antibiotic-free feed. Because they are kept in such close quarters, commercially raised meat and poultry are routinely fed antibiotics to help keep them healthy. The lack of antibiotics in your food could be an important issue to you.

While some organic (and commercial) producers may tout that their birds are "hormone-free," this is an empty phrase because hormones have been banned from all poultry since the 1950s. (This is not true of most American beef, where speedy growth is chemically enhanced, and is one of the reasons why some people choose to avoid red meat.) So is the term "all-natural," because there can be products in most commercial poultry feed that may be natural, but you still may not want them in your turkey's feed, knowing that they will of course end up in you, too. If an organic bird is labeled "all-natural," it has a bit more meaning, as the feed is likely to be vegetarian as well as organic, since often there are animal by-products in commercial feed.

"Free-range" turkeys, which are often organic, have been raised in a relatively spacious environment that gives them access to open spaces. But many turkeys that are not called free-range may have been raised in hen-houses with the same amount of space. Free-range means that the turkeys have access to the outdoors, usually through an open door in the henhouse. This is all well and good, except that turkeys are flocking birds, and the entire flock is usually quite happy staying inside—your free-range bird may have never ranged free by its own choice. These birds can be excellent, but they still need to be cooked carefully for fine results. They are significantly more expensive than ordinary fresh turkeys, and whether they are worth it is up to you. If your guests are all adults who love eating out at fancy restaurants, try an organic bird, whether it is free-range or not.

What are heritage turkeys?

By far, the turkeys that grace most tables on Thanksgiving are of the Large White or Broad Breasted Bronze breeds. These birds were developed to grow quickly and yield copious servings of white meat from their enormous breasts. Before the advent of these commercial turkeys, holiday birds were raised by local producers from old breeds like Beltsville Small White, Black, Standard Bronze, Narragansett, Slate, White Holland, Royal Palm, Jersey Buff, and Bourbon Red. Recently, some farmers have been reviving these retired "standard" breeds, and lovers of old-fashioned flavors have lined up to sample the wares. Heritage turkeys can be purchased at high-end markets or mail-ordered during the holidays, but as supplies are limited, reserve yours early.

I have found that it is best to find a current, local producer, putting you in direct contact with your source, which is easy to accomplish with an online search. Slow Food, an international culinary organization dedicated to preserving food traditions, has a state-by-state list at http://www.slowfoodusa.org/ark/turkeys.html. Freshness is key, because if the bird is hard-frozen for mail delivery across the country, the juiciness of the roasted bird will be compromised. Expect a bird with deep, old-fashioned flavor, and meat that is noticeably darker and firmer than a supermarket brand. Do not be alarmed if the bird has a humped breastbone or if the skin if freckled, which actually indicates its heritage status. As heritage turkeys are bred to retain their natural conformation, they will be on the relatively small side—do not expect to find any 25-pound heritage mega-birds.

My specialty butcher carries wild turkeys. What are they like?

Today, most wild turkeys are actually farm-raised. They are very full-flavored, but not gamy like hunter-bagged wild turkeys. (True wild turkeys are so chewy that some cooks roast only the tender breast, and stew or grind the tough dark meat.) I like to say they are to regular turkeys what sourdough bread is to white bread. Some people just like the complex flavor of the former better than the latter.

Wild turkeys look much different than regular ones, with a high, humped breastbone and freckled white skin. The freckling comes from the pigmentation in the feather quills—regular turkeys are bred with white feathers that leave no colored freckle when plucked. While wild turkeys may look meaty, they actually have a very low meat-to-bone ratio. Their weight ranges from only 6 to 12 pounds. Allow about 1½ pounds per person. Due to supply-and-demand problems, you may not get the exact size bird you ordered. More than once I have had to supplement a wild turkey with a small ham or another main dish because the butcher only had tiny birds available. They are very lean, and should be roasted only from 170° to 175°F or the meat will dry out. The dark meat may be a little pink, but it is safe to eat. If you prefer your dark meat more well done, just pop the sliced meat back into a 400°F oven for a few minutes—it will probably be cooked by the time you get around to serving the mashed potatoes.

My neighbor swears by kosher turkeys. What makes them different?

Kosher turkeys are raised free-range in a manner similar to organic turkeys and are fed antibiotic-free feed. They are slaughtered and salted according to Jewish dietary laws. Some cooks feel that the slaughtering gives the birds a fresher, cleaner taste. The salting seasons the turkeys and makes their meat somewhat firmer than that of regular birds. These extra steps are labor-intensive, so kosher turkeys always cost more. Many kosher turkeys are frozen, so defrost them properly to protect your investment.

Getting Ready

How much turkey should I buy?

Estimate 1 pound per person, which allows for a modest amount of seconds or leftovers. Larger toms are very chesty with lots of breast meat, so you will get more servings from a big bird.

My family likes white meat and we never have enough to go around. Any solutions?

Thanks to the year-round popularity of turkey, it's easy to buy individual parts to roast for extra servings. Most packaged parts have cooking instructions, but here are some general guidelines:

For extra white meat, buy turkey breast halves. (Turkey breast halves, with the skin and bone, are tastier than boneless, skinless breasts, and cook more quickly than whole breasts.) Place them in an oiled roasting pan, rub with softened butter, and season with salt and pepper. Add ½ cup broth or water to the pan. Roast in a preheated 350°F oven, basting occasionally, until a meat thermometer reads 170°F, 20 to 25 minutes per pound.

If you need extra drumsticks or wings, always a favorite with kids, they can be roasted in the same manner, allowing 1½ to 2 hours at 350°F to cook until tender.

I have a huge crowd coming, but I can't handle roasting and carving two turkeys. Now what?

You will need two ovens. In the first oven, roast a large tom to present as a centerpiece; it can be carved while everyone admires it. In the second oven, roast turkey parts as directed above. The turkey parts will only take an hour or two to roast. Cover them loosely with aluminum foil and keep them in a warm place until ready to serve. (The USDA advises not holding cooked poultry for longer than 1 hour.) The second oven will now be empty and available to bake all the side dishes.

What tools are essential for roasting the perfect turkey?

You'll need a high-quality roasting pan, a roasting rack, a meat thermometer, an oven thermometer, and a bulb baster.

A *high-quality roasting pan* makes all the difference in the world. A heavy, dark metal pan allows the drippings to brown beautifully, and turns gravy making into a snap. Buy the best roasting pan you can afford. Some of them may seem expensive, but you will probably never need to buy another one again. My favorite roasting pan measures 18 × 14 × 3 inches. Whether you choose a nonstick pan or not is a matter of personal choice. The dark surface of a nonstick pan absorbs heat and creates especially dark drippings, an advantage when it comes time to make the gravy. On the other hand, heavy pans with stainless steel interiors are excellent, and the smooth surface cleans easily. A turkey roasting pan should be fairly shallow so the air can circulate around the bird and promote browning. Choose the largest pan that fits your oven and accommodates the size turkey you roast most often. (I've heard many a tale about the turkey that wouldn't fit into the pan, or the pan that wouldn't fit into the oven.)

Old-fashioned speckled blue enamel turkey roasters only do a fair job. Those grooves in the bottom of the pan don't serve much purpose and are an obstacle at gravy-making time. The sides are too high and block the heat that makes for good browning. If you have a covered turkey roaster, don't use the lid—uncovered turkeys brown best.

I am no fan of disposable aluminum foil roasting pans. They buckle under the weight of most turkeys, and are almost impossible to make gravy in. The bright metal allows the oven heat to bounce off the pan's surface and inhibits the browning of both the turkey and the drippings. Roast a turkey in an aluminum foil pan and you are guaranteed wimpy-looking drippings that will make bland, beige gravy that needs to be colored with a gravy booster. Aluminum foil pans are too high to allow for proper heat and air distribution. Don't tell me that you prefer them to a good roasting pan because you only do a turkey once a year! Once you have a beautiful heavy pan, you'll find lots of uses for it all year long. If you *absolutely* have to use an aluminum foil pan, at least put it on a large baking sheet to make it easier to take in and out of the oven. Better yet, buy two and insert one inside of the other for increased stability. (You may even be able to pull off making gravy in a double-thick aluminum pan.)

Turkey should always be baked on a *roasting rack*. If the turkey is placed on the bottom of the pan, it can stick. Also, the back of the turkey simmers in the juices, so when you go to lift the bird out of the pan, the wings usually fall off (after all, they've been stewing in liquid for hours). Even though the turkey can be roasted on a flat rack, an adjustable roasting rack is more versatile, as it can be folded up into a V shape for cooking cylinder-shaped meat roasts, too. The racks that are permanently fixed in a wide, flat U shape are also good.

The best way to tell when any poultry or meat is done is with a *meat thermometer*. An old-fashioned meat thermometer is inserted into the poultry before it is put into the oven, and stays there throughout roasting. Its thick stem can make a large hole in the meat that releases juices. Most cooks prefer instant-read thermometers, which have thin stems and are used only when actually checking the temperature. In fact, never leave an instant-read thermometer in the oven or the plastic top will melt. My favorite is the *probe-style thermometer*, which is attached to a monitor outside the stove so you can easily check the progress without opening the oven door. You can also set the timer to sound when the desired internal temperature is reached, and some models have portable alarms so you don't even have to be in the kitchen to hear the beep. *Pop-up thermometers* are good indicators of doneness, but are not always reliable. It's not that they don't work, but sometimes they get glued shut by the basting juices. Always back up the pop-up with a reliable meat thermometer, and do not count on the pop-up alone.

An *oven thermometer* is the only way to determine your oven's true temperature. A turkey is one of the largest things that you will ever cook in the oven, and a few degrees' discrepancy can make a big difference. Never trust the thermostat dial. I have gotten in the habit of bringing my own oven thermometer with me when I cook at a friend's house, because every oven is off to some degree. Alcohol-filled glass thermometers are the most accurate, but spring thermometers are less expensive and work well, too.

Basting helps brown the bird, sealing the

skin and holding in juices. A *bulb baster* makes the job easy. Basters with metal syringes aren't worth the money, as the fat lubricates the metal and the rubber bulb slides off. The one I like best is made of plastic with a flat rubber bulb that allows the baster to stand straight up on the counter.

Any other goodies that I can pick up at the kitchenware store?

I use a *bamboo skewer* or a *thin metal skewer* to close the neck cavity. Just in case you have to tie the drumsticks together, get a ball of *cotton kitchen twine*. Many cooks like *turkey lifters*, which make it easier to remove the turkey from the pan, but take care to buy ones that won't tear the crisp turkey skin. You will need a *serving platter* big enough to hold the bird. And if you don't have a good *carving set*, with a long, thin-bladed, sharp knife and a meat fork, now's the time to get one.

How do I get the bird ready for roasting?

Take the bird out of its plastic wrapper and rinse it well, inside and out, under a thin stream of cold running water. This is not actually washing the bird, just refreshing it, and this step is optional. If you choose to rinse the bird, to avoid cross-contamination, take care not to splash any of the water on your kitchen counter. Place the bird onto a work surface and pat it completely dry with paper towels. Remove the neck from the body cavity, and *don't forget the package of giblets in the neck*! But if you ever do leave them in, don't worry, as they are packed in oven-safe materials and the cooked giblets won't hurt anyone. Pull out the lumps of pale yellow fat on either side of the tail area. Reserve the fat: It can be tossed into the roasting pan to increase the amount of drippings or added to the stockpot.

After preparing the bird, be sure to wash the cutting board, your hands, and any utensils well with soap and hot water.

What about that metal clip in the tail area?

Some poultry producers provide a metal or plastic clip, called a "hock lock," which secures the drumsticks in place. Don't remove it! It will save you the trouble of having to tie the drumsticks together with kitchen string. Sometimes, the producers cut a strap of skin near the end of the body cavity, which also acts to hold the drumsticks.

Cooking the Turkey

Sometimes my turkey breast turns out dry. Why?

Dry turkey is caused by overcooking. Admittedly, roasting a whole turkey is problematic. When was the last time you roasted *anything* that was 25 pounds? The main problem is the turkey itself. The white meat is done to perfection at 170°F, and above that temperature it begins to dry out and get stringy. On the other hand, the dark meat isn't tender until 180°F. It disturbs me to see recipes that suggest cooking the turkey to only 170°F. Granted, the white meat is cooked just right, but at that temperature the dark meat still looks pink and rare and hasn't developed a roasted flavor. Although the meat is safe to eat, it looks and tastes undercooked. Luckily, there are ways to "trick" the white meat into staying moist for the extra time it takes for the dark meat to cook that extra 10 degrees.

There are so many ways to roast a bird, it's hard to decide which is the best method for me. What are your favorites?

My Favorite Method. The Perfect Roast Turkey with Best-Ever Gravy on page 56 is my adaptation of the traditional method that uses a moderately low oven temperature of 325°F. Temperatures above that tend to shrink the turkey, and any temperature below 325°F is unsafe. My secret to avoiding dried-out meat? I tightly cover (not just tent) the breast area with aluminum foil, which traps the steam and keeps the breast moist. During the last hour of roasting, I remove the foil to allow the skin to brown.

Bottom Line. This time-tested method doesn't call for any special skills, and roasts a wonderful, juicy turkey with an old-fashioned flavor. It also makes a picture-perfect bird that looks like a Norman Rockwell magazine cover. The only drawback is that it takes time, but sometimes patience is its own reward.

High-Oven Method. The turkey is roasted in a very hot oven, sealing the skin and holding in the juices. This method gives a richly colored, moist bird with a deep, roasted flavor in just a couple of hours. You'll find it detailed in Oven-Blasted Turkey on page 57. Be sure your oven is impeccably clean before roasting, and be warned that it will certainly need to be cleaned afterward. You must use a heavy roasting pan and a fresh bird that hasn't been injected with any moistening agents. The hot turkey must be turned from side to side to get it evenly roasted—this calls for an agile, strong cook. Also be aware that the drippings can be burned beyond repair, leaving you to make a sauce on the side.

Bottom Line. The bird is delicious made this way and cooks in record time, but it's a method for experienced cooks with self-cleaning ovens, lots of oven cleaner, or hired help.

Brine Method. Proponents of the brine method (which is used to make the Herb-Brined Roast Turkey on page 59) report that soaking the turkey in salted water makes it juicier and better seasoned. However, the added moisture is not actually turkey juices, just salt water, so don't be fooled. You must have a large receptacle to soak the bird and a place to keep it chilled overnight. Most people don't have a refrigerator big enough to hold a huge stockpot. The most convenient place to brine turkey is in an ice chest. The brining does increase the moistness, but it also firms and seasons the flesh in a way that some people may not like.

Bottom Line. If your goal is a juicy bird, this method is a worthwhile effort, once you surmount the logistical problems of chilling the soaking bird. Just be prepared for some guests who might not like the flavor and texture change of the "enhanced" turkey. My recipe for The Perfect Roast Turkey with Best-Ever Gravy (page 56) produces such a moist bird that I find brining entirely extraneous.

Grilled Turkey. Grilling is fast becoming the preferred method of Thanksgiving cooks who love to cook outdoors. Weather can be an issue, but such a little thing doesn't deter dedicated grillmasters. Grilling gives a smoked-scented bird with a deep brown skin. This method (which is used in the recipe for Smoked, Cider-Basted Turkey on page 61) works best with birds no larger than 12 pounds. No one believes me when I say this, but please trust me. The drippings may be too smoky to make gravy, so plan to serve a sauce or salsa on the side.

Bottom Line. If the weather is cooperating (while I have grilled in the snow, I don't recommend it), and your family and friends enjoy nontraditional flavors, grill the bird.

Deep-fried Turkey. A contender for the "What a great turkey, but . . ." award. A favorite of Cajun cooks (see Bayou Deep-fried Turkey on page 64), the turkey is deep-fried in only

45 minutes. The skin turns out golden and crispy, and the meat is deliciously juicy. If you have a 10-gallon stockpot with a deep-frying basket, a 125,000-BTU propane ring burner, a full tank of propane, and 5 gallons of cooking oil handy, this could be the bird for you. But only if you have nerves of steel and an old set of clothes that you are willing to get oil-splattered, and are willing to forgo the stuffing and gravy. The method works best with smaller birds, so don't plan to feed a crowd.

Bottom Line. I'm not saying this method isn't good, I'm only saying it is more work than most of us are willing to do. And it can be very dangerous, so keep your wits about you. Note that the Underwriters Laboratories, which test and set standards for appliances, have declined to give their approval to any model of turkey fryer. If that doesn't tell you something . . .

What are some of your least favorite methods for cooking turkey?

I am almost loath to mention these methods, because if your mom's turkey is criticized, I'm asking for trouble. But remember that I cook turkeys all year long, not just one day a year. I have taken a good, hard, objective look at roasting turkeys, and I think it's best to steer you away from potential disaster.

Upside-down Turkey. Some cooks believe that roasting the bird upside down allows the juices to run into the breast and keep it moist. During the last hour of roasting, the bird is turned right side up. I remember the year that my friend Michelle and I tried this method. The person who gave us the instructions forgot to mention putting the bird on a rack, and when we went to turn the bird right side up, about half of the breast stuck to the pan. In subsequent, nonholiday kitchen tests, the turning always made for some kind of disaster (usually the skin tears around the drumsticks) and the bird ended up looking as if it had been in an accident. If you have ever tried to turn a hot, greasy 25-pound turkey right side up, especially after having downed a Bloody Mary, you know it is a job not to be taken lightly. There are easier ways to keep the breast moist.

Cheesecloth Turkey. The oiled turkey is covered with cheesecloth dipped in melted butter. I have no idea what advantage it provides—could the cheesecloth act as a wick, drawing the juices over the breast? The cheesecloth is pulled off during the last hour of roasting, but mine always seems to stick to the skin. If you can discern any improvement of flavor or moisture, you are better than I am.

Paper Bag Turkey. I haven't been able to try this method recently, even though it was popular when I was growing up. These days, it's hard to find paper bags that are large enough, and most supermarkets have converted to plastic bags. I wouldn't advise roasting a turkey in today's chemical-loaded recycled paper bags anyway.

Roasting Bag Turkey. The concept of the paper bag turkey generally has been replaced by cooking the turkey in the modern roasting bag. The bird turns out steamed, not roasted, and a pale steamed turkey isn't my idea of a terrific Thanksgiving centerpiece. The turkey tends to fall apart when you take it out of the bag (that is, when the bag doesn't stick to the bird). If you decide to try this method, and it is a timesaver, note that the instructions that come with the bag do not say to season the turkey. When I called the company's consumer hotline to ask about this, the person I spoke with said the company assumes that most people who use their product will be using defrosted frozen self-basting turkeys that are already seasoned from the moistening agents. Season birds that are not self-basting. My Thanksgiving nightmare turkey would be a self-basted bird in a roasting bag. I know a lot of people cook their turkey this way, but it sure doesn't taste like roast turkey to me!

Foil-Wrapped Turkey. Again, the bird ends up steamed, not roasted, and lacks flavor and color. But again, it saves time.

Overnight Turkey. Never try to roast a turkey overnight at low temperatures. It is a very unsafe method that creates the warm, moist atmosphere that can turn the inside of your turkey into a Petri dish. And never partially roast the turkey, refrigerate it, and try to finish the cooking later. It is equally dangerous.

I have a convection oven, but I am nervous to try convection on my holiday turkey. What to do?

Don't be nervous! The vast majority of cooking schools, where I perfected these recipes, have convection ovens, and I use them more often than not. (However, the estimated cooking times in this book are for conventional ovens.) The circulating hot air of a convection oven gives the turkey an evenly browned surface, but with the added advantage of reducing the estimated roasting time. The common rule of conversion from conventional roasting to convection heat is to reduce the temperature by 25°F, and to cut the time by one-third. I follow the temperature adjustment when I am making smaller items like baked goods, but for a large turkey, I keep the temperature at 325°F, and leave it at that. If the turkey is done a bit ahead of time, so much the better.

What about stuffing the bird?

In recent years, this issue has become quite a hot potato, as some cooks are concerned about the stuffing encouraging dangerous bacterial growth inside the bird. If you follow the guidelines on how to stuff the bird safely, you'll have no problems. The only time I consider not stuffing the bird is to save time. An unstuffed turkey weighs less and cooks more rapidly. The bird is just as tasty without the stuffing. (Whether the stuffing is as tasty cooked outside of the bird is a matter of personal taste.)

If you choose not to stuff the turkey, there are two excellent ways to add flavor to the bird and drippings. I usually replace the stuffing with a vegetable seasoning: Chop 1 large onion, 1 large carrot, and 1 large celery rib with leaves. Mix with 2 tablespoons chopped parsley, 1 tablespoon poultry seasoning (preferably Homemade Poultry Seasoning on page 79), 1 teaspoon salt, and 1/4 teaspoon freshly ground black pepper. The vegetables are only a seasoning—don't serve them as a side dish.

Or stuff the neck and body cavities with fresh herbs. I use about 2 packed cups mixed fresh thyme, sage, rosemary, parsley, and marjoram sprigs for a 20-pound bird. This potpourri adds an incredible scent to the turkey and makes the gravy terrific.

If you don't stuff the turkey, at the end of the roasting period, tilt the bird so the juices that have collected in the cavity run into the pan drippings, where they will add flavor.

If I stuff the bird, do I have to sew up the openings to hold it in?

It is unnecessary to sew up a bird. To hold the neck stuffing in place, skewer the neck skin to the back skin with a bamboo or thin metal skewer. To protect the exposed stuffing from overbrowning, just cover it loosely with a small piece of foil. But if your grandma taught you to sew up the stuffing in the bird, and you have good tailoring skills, go right ahead. Use a strong mattress or sailing-canvas needle, available at sewing stores, for the job. These also have eyes big enough to thread thick kitchen twine.

Do you have to truss a turkey with string?

A trussed bird is more evenly roasted and holds its shape. Many cooks truss their birds with crisscrosses of string, but I never tie up my bird more than necessary. To secure the wings, fold them back ("akimbo") behind the turkey's shoulders. If the wings are too big to be folded back, then tie them alongside the body with string. To hold the drumsticks, insert them into the hock lock. If the bird doesn't have a hock lock or a strap of skin to hold the drumsticks, tie them together with string. If you are out of string, use unwaxed dental floss (I don't have to say "unflavored," do I?).

With the oven-blasted method, the turkey is easier to turn if it is trussed in the classic French manner, so instructions are included with that recipe.

What do you put on the outside of your turkey?

Not much—butter, salt, and pepper. I massage the bird with softened unsalted butter, but you can also brush it with melted butter. The butter melts to ensure drippings for basting and the gravy, and its dairy proteins promote browning. Vegetable oil or margarine do not work as well. I season the bird with salt and pepper, nothing else. If the bird is seasoned on the outside with herbs, they often scorch during the long roasting period. Some cooks slip fresh herbs or an herb butter under the breast skin to add flavor. That it does, but during roasting, the herbs turn dark and look unappetizing. Paprika, which some people use on the bird as a browning agent, is particularly extraneous. When the correct oven temperature is used, your bird will be a gorgeous golden brown, even without paprika.

Generally, I don't glaze the bird, as some of the glaze always drips into the roasting pan and ends up in the gravy.

Do you like to baste the turkey?

Basting promotes browning, and the hot drippings help seal the skin and hold in the juices. Baste every 45 minutes or so, and do it quickly so the temperature doesn't fall while the oven door is open.

At the beginning of roasting, I pour turkey stock into the roasting pan. The stock adds moisture to the oven interior (again, helping keep that turkey moist), and gives me something to baste *with*. Experienced cooks know that it takes quite a while for a turkey to release enough juices and rendered fat to create enough drippings for basting. As the stock evaporates, its flavor concentrates and enriches the drippings.

That being said, there have been times when I simply forgot to baste the turkey until the very end of the roasting. You know what? It still turned out fine. My conclusion is, baste when you remember to, and don't make too big a deal over it.

My mom always tents the bird with aluminum foil. What does that do?

Tenting is another Great Thanksgiving Myth. Loosely tenting the bird at the beginning of roasting doesn't do much. If you want to keep the turkey from drying out, the breast area must be *tightly* covered with foil, as directed in the recipe for Perfect Roast Turkey with Best-Ever Gravy (page 56). Some cooks tent the turkey if it seems to be browning too much. But if your oven is at the right temperature (325°F), the turkey will brown at the correct rate and not need tenting.

Why are turkey roasting times always approximate?

There are a number of factors that determine how turkeys cook.

- The bigger the bird, the more meat on the bones. It takes less time for oven heat to pass through soft muscle than hard bone. Therefore, it takes more time per pound to roast a small hen than a large tom. Factor in the various conformations of the birds, and you can see why a certain leeway is needed.

- The differences in oven temperatures. Use an oven thermometer!
- Sporadic heat loss from opening the oven door. Don't baste more often than every 45 minutes, if at all. You can wait until the last hour to baste, if you wish.
- The exact temperature of the turkey when it goes in the oven. Unless the recipe says otherwise, the timings are always for refrigerator-temperature turkeys.

When you estimate your cooking time, err on the long side, because if the turkey is done early, it will stay warm for up to an hour. In fact, turkey *should* rest for at least 20 minutes before carving anyway.

Start testing your bird for doneness about 30 minutes before the end of the estimated roasting time, just to be sure the turkey doesn't overcook. Remember, an overcooked bird is a dry bird.

How can you tell when the turkey is done?

The best way is tell is with a meat thermometer, preferably an instant-read probe model. Inserted into the thickest part of the thigh, but not touching a bone (which conducts heat and would give an incorrect reading), it should register 180° to 185°F. This exact spot is somewhat difficult to determine, but if you picture the turkey's imaginary "panty line" (that is, the area where the thigh and the drumstick converge), you'll have a good idea. Also, the thigh and drumstick will feel tender when pressed with a finger. Do not cook the turkey until the drumstick jiggles, meaning that the collagen in the joints has completely dissolved, and indicating that the bird is overcooked. The turkey will have released a lot of juices into the bottom of the pan that probably weren't there the last time you looked.

Serving the Turkey

What kind of wine should I serve with turkey?

Turkey can be served with just about any wine, and it really boils down to personal preferences. Often, I consider the seasonings in the side dishes to help me make my decision. Spicy flavors would be better complemented by a Gewürztraminer than a Pinot Grigio. If I want to serve the same wine throughout the meal, my favorite white is a full-bodied Chardonnay, because it also complements many soups and salads. When your first course is creamy, you may want a crisp, slightly sharp Sauvignon Blanc to balance the richness. For a red wine, I usually choose a light-bodied varietal, maybe one of the current Beaujolais Nouveau, which have just arrived in early November. To my taste, full-bodied reds are just too much to handle at the typical Thanksgiving spread with lots of contrasting flavors. But with a deep-flavored heritage or wild turkey, I'd pour a richer Pinot Noir. One of my favorite Thanksgiving dinner beverages is a hard, dry apple or pear cider. Served well chilled, it is very refreshing.

Are there any special ways to garnish the turkey?

Usually, a beautiful serving platter is all that a turkey needs. If you don't have one, you'll have to improvise. One year, visiting friends in the country, I forgot to bring my turkey platter, so we used a broiler pan—heavily garnished, but it worked.

Even with an heirloom platter, you may want to gild the lily. Dark curly kale makes an attractive bed for nestling the golden-brown bird. Surround the turkey with small gourds, tiny ears of dried Indian corn, bouquets of fresh herbs, or nuts in their shells. Many fresh fruits make beautiful decorations. Try clusters of grapes or kumquats with their leaves, miniature Lady Apples or Seckle or Forelle pears, or a scattering of fresh cranberries, all of which are in season during the holiday season. If you plan to carve the bird at the table, have an empty bowl handy to hold the garnishes—while they look lovely, they can get in the way of carving. Fresh fruits can be rinsed, dried, and returned to the fruit bowl to serve later in the meal.

I'm nervous about carving the bird. Help!

Let the turkey stand for at least 20 minutes before carving. The bird will stay perfectly hot for up to 1 hour. You may cover the turkey with aluminum foil and a kitchen towel to help retain the heat, but I find this is unnecessary, and it softens the skin. Once I timed how long it took a 25-pound, hot-out-of-the-oven, 180°F turkey to cool off, and it took 3 hours. This short rest period of 20 minutes allows the juices, which have been forced by the oven heat to the center of the bird, to retract back into the meat, helping retain moisture and firming the meat for easy carving. Most people are so thrilled to have the turkey done that they rush it to the table for carving. The juices run out of the turkey and all over the tablecloth.

Carving is simple with a long, thin, very sharp knife and a sturdy meat fork. An electric knife is a very good investment, even if you only use it on holidays. As odd as it seems, think of the turkey in terms of human anatomy—that is, the leg is connected to the thigh; the turkey's wing is its arm, which connects to the shoulder joint; and so on—it will help you figure out what you're doing.

Have an empty platter nearby to hold the sliced meat. If you are carving for a crowd, you may want two platters, one for dark and one for white. Try to avoid carving for each individual in turn, as you will have to alternate carving the light and dark meat, and that gets crazy. Carve the entire bird, then serve it. Before you get started, scoop all of the stuffing out of the cavity and place it in a serving dish.

Here are the steps for carving a turkey:

1. Remove the drumsticks to make the breast easier to reach and carve. Cut off each drumstick at the knee joint. If the turkey is properly cooked (to at least 180°F), they will pull away without any trouble, making the joints easy to sever. Do not remove the thighs at this point or the bird will roll around the platter while you try to carve it. Transfer the drumsticks to a platter. To allow more people to enjoy the dark meat, tilt each drumstick, holding it from the foot end, and cut downward along the bone to slice the meat.

2. Hold the breast firmly with the meat fork. One side at a time, make a deep incision and cut parallel to the table down near the wing into the rib cage.

3. Cut down along the side of the breast to carve it into thin slices. Every slice will stop at the parallel cut. Transfer the sliced breast to the platter. Turn the turkey around to carve the other side.

4. Pry the thighs away from the hips to reveal the ball joints, and sever at the joints. Transfer the thighs to the platter. To carve each thigh, hold the thigh with a meat fork and carve the meat parallel to the bone.

5. Pry the wings away from the shoulder joints and sever at the joints. Transfer to the platter.

If you still feel nervous about carving in front of your guests, present the whole roast bird at the table in all its glory. Then hightail it back into the kitchen and carve the meat where no one is looking.

As a final fillip, pour a ladle of piping-hot turkey stock over the sliced turkey. The hot stock will help heat up any meat that might have cooled, and make the platter look irresistibly juicy. Yes, it's cheating, but I won't tell.

After Thanksgiving dinner, I need a nap. Is there something in turkey that makes me tired?

If you are so full after dinner that you need to lie down, don't blame the turkey! Recent studies show that a carbohydrate-rich Thanksgiving dinner is the culprit, as the carbs increase the number of tryptophans in the brain. It's not a normal meal that includes so many carbohydrates, with mashed potatoes, sweet potatoes, stuffing, and gravy, just for starters.

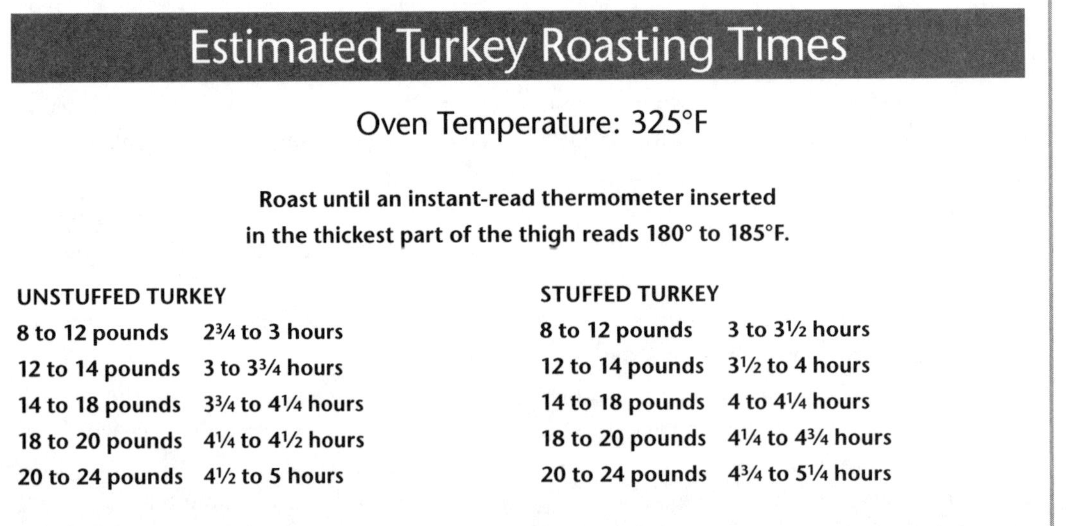

Estimated Turkey Roasting Times

Oven Temperature: 325°F

Roast until an instant-read thermometer inserted in the thickest part of the thigh reads 180° to 185°F.

UNSTUFFED TURKEY	
8 to 12 pounds	2¾ to 3 hours
12 to 14 pounds	3 to 3¾ hours
14 to 18 pounds	3¾ to 4¼ hours
18 to 20 pounds	4¼ to 4½ hours
20 to 24 pounds	4½ to 5 hours

STUFFED TURKEY	
8 to 12 pounds	3 to 3½ hours
12 to 14 pounds	3½ to 4 hours
14 to 18 pounds	4 to 4¼ hours
18 to 20 pounds	4¼ to 4¾ hours
20 to 24 pounds	4¾ to 5¼ hours

It's Not Thanksgiving Without . . . Turkey

It is assumed that wild turkeys were served at that first Thanksgiving in 1621. The firsthand accounts of the menu only mention "fowl." As main courses go, we do know that the Pilgrims had venison, cod, and lobster on the table. So why don't we have surf-and-turf instead of turkey?

The turkey is an impressive bird, with its bronze feathers, unusual head markings, and showy tail.

The wild turkey was native to North and Central America, and domesticated by the Aztecs. No one knows when the first turkey traveled to Europe, but the birds seem to have been brought to Spain by conquistadors in the early 1500s. The turkey quickly established itself as *the* bird to serve at festive occasions, especially in Italy, France, and England, and was bred into a plumper version. This new, improved turkey was brought back to the Americas, where it cross-bred with its wild cousin to make the breed we know today. The Pilgrims were well acquainted with the bird, and must have been relieved to find a familiar food in this strange land.

No one really knows how the turkey got its name. Some think that early explorers, thinking they were close to India, misidentified the bird and called it *tuki*, or Indian for peacock. Because it also resembled a guinea fowl, which came from Africa via Turkish merchants, it could have picked up the name by another misappropriation of origin. (Guinea fowl were also called turkeys.) It could have gotten its name from one of its calls, which sounds like "turk, turk, turk."

Because turkeys were so abundant in colonial America, they were a major source of nourishment for our country's forefathers. In a well-known letter to his daughter, Benjamin Franklin expressed his dismay over the eagle's being chosen as the official United States bird. Referring to the eagle's "bad moral character," he went on to say, "I wish that the bald eagle had not been chosen as the representative of our country! The turkey is a much more respectable bird, and withal a true original native of America."

While about 675 million pounds of turkey are served each Thanksgiving, in recent years its healthy profile and versatility have changed the turkey from a holiday bird to one that competes with other meat and poultry on a year-round basis. Surprisingly, Americans do not eat the most turkey. The Israelis usually come in first in the turkey-eating lineup, at about 27 pounds per capita, while we weigh in at around 18.5 pounds. In third place is France, at approximately 13.5 pounds.

Most turkeys are of the White Holland variety, which have a lot of white breast meat, which over 70 percent of Americans prefer. In fact, turkeys are so chest-heavy that they cannot get close enough to mate. All commercially raised turkeys are artificially inseminated.

Perfect Roast Turkey with Best-Ever Gravy

After trying every turkey roasting method under the sun, this is the one I come back to, and the one I always teach at my cooking classes and use in my magazine articles. Its main feature is the trick of protecting the breast with aluminum foil to keep it nice and juicy. This method is especially useful with organic or heritage turkeys, which can be leaner than mass-produced birds. Instructions here are for an average-sized 18-pound turkey, but the instructions can expand or reduce depending on the size of your bird. Read the information about stuffing and gravy on pages 81 and 117. If you prefer to roast an unstuffed turkey, use the vegetable seasoning on page 50.

Makes about 18 servings, with about 7 cups gravy

One 18-pound fresh turkey
About 12 cups of your favorite stuffing
8 tablespoons (1 stick) unsalted butter, at room temperature
Salt and freshly ground black pepper
2½ quarts Homemade Turkey Stock 101 (page 34), as needed
Melted unsalted butter, if needed
¾ cup all-purpose flour
⅓ cup bourbon, port, or dry sherry, optional

1. Position a rack in the lowest position of the oven and preheat the oven to 325°F.

2. Reserve the turkey neck and giblets to use in gravy or stock. Pull out the pad of yellow fat on either side of the tail and reserve. (These are sometimes already removed by the processor, so don't worry if they aren't present.) If you wish, rinse the turkey inside and out with cold water. Pat the turkey skin dry. Turn the turkey on its breast. Loosely fill the neck cavity with stuffing. Using a thin wooden or metal skewer, pin the turkey's neck skin to the back. Fold the turkey's wings akimbo behind the back (the tips will rest behind the turkey's "shoulders") or tie them to the body with kitchen string. Loosely fill the large body cavity with stuffing. Loosely cover the exposed stuffing with a piece of aluminum foil. Place any remaining stuffing in a lightly buttered casserole, cover, and refrigerate to bake as a side dish. Place the drumsticks in the hock lock or tie together with kitchen string.

3. Rub the turkey all over with the softened butter. Season with the salt and pepper. Tightly cover the breast area with aluminum foil. Place the turkey, breast side up, on a rack in the roasting pan. Place the reserved fat in the pan—it will melt during roasting and add to the drippings. Pour 2 cups of the turkey stock into the bottom of the pan.

4. Roast the turkey, basting all over every 45 minutes with the juices on the bottom of the pan (lift up the foil to reach the breast area), until a meat thermometer inserted in the meaty part of the thigh (but not touching a bone) reads 180°F and the stuffing is at least 160° F, about 4¼ hours. (See Estimated Turkey Roasting Times on page 54.) Whenever the drippings evaporate, add broth to moisten them, about 1½ cups at a time. Remove the foil during the last hour to allow the skin to brown.

5. Transfer the turkey to a large serving platter and let it stand for at least 20 minutes before carving. Increase the oven temperature to 350°F. Drizzle ½ cup turkey stock over the stuffing in the casserole, cover, and bake until heated through, about 30 minutes.

6. Meanwhile, pour the drippings from the roasting pan into a heatproof glass bowl, measuring cup, or fat separator. Let stand for 5 minutes; then skim off and reserve the clear

yellow fat that rises to the top (for a separator, pour off the drippings and reserve both drippings and fat). Measure ¾ cup fat, adding melted butter, if needed. Add enough turkey broth to the skimmed drippings to make 8 cups total.

7. Place the roasting pan over two stove burners on low heat and add the turkey fat. Whisk in the flour, scraping up the browned bits on the bottom of the pan, and cook until lightly browned, about 2 minutes. Whisk in the turkey stock and the optional bourbon. Cook, whisking often, until the gravy has thickened and no trace of raw flour flavor remains, about 5 minutes. Season with salt and pepper. Transfer the gravy to a warmed gravy boat, straining the gravy, if desired, through a wire sieve. Carve the turkey and serve the gravy alongside.

Oven-Blasted Turkey

In the late 1990s, there was a fad for turkeys roasted at a very high oven temperature. The method was introduced to mainstream America in Barbara Kafka's cookbook *Roasting*. When it was promoted one year as "the" turkey recipe in the *New York Times*, it guaranteed that thousands of people would try it. Plenty of kitchen smoke alarms went off that year. This recipe is at opposite ends of the roasting spectrum from my Perfect Roast Turkey with Best-Ever Gravy (page 56), which uses a relatively slow temperature to discourage shrinkage. The high-temperature method blasts the outside of the bird with very hot air to seal the skin to hold in juices, and it does make a very tasty bird with a rich, roasted flavor. But here are some things to watch out for:

- **Unless you have an excellent kitchen ventilation system, do not attempt this recipe, as there will be some smoke no matter what you do. The oven must be very clean before roasting, as any old splatters will burn and really smoke up the kitchen.**
- **The original high-roast turkey recipes called for trussing the turkey, turning it often during roasting, and other chores. I just roast it on a rack without turning, and the results are excellent.**
- **You must use a heavy, high-quality roasting pan. The thinner the pan, the more likely the drippings are to burn. Do not use a disposable aluminum foil pan.**
- **The bird should be around room temperature to cook most quickly. However, never let an uncooked turkey stand out of the refrigerator for longer than 1 hour. To bring down the temperature, rinse the bird under lukewarm water for about 20 minutes.**
- **For the most even cooking, use a small (12- to 14-pound) turkey, allowing about 8 minutes per pound for an unstuffed bird. If you use a larger bird, the drippings will certainly burn beyond repair during the longer roasting period.**
- **I use this method when I am in a hurry, and as unstuffed turkeys cook more quickly than stuffed ones, I don't weigh the bird down by stuffing it. Instead, I used a light, chopped vegetable and fresh herb mixture that serves to season the juices. You can stuff the turkey with your favorite dressing, if you wish, allowing an extra 2 minutes per pound of turkey.**
- **It's difficult to predict whether the roasting pan drippings will be too dark to use for gravy or if they'll be fine. (The thickness of the pan and whether it is dark or shiny are**

some factors that affect the drippings' color.) As a safety precaution against burned drippings, prepare Head Start Gravy (page 120). If the drippings taste all right, stir the gravy base into the degreased drippings and reheat in the pan. If they have burned, discard them and reheat the previously prepared gravy base without the drippings to serve instead. Either way, you won't be left with an empty gravy boat.

Makes 10 to 12 servings

One 12- to 14-pound fresh turkey, neck and giblets reserved for another use, and fat at tail area discarded
1 medium onion, chopped
1 medium celery rib with leaves, chopped
2 tablespoons chopped fresh rosemary
2 tablespoons chopped fresh sage
2 tablespoons chopped fresh thyme
1¼ teaspoons salt
1 teaspoon freshly ground black pepper
4 tablespoons (½ stick) unsalted butter, melted
4 cups Head Start Gravy (page 120)

1. Position a rack in the lower third of the oven and preheat the oven to 425°F.

2. Place the turkey in a large bowl and then in the sink, directly under a thin stream of lukewarm water. Let the water run over the turkey until the turkey has lost its chill, about 15 minutes.

3. Drain the turkey and pat the skin dry. Turn the turkey on its breast. Mix the onion, celery, rosemary, sage, thyme, ½ teaspoon of the salt, and ½ teaspoon of the pepper in a medium bowl. Fill the neck cavity with the vegetable-herb mixture. Using a thin metal skewer, pin the turkey's neck skin to the back. Fill the large body cavity with the remaining vegetable-herb stuffing. Place the turkey on a roasting rack in a heavy-duty roasting pan. Brush the turkey all over with the melted butter, then season with the remaining ¾ teaspoon salt and ½ teaspoon pepper.

4. Roast the turkey, basting with the pan juices after 45 minutes, until a meat thermometer inserted in the thickest part of the thigh reads 180°F, about 1¾ hours.

5. Transfer the turkey to a serving platter and let stand for at least 20 minutes before carving. If the drippings are black and taste burned, discard them and serve the turkey with the reheated gravy. If the drippings look and taste fine, pour them into a separator cup, leaving the browned bits in the pan. Let stand for 5 minutes, then pour off, reserving the drippings and discarding the fat. Return the dark drippings to the pan and place the pan on two burners over medium-high heat. Add the gravy and bring to a boil, scraping up the browned bits in the pan with a wooden spatula. Simmer until the gravy thickens. Strain and transfer to a warmed gravy boat.

6. Carve the turkey and serve with the gravy.

Herb-Brined Roast Turkey

Brined turkey first made a splash a few years ago in the pages of *Cook's Illustrated* magazine, whose editors, in turn, derived their recipe from a Portuguese version in Jean Anderson's *The Food of Portugal* (with a few tips from kosher butchers along the way). The brining idea is a good one, as the bird soaks up moisture and seasoning (I include herbs for added flavor), but the logistics can be daunting. I have done my best to simplify the procedure.

- When I teach this method in my classes, it is not universally loved. The public has become salt-conscious, if not salt-phobic. Some people don't like the extra seasoning, and find the turkey meat too salty. And the brine firms the meat to give it a texture that some find odd. Don't kid yourself—brining does not make a juicier bird. It is salted water that you taste, not turkey juices. Critics of the brining method argue that you might as well buy a frozen bird, which has also been treated with salted water. But brining is insurance against a dry bird.
- This method only works with fresh turkeys—self-basting, frozen, or kosher turkeys have already been salted, so don't use them. If you are spending the money on a beautiful, organically raised turkey, I would think twice about brining because it changes the natural flavor of the bird. I like this method best for supermarket-quality, commercially raised fresh turkeys.
- You'll need a container big enough to hold your turkey. You will see recipes that require a huge (minimum 5-gallon) stockpot, but few home cooks have such a utensil. Also, the combined weight of the turkey, brine, and pot could challenge your refrigerator shelf, especially if it is plastic. I enclose the turkey and brine in jumbo oven-roasting bags, then keep the brined turkey chilled in an ice chest.
- To estimate the amount of brine, place the turkey in the bags in the ice chest, and measure the cold water needed to cover the bird completely. The proportions in the recipe are for 2 gallons water, but the amount of brine can be adjusted as needed. For each 2 quarts water, use 1/4 cup plain salt; 1/4 cup sugar; 1 1/2 teaspoons each rosemary, thyme, and sage; and 3/4 teaspoon each marjoram, celery seed, and peppercorns.
- Use plain, noniodized table salt for the brine. Kosher salt is problematic because the crystal size changes from brand to brand. If you wish, use twice as much kosher salt by volume, or 2 cups kosher salt for 1 cup plain salt. Fine sea salt often has a finer grain than the iodized salt, so you need slightly less (about 3/4 cup plus 2 tablespoons) if you substitute for plain salt. I know that many cooks have their favorite salt, but in this case I find that for consistency's sake, plain salt is the best choice, and that a particular salt's subtleties are muddled with the flavors of the turkey and herbs.
- The turkey must be well chilled during brining. Surround the brined turkey in its bag with lots of ice cubes (buy bags of ice if you don't want to deplete your freezer's supply), or use frozen "blue-ice" packs.
- Don't run the risk of the risk of stuffing the turkey, as the salty juices could ruin it. Instead, loosely fill the cavities with seasoning vegetables and bake the stuffing on the side.
- As the pan drippings will be seasoned by the brine as well, they could be too salty to guarantee palatable gravy. It's a good idea to

prepare Head Start Gravy (page 120), and add the degreased drippings as needed to color and season it, stopping when the gravy is salted to taste.

Makes 12 to 16 servings

BRINE

1 cup plain (noniodized) table salt
1 cup packed light brown sugar
2 tablespoons dried rosemary
2 tablespoons dried thyme
2 tablespoons dried sage
1 tablespoon dried marjoram
1 tablespoon celery seed
1 tablespoon whole black peppercorns
6 quarts ice water

One 14- to 18-pound turkey, neck and giblets reserved for another use, and fat at tail area discarded
1 medium onion, chopped
1 medium carrot, chopped
1 medium celery, chopped
6 tablespoons (¾ stick) unsalted butter, at room temperature
4 cups Head Start Gravy (page 120)

SPECIAL EQUIPMENT

2 jumbo (turkey-sized) oven-roasting bags
A large ice chest, to comfortably hold the brined turkey
About 10 pounds ice cubes or 2 "blue-ice" packs, frozen

1. To make the brine, in a large stockpot, mix 2 quarts water with the salt, sugar, rosemary, thyme, sage, marjoram, celery seed, and peppercorns. Bring to a boil over high heat, stirring until the sugar and salt are dissolved. Remove from the heat. Add the ice water and stir until the ice melts and the brine is very cold.

2. Place the turkey in a roasting bag, then slip the bagged turkey into the second bag to make a double thickness. Place the turkey in the ice chest. Pour the brine into the bag. Close the bag, being sure that the turkey is completely covered with brine, and with a rubber band. Surround the bagged turkey with ice cubes or blue-ice packs. Close the chest and let the turkey stand for 10 to 16 hours. Do not brine the bird for longer than 16 hours or the flavor and texture will be compromised.

3. Position a rack in the lower third of the oven and preheat the oven to 325°F. In a small bowl, mix the onion, carrot, and celery.

4. Remove the turkey from the brine and rinse well, inside and out, under cold running water. Pat the skin and body cavities dry with paper towels. Turn the turkey on its breast. Loosely fill the neck cavity with the onion mixture. Using a wooden or metal skewer, pin the turkey's neck skin to the back. Fold the turkey's wings akimbo behind the back or tie to the body with kitchen string. Loosely fill the large body cavity with the remaining onion mixture. Place the drumsticks in the hock lock or tie together with kitchen string.

5. Place the turkey, breast side up, on a rack in the roasting pan. Rub all over with the butter. Pour 2 cups water into the bottom of the pan.

6. Roast the turkey, basting all over every 45 minutes with the juices on the bottom of the pan, until a meat thermometer inserted in the meaty part of the thigh (but not touching a bone) reads 180°F and the stuffing is at least 160°F, about 4½ hours. (See Estimated Turkey Roasting Times, page 54.) Whenever the drippings evaporate, add more water, about 1½ cups at a time.

7. Transfer the turkey to a large serving platter and let it stand for at least 20 minutes

before carving. Pour the pan drippings into a separator cup, leaving the browned bits in the pan. Let stand for 5 minutes, then pour off and reserve the drippings and discard the fat. Place the roasting pan on two burners over medium-high heat. Add the gravy and bring to a boil, scraping up the browned bits in the pan with a wooden spatula. Gradually add the dark, degreased pan drippings until the gravy is salted to taste. Simmer until the gravy thickens. Strain and transfer to a warmed gravy boat.

8. Carve the turkey and serve the gravy alongside.

Smoked, Cider-Basted Turkey

Smoking adds a robust flavor to turkey. The turkey is cooked by the indirect method, where the bird is cooked by the radiating heat supplied by a bank of coals. Of course, the bird can be cooked on a gas grill, too, but I much prefer the deeper flavor provided by charcoal.

- **This method smokes the turkey in a standard 22½-inch charcoal grill. The turkey can also be smoked on a gas grill, but the recipe was not designed for use in a water smoker, which should be used according to the manufacturer's instructions.**
- **Two accessories, available to owners of Weber charcoal grills, will help simplify indirect cooking. One is a hinged cooking grate that makes it easier to add the ignited coals to the grill. To hold the charcoal in a mound and concentrate its heat, use a basket-shaped charcoal holder. If your grill didn't come with these accessories, you may want to mail-order them from Weber-Stephen Products at 1-847-934-5700, or call other manufacturers to see if they have similar products.**
- **Allow about 15 minutes per pound of turkey. If the grill temperature fluctuates, adjust the timing.**
- **Smoke the turkey in a disposable aluminum foil roasting pan. The smoke will discolor the pan, so you won't want to use your best roaster.**
- **Maintain a grill temperature of about 325°F. With a charcoal grill, you will need to add coals every 40 minutes or so to keep up the heat.**
- **Even with a gas grill, it is a challenge to maintain an even temperature. The weather is a factor (cold breezes can chill the outside of the grill and affect the inner temperature, too), as well as the kind of charcoal used (briquettes burn more evenly and slowly, while hardwood charcoal burns very hot and quickly, and I often mix the two to get the best from each). If you can, cook the turkey in a grill that has a thermometer in the lid. Otherwise, place an inexpensive oven thermometer next to the turkey on the grill to monitor the temperature, or insert a prong-style deep-frying thermometer in the lid vent. Don't open the lid too often because the heat will escape.**
- **Smaller 12- to 14-pound turkeys cook best on the average grill. It's risky to cook big turkeys outside, because a big bird won't even fit onto a typical gas grill. (A Weber gas grill can cook a turkey up to 18 pounds. The unique design has burners that go front-middle-back, instead of side by side, and they have more cooking space. To fit the burner configuration, choose a turkey with an elongated, not round, shape.) If you insist on**

barbecuing a large bird, grill it with plenty of wood chips for about 1½ hours to get it nice and smoky. Then, transfer it to a solid metal roasting pan and continue cooking it indoors in a preheated 325°F even for the rest of the time.

- **Smoke-cooking gives the turkey a very dark brown skin. If the bird is getting too dark, tent it with foil. Also, there will be a thin layer of pink under the skin, caused by the smoke, which is harmless and does not indicate that the turkey is undercooked.**

- **To my taste, regular stuffing gets oversmoked inside a barbecued bird. I substitute a seasoning mixture of apples and onions. My favorite dressing, baked separately, is Southwestern Chorizo Dressing (page 84).**

- **For real Western flavor, serve the turkey with Cranberry-Pineapple Salsa (page 114). If you want gravy, be flexible, as the condition of the pan drippings is unreliable. With a charcoal grill, ashes from the coals could blow into the drippings. Even if they are clean, or you have cooked the bird in a gas grill, they can be too smoky. Make Head Start Gravy on page 120. Pour the drippings into a separator cup, leaving the browned bits in the pan. Discard the fat from the cup and taste the drippings. If they aren't too smoke-flavored or gritty with ashes, stir the hot gravy into the pan, scraping up the browned bits with a wooden spoon (you won't be able to place the aluminum foil pan on the stove, so just scrape up what you can), then pour in the drippings to color the gravy. If the drippings aren't usable, just serve the Head Start Gravy without the drippings.**

Makes 8 to 12 servings

CIDER BASTE

4 tablespoons (½ stick) unsalted butter
⅓ cup finely chopped shallots or red onion
2 garlic cloves, minced
1 tablespoon chili powder
One 12-ounce bottle hard dry apple or pear cider
1 teaspoon dried rosemary
1 teaspoon dried sage
½ teaspoon salt

1 medium apple, peeled, cored, and chopped
1 small onion, chopped
2 garlic cloves, minced
1½ teaspoons chili powder
½ teaspoon dried rosemary
½ teaspoon dried sage
½ teaspoon salt
One 12- to 14-pound turkey, neck and giblets reserved for another use, fat from tail area discarded
Cranberry-Pineapple Salsa (page 114)

6 cups mesquite or applewood chips, soaked in water for at least 30 minutes, drained

1. To make the cider baste, melt the butter in a medium saucepan over medium heat. Add the shallots and garlic and cook, stirring often, until softened, about 1 minute. Add the chili powder, and stir for 30 seconds. Add the cider, rosemary, sage, and salt. Bring to a simmer and reduce the heat to very low. Simmer for 10 minutes. Cool completely.

2. In a small bowl, mix the apple, onion, garlic, chili powder, rosemary, sage, and salt. Turn the turkey on its breast. Loosely fill the neck cavity with the apple mixture. Using a thin wooden or metal skewer, pin the turkey's neck skin to the back. Fold the turkey's wings akimbo behind the back or tie to the body with kitchen string. Loosely fill the large body cavity with the remaining apple mixture. Place the drumsticks in the hock lock or tie together with

kitchen string. Place the turkey on a roasting rack in a large disposable aluminum foil pan. Set aside while you light the grill.

3. *For a charcoal grill*, light 3 pounds of charcoal briquettes on one side of a grill and let burn until covered with white ash. Place the roasting pan on the cooking grate on the empty side of the grill opposite the coals. Sprinkle a handful of drained wood chips over the coals. *For a gas grill*, preheat the grill on High. Wrap a handful of dried wood chips in a packet of aluminum foil. Tear open the top of the packet to expose the chips. Place the packet directly on the source of heat. With the grill lid open, let the chips ignite (this may take about 10 minutes). Turn one burner off, and adjust the other(s) on Medium to Low to regulate the heat to 325°F. Place the roasting pan in the cool (off) part of the grill.

4. Pour 2 cups water into the roasting pan. Baste the turkey with some of the cider mixture. Cover the grill and cook until a meat thermometer inserted in the thickest part of the thigh reads 180°F, 3 to 3½ hours. *For a charcoal grill,* add more briquettes and drained wood chips every 40 minutes or so to maintain a temperature of about 325°F, and baste the turkey. *For a gas grill,* add a handful of drained wood chips every 40 minutes to the foil packet. *For both grills,* as the liquid in the pan

The Great Blackened Turkey (Almost) Disaster

My mom and dad called me for a recipe for grilled turkey. While relating it, I warned them that a big bird really doesn't fit on a regular grill. Of course, they listened politely, and then went right out and bought their usual bird—which is about the size of a '64 Volkswagen.

Dad got up early and stuffed the bird into his Weber. Like most California men over the age of eighteen, my father is a grilling expert, specializing in burgers and ribs (the barbecuing gene is part of our family's DNA makeup). But he didn't know what to expect from a whole turkey.

My folks' patio is right outside their dining room. Relaxing at the table, sipping his Bloody Mary, Dad calmly glanced out to see that the grill had so much smoke coming out of it, it looked like Mount Saint Helens. He ran outside to find that the bird, one side of which was hanging over the coals, was burned black.

Well, Dad wasn't about to throw out a turkey and start all over from scratch. So, after a consultation with Mom, he decided to protect the blackened parts of the bird with foil and finish roasting it in the oven. The rest of my family took the situation in stride—after all, the prized breast meat was unscathed.

When the bird was served, everyone swore it was the best bird they ever had. And the "blackened" parts of the bird were fought over by relatives who like crispy skin. They said it was the best turkey they ever had.

evaporates, add more water to keep the drippings from burning. If the turkey is getting too brown, tent it with foil.

5. Transfer the turkey to a serving platter and let stand for 20 minutes before carving. Carve and serve with the salsa.

Bayou Deep-fried Turkey

Every time I turned around, another person was telling me about how deep-frying turkey was the best method known to man. A quick Internet search revealed hundreds of deep-fried turkey sites, all with guaranteed recipes, some only a couple of paragraphs long, to describe what is not a procedure for inexperienced cooks. (The most detailed was from my friend "Hoppin' " John Taylor, from his *The Fearless Frying Cookbook.*) Some of my guests did love the crisp golden skin and moist, tender meat. It certainly is the quickest way to cook a bird—about 3 minutes a pound.

For years it has been a staple at Cajun-country cookouts, where it makes sense. In Louisiana, at church suppers where they are cooked outdoors in 10-gallon pots with the same equipment used for fish fries, deep-fried turkeys are no hassle. Outside of the Bayou, I have my reservations. When I first started frying turkey, I had to gather a battery of equipment, including a 10-gallon stockpot with a fryer insert and a propane ring, at a professional restaurant supplier. Now you can buy inexpensive outdoor deep-fryer kits just about anywhere.

- **Of all the turkey cooking methods, this takes the most organization. You must keep your wits about you, so stay out of the Bloody Marys. Also, discourage kids and pets from coming around the pot.**

- **Place the propane burner on a level dirt or grass surface. There are heatproof protectors (they look like big doormats) designed for grills that also work for deep-fryers. Splattering oil will stain concrete driveways, and wood decks could catch fire. Do not fry turkeys in attached buildings, such as garages, or near bushes. Of course, in inclement weather, the area must be covered. Do not leave the burner, not even for a second. I made this mistake, and when I returned, found that some paper had blown into the burner and started a scary fire. Have a fire extinguisher or baking soda nearby.**

- **You *will* get oil on your clothes, so wear old ones. An apron is not enough protection.**

- **Many of those Internet recipes from pseudo-gourmets call for cooks to inject the bird with spicy liquid seasonings from a marinating syringe, although the herbs and spices in the recipe I tried wouldn't go through the tiny nozzle. Anyway, this seasoning detracts from the natural turkey flavor. It does absolutely no good to season the bird with salt, pepper, spice rubs, or the like, as they wash off into the oil. Also, additional moisture will only increase the chances of the oil bubbling over. (A brined turkey, with all that extra liquid, could cause the same dangerous scenario.) Allow each person to season his own serving with salt, pepper, and hot red pepper sauce. A squeeze of fresh lemon juice is also an excellent accent.**

- **Buy the vegetable oil at a wholesale price club or Asian grocer for the best price. Because of its high smoke point, many cooks suggest expensive peanut oil; regular vegetable oil works just as well. Save the oil container, as you will probably need it to dispose of the used oil. Let the oil stand overnight in the pot to cool completely, then funnel it back into its container for disposal.**

- **Do not even think about using the oil again. It is very easy for previously used oil to catch fire when reheated. You must factor the oil into your budget. And seriously consider how you will dispose of the dirty cooking oil. My township's health department told me to flush it but I don't have a septic system.**

- **Heat the oil to 390°F, using a long-stemmed deep-frying thermometer to gauge the heat. Watch the oil carefully because if it begins to smoke (usually around 410°F), the turkey will have an off flavor. When the turkey is added to the hot oil, the temperature will drop. Adjust the heat as needed to keep the oil around 365°F.**

- **The amount of oil called for here works for a 10-pound turkey. To double-check the amount of oil needed, place the turkey in the pot and fill the pot with water until it reaches 1 to 2 inches above the turkey. To allow for the inevitable oil bubbling, the pot must never be more than two-thirds full. Remove the turkey and measure the amount of water. Dry the turkey and the pot very well to reduce splattering.**

- **The frying basket keeps the turkey from touching the bottom of the pot, where it could burn. It is not an optional tool. If you can't locate a basket, place a large collapsible metal vegetable steamer or colander in the pot before adding the oil. Some deep-fried turkey equipment suppliers sell a turkey holder, a kind of hook that looks like a fireplace holder, that can be used to lower the bird into the hot oil.**

- **Small 10- to 14-pound turkeys work best. If you have a lot of guests, cook two birds. After cooking the first bird, cover it loosely with aluminum foil to keep warm as the second bird fries. A better solution is to roast a second bird because cold fried turkey isn't very tasty.**

- **Do not stuff turkeys for deep-frying. Bake the Sausage Gumbo Dressing (page 84) on the side for the perfect partner.**

- **If you want gravy, use Head Start Gravy on page 120, perhaps spiked with 1 tablespoon bourbon for every 1 cup liquid, and well seasoned with hot red pepper sauce.**

- **Be sure your propane tank is full. You don't want to run out of gas in the middle of frying.**

Makes 10 to 12 servings

One 10- to 14-pound fresh turkey, neck and giblets reserved for another use, and fat from the tail area discarded
5 gallons vegetable oil, as needed
Salt, pepper, hot red pepper sauce, and fresh lemon wedges, for serving

SPECIAL EQUIPMENT

One 10- to 12-gallon stockpot
Large deep-frying basket insert for stockpot
A 12-inch propane gas burner with at least 100,000 BTUs (an electric hot plate will *not* work)
A long-pronged deep-frying thermometer for outdoor frying, or a conventional deep-frying thermometer attached to a long piece of flexible wire
Oven mitts
A large roasting pan

1. Rinse the turkey well, inside and out, with lukewarm water to help remove the chill from the bird. Pat the turkey completely dry, inside and out, with lots of paper towels. If the turkey is too cold or has any moisture at all on its surface, the oil will splatter dangerously when the turkey is added to the pot. Fold the turkey wings akimbo behind the shoulders.

Remove the hock lock and do not tie the drumsticks together. Place the turkey on a large wire rack and let it stand while the oil is heating.

2. Place the stockpot on the burner and add enough oil to reach two-thirds up the sides of the pot. Attach the deep-frying thermometer. (If using a conventional thermometer, attach it to the pot handle with thin, flexible wire so its tip is submerged 1 to 2 inches into the oil.) Light the fire and heat the oil to 390°F. This will take about 30 minutes, depending on the burner's efficiency. Be sure that the flames are not licking the outside of the pot.

3. Place the well-drained turkey, breast first, in the basket. Wearing oven mitts, carefully lower the basket into the oil. The oil will bubble up dramatically, so don't be surprised. Lift up the turkey, and dip it again into the oil three or four times before leaving it in the pot. This allows the oil temperature to gradually adjust to the turkey and reduces the initial bubbling. Fry the turkey, allowing about 3½ minutes per pound, until golden and a meat thermometer inserted in the thickest part of the thigh registers 175°F (the temperature will rise 5° to 10°F while the turkey stands), about 45 minutes. Adjust the heat as needed to maintain the oil temperature at 365°F.

4. Lift the basket out of the oil and transfer to the roasting pan. Drain the turkey completely, especially the body cavity, allowing the oil to drain into the pan. Let the turkey stand for at least 20 minutes before carving. Carve and serve, letting each guest season the turkey with salt, pepper, hot pepper sauce, and lemon juice.

French Boned Turkey with Pâté Stuffing

This is one of the most elegant and flavorful ways to serve the holiday bird. This is the kind of turkey you would find on many French tables at Christmastime. It translates well to our Thanksgiving. Sure, it takes ingenuity to bone a turkey, but it's not really hard to do—given you have a good sharp boning knife. Some people may find the sauce, called *demi-glace* by French cooks, easier to make than old-fashioned gravy. Because it is no more than concentrated stock, it must be the very best homemade variety.

- **While boning the turkey, try keep the skin as intact as possible. If you do make a couple of holes, they can be sewn shut with kitchen twine. After the turkey is roasted and the twine pulled out, no one will know.**
- **Boned turkey gives you lots of turkey parts that should be turned into stock. Save the neck, giblets, wing tips, thigh bones, carcass, and any trimmings. Chop the neck and carcass into manageable pieces. Make Homemade Turkey Stock 101 (page 34), using only 1 turkey wing and substituting the turkey pieces for the remainder of the wings.**

Makes 8 to 10 servings

Make Ahead: The turkey can be boned up to 1 day ahead, covered, and refrigerated.

STUFFING

½ cup diced (½-inch) pitted dried plums (prunes)
½ cup Madeira or tawny port
2 tablespoons unsalted butter
½ cup finely chopped shallots
1 pound ground pork
1 pound ground turkey or ground veal

¾ cup fresh bread crumbs, made from day-old crusty bread
¼ cup coarsely chopped shelled pistachios
¼ cup chopped fresh parsley
1 large egg plus 1 large egg yolk
2 teaspoons salt
1 teaspoon dried thyme
½ teaspoon freshly ground black pepper

One 11-pound fresh turkey, neck and giblets reserved for another use, fat from tail area discarded
2 tablespoons unsalted butter, melted
Salt and freshly ground black pepper
About 2 quarts Homemade Turkey Stock 101 (page 34)

SPECIAL EQUIPMENT

A sharp, thin-bladed boning knife
Kitchen twine
A sturdy, large (mattress or sailing) needle

1. To make the stuffing, place the prunes and Madeira in a small bowl, and let stand for 1 hour. (Or cover with plastic wrap and microwave on High for 1 minute, carefully uncover, and let stand for 10 minutes.)

2. In a medium skillet, melt the butter over medium-low heat. Add the shallots and cook, stirring often, until softened, 1 to 2 minutes. Transfer to a large bowl and cool slightly. Add the ground pork, ground turkey, dried plums and Madeira, bread crumbs, pistachios, parsley, egg, egg yolk, salt, thyme, and pepper. Mix well. Cover and refrigerate until ready to use.

3. To bone the turkey, use a heavy cleaver or large knife to chop off the first two joints of each wing (the tip and the center bone), and reserve for the stock. Place the turkey, breast side down, on the work surface. Using the boning knife, make an incision down the backbone. Keeping the point of the knife pointed toward the bones, make short slashes down one side of the rib cage until you reach the ridge of the breastbone. Repeat the procedure on the other side. Cut the carcass away from the turkey at the breastbone (be careful, it's close to the skin). To remove the thick silver tendon running down each breast, make a cut to reveal the wide end of the tendon and hold it. Pulling the tendon, scrape it with the knife to release it from the flesh.

4. Bend the thigh back to reveal the ball joint, and sever the ball joint. Holding the ball joint, scrape along the thighbone to reach the drumstick joint. Sever the drumstick joint and remove the thighbone, leaving the drumstick bone intact. Repeat with the other thigh. Remove the spatula-shaped collarbone. Leave the wing joints intact. (The turkey can be boned up to 1 day ahead, covered tightly, and refrigerated.)

5. Position a rack in the center of the oven and preheat the oven to 350°F.

6. Place the boned turkey, skin side down, on the work surface. Form the stuffing into a loaf shape and place down the center of the turkey. Bring both sides of the boned turkey up to enclose the stuffing. Using kitchen twine and a mattress needle, sew up the turkey. Tie the turkey crosswise in several places to form it into an elongated shape.

7. Place the turkey on a long roasting rack (or use two overlapped wire cake racks) in a roasting pan. Brush with the melted butter and season with ½ teaspoon salt and ¼ teaspoon pepper. Pour 2 cups of the broth into the pan.

8. Roast, basting occasionally with the pan juices, until a meat thermometer inserted in the thickest part of the turkey reads 175°F, about 3 hours. If the drippings evaporate and threaten to burn, moisten then with 2 cups additional stock. (With a boned turkey, the dark-meat area will not look undercooked at this temperature, as it does with bone-in turkey.) Transfer the

turkey to an oval serving platter, and tent with aluminum foil to keep warm. Let the turkey stand for 20 minutes before slicing.

9. Pour the pan drippings into a separator cup. Let stand 5 minutes, then pour off and reserve the drippings and discard the fat. Place the roasting pan on two burners over high heat. Pour the drippings into the pan. Pour in 1 quart of stock. Bring to a boil, scraping up the browned bits in the pan with a wooden spoon. Boil until syrupy and reduced to ¾ cup, about 12 minutes. Season to taste with salt and pepper. Pour the sauce into a warmed sauceboat.

10. Remove the strings. Carve the turkey crosswise into thick slices. Serve, drizzling a bit of sauce over each portion.

Whole Turkey Breast with Walnut-Raisin Stuffing

By no means are my Thanksgiving guest lists predictable. Sometimes it's dinner for twenty, and sometimes for six. One year, I decided a whole bird wasn't necessary for our small gathering, and as I was leaving the next day on a trip, I didn't want to worry about a lot of leftovers. We had this whole turkey breast, stuffed under the skin with a walnut-raisin dressing. My guests loved its traditional flavors in a contemporary setting, and I appreciated its easy preparation.

Makes 6 to 8 servings

Make Ahead: Stuff and roast the turkey breast just before serving.

STUFFING

12 tablespoons (1½ sticks) unsalted butter
½ cup finely chopped leeks (white and pale green parts)
1 medium carrot, finely chopped
1 medium celery rib, finely chopped
¼ teaspoon salt
¼ teaspoon freshly ground black pepper
6 cups seasoned bread stuffing cubes (about 11 ounces)
1½ cups Homemade Turkey Stock 101 (page 34)
½ cup raisins
½ cup toasted, coarsely chopped walnuts
1½ teaspoons poultry seasoning, preferably homemade (see page 79)

One 7-pound whole turkey breast
2 tablespoons unsalted butter, melted
Salt
Freshly ground black pepper
About 3⅓ cups Homemade Turkey Stock 101 (page 34)
⅓ cup all-purpose flour

1. To make the stuffing, in a medium skillet, melt 2 tablespoons of the butter over medium-low heat. Add the leeks, carrot, and celery, and cover. Cook, stirring occasionally, until tender, about 10 minutes. Season with the salt and pepper, and transfer to a large bowl. Add the remaining 10 tablespoons butter to the skillet and melt. Pour into the bowl. Add the stuffing cubes, stock, raisins, walnuts, and poultry seasoning, and mix well.

2. Position a rack in the center of the oven and preheat the oven to 325°F.

3. Rinse the turkey breast under cold water and pat dry. Slip your fingers underneath the skin to loosen it from the breast. Spread about one-third of the bread mixture under the skin, smoothing it to an even thickness. Place the remaining stuffing in a buttered casserole and cover to bake later as a side dish. Place the turkey breast on a roasting rack in a roasting pan. Brush with the melted butter and season

with ½ teaspoon salt and ¼ teaspoon pepper. Pour 2 cups water into the pan.

4. Roast, basting occasionally, until a meat thermometer inserted in the thickest part of the breast reads 170°F, about 2¼ hours. During the last 30 minutes, drizzle the reserved stuffing with ⅓ cup broth and bake with the breast to reheat.

5. Transfer the breast to a serving platter and set aside. Meanwhile, pour the drippings from the roasting pan into a separator cup. Let stand 5 minutes; then pour off the drippings and reserve the drippings and fat. Measure ⅓ cup fat, adding melted butter, if needed. Add enough turkey stock to the drippings (there won't be many) to make 3 cups total.

6. Place the roasting pan over a stove burner on low heat. Add the reserved turkey fat. Whisk in the flour, scraping up the browned bits on the bottom of the pan, and cook until lightly browned, about 2 minutes. Whisk in the turkey stock. Cook, whisking often, until the gravy has thickened and no trace of raw flour flavor remains, about 5 minutes. Season the gravy with salt and pepper. Transfer the gravy to a warmed gravy boat.

7. Carve the turkey and serve with the stuffing and gravy.

Wild Turkey with Wild Rice and Cherry Stuffing

An 11-pound wild turkey will feed only six to eight people. The meat a wild turkey does have is firm and full-flavored, but don't expect it to come cheaply. If your investment is cooked beyond 175°F, it will dry out, so keep an eye on the meat thermometer. Be sure to special-order your wild turkey, and be prepared for it to be a different weight than you expected. Small-scale turkey farms cannot always supply exact orders. Adjust the timing as needed, allowing about 15 minutes per pound for a stuffed turkey; 12 minutes per pound if unstuffed.

Makes 6 to 8 servings

Make Ahead: The wild turkey stock can be made up to 1 day ahead, cooled, covered, and refrigerated.

One 11-pound wild turkey, neck and giblets (except the liver) reserved
1 tablespoon vegetable oil
2 quarts Homemade Turkey Stock 101 (page 34)
Wild Rice, Dried Cherries, and Almond Stuffing (page 86)
4 tablespoons unsalted butter, softened, plus 2 tablespoons unsalted butter, chilled
Salt and freshly ground black pepper
2 teaspoons cornstarch
⅓ cup tawny or ruby port

1. At least 2 hours before roasting the turkey, chop the turkey neck into 1-inch pieces. Heat the oil in a medium saucepan over medium heat. Add the neck, turkey heart, and gizzard. Cook, stirring occasionally, until the turkey pieces are well browned, about 10 minutes. Add the stock, bring to a simmer over medium-high heat, scraping up the browned bits in the pan. Reduce the heat to very low and simmer for 2 hours. Strain the stock and set aside. Let stand 5 minutes and skim off any fat that rises to the surface. You should have 1½ quarts stock; add water to the stock, if needed. (The stock can be prepared up to 1 day ahead, cooled, covered, and refrigerated.) Set aside.

2. Position a rack in the lower third of the oven and preheat the oven to 325°F. Turn the turkey on its breast. Loosely fill the neck cavity with stuffing. Using a thin wooden or metal

skewer, pin the turkey's neck skin to the back. Fold the turkey's wings akimbo behind the back or tie to the body with kitchen string. Loosely fill the large body cavity with some of the stuffing, and cover the stuffing with foil. Place any remaining stuffing in a lightly buttered casserole, cover, and refrigerate to bake as a side dish. Tie the drumsticks together with kitchen string.

3. Place the turkey, breast side up, on a rack in the roasting pan. Rub all over with the 4 tablespoons softened butter. Season with ½ teaspoon salt and ¼ teaspoon pepper. Tightly cover the breast area with aluminum foil. Pour 2 cups stock into the bottom of the pan.

4. Roast the turkey, basting all over every 40 minutes with the juices on the bottom of the pan (lift up the foil to reach the breast area), until a meat thermometer inserted in the meaty part of the thigh (but not touching a bone) reads 170°F and the stuffing is at least 160°F, about 3 hours. Whenever the drippings evaporate, add water to moisten them (about 1½ cups at a time). During the last 45 minutes, remove the foil and baste a couple of times to brown the skin.

5. Transfer the turkey to a large serving platter and let it stand for at least 20 minutes before carving. Increase the oven temperature to 350°F. Cover and bake the stuffing until heated through, about 20 minutes.

6. Meanwhile, pour the drippings from the roasting pan into a separator cup. Let stand 5 minutes; then pour off and reserve the drippings and discard the fat. Return the drippings with the remaining 1 quart stock to the roasting pan. Place the roasting pan over two burners on high heat, and bring the stock to a boil, scraping up the browned bits on the bottom of the pan with a wooden spatula. Boil until the liquid is reduced to 2 cups, 10 to 15 minutes.

7. In a small bowl, sprinkle the cornstarch into the port and stir to dissolve. Stir into the pan and cook until the sauce is lightly thickened. Remove from the heat. One tablespoon at a time, whisk in the remaining 2 tablespoons butter until melted. Season with salt and pepper. Strain the sauce and pour into a warmed sauceboat.

8. Carve the turkey and serve with the stuffing and gravy. If the dark meat seems a bit pink, do not be concerned, because it is safe to eat. If you want it cooked longer for aesthetic reasons, cut the thighs and drumsticks from the carcass, and bake them at 350°F for a few minutes until the meat shows no sign of pink. Or microwave on High at 30-second intervals until the meat looks well done.

Turkey Breast with Wild Mushroom Stuffing and Marsala Sauce

Need a great low-fat Thanksgiving entrée? Look no further. A combination of fresh and dried mushrooms gives hearty flavor to the mild turkey breast, and it's further enhanced by a Marsala wine sauce. It meets the criteria for any good recipe, low-fat or not, and I serve it throughout the year at dinner parties, as well.

Makes 8 to 10 servings

Make Ahead: The breasts can be stuffed up to 4 hours ahead, covered, and refrigerated.

WILD MUSHROOM STUFFING

1 cup boiling water
1 ounce (about 1 cup) dried porcini mushrooms
8 ounces fresh mushrooms, preferably cremini
1 tablespoon unsalted butter
¼ cup finely chopped shallots
1 garlic clove, minced
1½ teaspoons chopped fresh rosemary or 1 teaspoon dried rosemary

½ teaspoon salt
¼ teaspoon freshly ground black pepper
½ cup fresh bread crumbs, preferably from day-old crusty bread
1 large egg white, beaten until foamy

Two 1½-pound boneless, skinless turkey breast roasts
Nonstick vegetable oil spray
Salt and freshly ground black pepper
1½ cups Homemade Turkey Stock 101 (page 34) or canned reduced-sodium chicken broth
1 teaspoon cornstarch
¼ cup dry Marsala
1 tablespoon unsalted butter, chilled

1. To make the stuffing, combine the boiling water and dried mushrooms in a small bowl. Let stand until the mushrooms soften, about 30 minutes. Lift the mushrooms out of the water, rinse under running water, and chop coarsely. Strain the cooking liquid through a wire sieve lined with a moistened paper towel set over a small bowl. Reserve the liquid.

2. In a food processor, pulse the fresh mushrooms until finely chopped. Set aside.

3. In a large skillet, heat the butter over medium heat. Add the shallots and garlic, and cook, stirring often, until softened, about 1 minute. Add the fresh mushrooms, soaked mushrooms, soaking liquid, rosemary, salt, and pepper. Cover and cook until the fresh mushrooms release some liquid, about 3 minutes. Uncover and cook over high heat until the liquid evaporates, about 10 minutes. Transfer to a medium bowl and cool completely. Stir in the bread crumbs and egg white.

4. Place a turkey breast, skin side down, on a work surface. Using a sharp knife, cut a deep, diagonal incision into the thickest part of the breast from the center of the roast almost to the edge, being careful not to cut completely through to the skin. Open this flap like a book. Make another cut on the other side, to butterfly the other side of the roast, and fold out in the other direction. Pound gently with a meat mallet, rolling pin, or empty wine bottle to flatten to an even thickness. Repeat with the other breast.

5. Spread half of the filling over one breast. Starting at a long side, roll up into a thick cylinder. Tie the breast crosswise in several places with kitchen string. Repeat with the remaining stuffing and breast. (The turkey breasts can be prepared up to this point 4 hours ahead, covered with plastic wrap, and refrigerated.)

6. Position a rack in the center of the oven and preheat the oven to 350°F. Spray a flameproof baking dish large enough to comfortably hold the turkey breasts with nonstick spray.

7. Spray a large nonstick skillet with nonstick spray and heat over medium heat until very hot. Season the turkey with ¼ teaspoon salt and ⅛ teaspoon pepper. Add the turkey breasts and cook, turning occasionally, until browned on all sides, about 6 minutes. Transfer the turkey to the prepared dish. Pour the broth into the dish and cover loosely with aluminum foil. Bake until a meat thermometer inserted in the centers of the breasts reads 165°F, about 40 minutes. Transfer the breasts to a serving platter and cover with aluminum foil to keep warm.

8. Place the roasting pan on top of the stove and bring the liquid to a boil over high heat. Boil until reduced to about ½ cup, about 8 minutes. In a small bowl, sprinkle the cornstarch into the Marsala, and stir to dissolve. Whisk into the pan and cook until lightly thickened. Remove from the heat and whisk in the butter until melted. Season with salt and pepper.

9. Discard the kitchen string. Slice the turkey into ½-inch thick slices. Serve immediately, drizzling each serving with the sauce.

Turkey Roulades with Prosciutto and Sage in Cranberry–Red Wine Sauce

There were only four of us for dinner that Thanksgiving. We had a full schedule of visiting friends, but we wanted to have dinner at home during a three-hour period between visits. Without any fuss, I prepared this spin on Italian saltimbocca, usually made with veal cutlets. *Saltimbocca* means "jump in mouth," which is exactly what these tender morsels will do.

- **Some turkey cutlets are one beautiful slice of turkey breast that is easy to roll. Other cutlets may look whole in the package, but separate into two or more pieces when taken out. Don't worry. Just overlap the slices back into a cutlet shape on a piece of moistened wax paper. Top with another piece of moistened wax paper, and lightly pound the edges together with a flat meat mallet or rolling pin to help them adhere. When the cutlets are rolled and cooked, any irregularities will disappear.**
- **Turkey cutlets are lean, and should be cooked over moderate heat, for they toughen if browned over the high heat we typically use for other meats and poultry.**
- **If you want to double the recipe, use two 12-inch skillets—the cutlets should not be crowded in the pan.**

Makes 4 servings

Make Ahead: The turkey cutlets can be rolled up to 8 hours ahead.

1½ cups (6 ounces) dried cranberries
½ cup hearty red wine, such as Chianti or Zinfandel
3 ounces sliced prosciutto, cut into pieces (about 1 × 2 inches) to fit each cutlet
8 turkey breast cutlets (about 2 pounds)
4 teaspoons chopped fresh sage
Wooden toothpicks, to secure roulades
1 tablespoon vegetable oil
Salt and freshly ground black pepper
3 tablespoons unsalted butter
2 tablespoons finely chopped shallots
¾ cup Homemade Turkey Stock 101 (page 34)
2 tablespoon balsamic vinegar
1 teaspoon light brown sugar
⅛ teaspoon crushed hot red pepper flakes

1. Place the cranberries in a wire sieve and rinse well under hot water to remove excess sugar. Drain well, place in a small bowl, and add the wine. Let stand for 1 hour. (Or cover with plastic wrap, microwave on High for 1 minute, carefully uncover, and let stand for 10 minutes.)

2. Place a piece of prosciutto on each cutlet and sprinkle with ½ teaspoon fresh sage. Roll up each cutlet into a cylinder and secure with a wooden toothpick. Place the roulades on a wax paper–lined plate and cover with plastic wrap. (The turkey cutlets can be prepared up to 8 hours ahead, covered, and refrigerated.)

3. In a 12-inch nonstick skillet, heat the oil over medium heat until very hot but not smoking. Season the roulades with ¼ teaspoon salt and ¼ teaspoon pepper. Add the roulades and cook, turning once, until lightly browned on both sides, about 4 minutes. Reduce the heat to medium-low. Cook gently until the roulades are cooked through and show no sign of pink when pierced in the center with the tip of a sharp knife, about 8 minutes. Transfer to a warmed serving platter and tent with aluminum foil to keep warm while making the sauce.

4. Return the skillet to medium heat. Add and melt 1 tablespoon of the butter. Add the shallots and cook, stirring often, until softened, about 1 minute. Add the cranberries with their wine, the stock, balsamic vinegar, brown sugar, and hot red pepper flakes. Bring to a boil over high heat and cook until the liquid reduces by half, about 3 minutes. Remove from the heat and whisk in the remaining butter, 1 tablespoon at a time. Season with salt.

5. Remove the toothpicks. Serve the roulades immediately, spooning the sauce over each serving.

Smoked Ham with Zinfandel-Orange Glaze

Sometimes you need to make your groaning board groan just a little more. A baked ham is a carefree and tasty way to feed a crowd, and it's a natural partner to turkey. A bone-in smoked ham has the best flavor, which can still be improved by bringing it to a simmer in a large pot of water to extract the excess salt. Basted with a not-too-sweet marinade, this gets a light glaze that goes with just about any menu. In fact, this has become one of my favorite dishes for any buffet, and from the amount of requests I get for this recipe, my friends must agree.

Makes about 16 servings

Make Ahead: The ham must marinate for 8 to 16 hours.

One 6½- to 7½-pound smoked ham
One 12-ounce jar bitter orange marmalade
½ cup hearty red wine, such as Zinfandel
½ cup fresh orange juice
2 garlic cloves, crushed under a knife

1. Place the ham in a large kettle and add enough cold water to cover. Bring to a simmer over medium-high heat. (This could take up to 45 minutes.) Drain the ham and cool completely.

2. In a medium bowl, whisk the orange marmalade, wine, orange juice, and garlic. Place the ham in a jumbo self-sealing plastic bag or oven roasting bag, then pour in the marinade. Close the bag and place in a large bowl. Marinate for at least 8 and up to 16 hours, turning occasionally.

3. Position a rack in the center of the oven and preheat the oven to 350°F. Line a roasting pan with aluminum foil.

4. Remove the ham from the marinade, scraping off any bits of orange marmalade. Strain the marinade and set aside. Place the ham on a roasting rack in the pan. Bake, basting occasionally with the marinade, until a meat thermometer inserted in the thickest part of the ham without touching a bone registers 140°F, about 1½ hours. (Allow about 15 minutes per pound.)

5. Transfer to a carving board or platter. Let stand for 15 minutes before carving.

Holiday Meatball Lasagna

For Italian-American families, pasta must be a part of the Thanksgiving menu, and usually lasagna plays just as big a starring role as turkey. Here, the meat for the sauce is rolled into little meatballs to make the dish extra special. It's a simple process, and you don't have to brown the meatballs—drop them into the simmering herb-scented tomato sauce.

Makes 8 to 12 servings

Make Ahead: The sauce can be prepared up to 2 days ahead, cooled, covered, and refrigerated; the lasagna can be prepared up to 1 day ahead and refrigerated. Both can be frozen for up to 1 month.

SAUCE AND MEATBALLS

2 tablespoons olive oil
1 large onion, chopped
3 garlic cloves, minced
1 cup dry red wine
One 28-ounce can tomatoes with added thick puree
Two 6-ounce cans tomato paste
One 8-ounce can tomato sauce
1½ teaspoons dried basil
1 teaspoon dried oregano
¼ teaspoon crushed hot red pepper flakes
1 pound ground round
1 pound ground pork
½ cup Italian-seasoned dried bread crumbs
2 large eggs, beaten
1½ teaspoons salt
½ teaspoon freshly ground black pepper

1 pound lasagna noodles
One 32-ounce container ricotta cheese
1½ cups (about 6 ounces) freshly grated Parmesan cheese
2 large eggs, beaten
⅓ cup chopped fresh basil or parsley
1 teaspoon salt
¼ teaspoon freshly ground black pepper
1½ pounds mozzarella cheese, thinly sliced

1. In a large Dutch oven, heat the oil over medium heat. Add the onion and cook, stirring often, until golden, about 5 minutes. Add the garlic and stir until fragrant, about 1 minute. Add the wine and bring to a boil. Stir in the tomatoes with their puree, 1 cup water, the tomato paste, tomato sauce, basil, oregano, and hot red pepper flakes. Bring to a boil, and reduce the heat to low. Simmer, uncovered, stirring occasionally, until slightly thickened, about 10 minutes.

2. In a large bowl, mix the ground round, ground pork, bread crumbs, eggs, salt, and pepper. Using about 1½ teaspoons for each, roll the mixture into small meatballs and place on a wax paper–lined baking sheet.

3. A few at a time, gently stir the meatballs into the simmering sauce. Return to the simmer and cook, stirring occasionally, until the sauce has thickened and the meatballs show no sign of pink when pierced in the center, about 20 minutes. Set the sauce aside. (The sauce can be prepared up to 2 days ahead, cooled, covered, and refrigerated, or frozen in airtight containers for up to 1 month.)

4. Meanwhile, bring a large pot of lightly salted water to a boil over high heat. Add the lasagna noodles, 2 or 3 at a time, and stir well. Boil, stirring occasionally to be sure the noodles don't stick to each other, just until tender, about 10 minutes. Drain and rinse under cold running water. (The noodles can be prepared up to 2 hours ahead, tossed with 1 tablespoon olive oil, and stored at room temperature.)

5. Position a rack in the center of the oven and preheat the oven to 375°F. Lightly oil a

10 × 15-inch baking dish. In a medium bowl, mix the ricotta, 1 cup of the Parmesan, the eggs, basil, salt, and pepper. Set aside.

6. Using a large skimmer or slotted spoon, transfer the meatballs to a large bowl. Coat the bottom of the prepared dish with ¼ cup of the tomato sauce. Arrange 5 lasagna noodles (4 horizontally and 1 vertically), slightly overlapping and cut to fit, in the dish. Spread half of the ricotta filling over the noodles. Cover with half of the mozzarella slices. Scatter half of the meatballs over the cheese, then top with one-third of the remaining tomato sauce. Arrange another 5 noodles in the dish. Cover with the remaining ricotta filling, remaining mozzarella, remaining meatballs, then half of the remaining sauce. Top with the remaining noodles, and spread with the remaining tomato sauce. Sprinkle with the remaining ½ cup Parmesan. Cover with aluminum foil. (The lasagna can be prepared up to 1 day ahead, cooled, covered, and refrigerated, or frozen, wrapped airtight, for up to 1 month.)

7. Bake for 30 minutes. Remove the foil and bake until bubbling throughout, about 30 minutes more. (If baking frozen lasagna, increase the initial baking time to 45 minutes, then uncover and bake for about 30 more minutes.) Let stand for 10 minutes before serving.

Butternut Squash and Rice Tian

Here's a terrific dish that serves two purposes. It is a substantial main course for vegetarians in the group, and it can be a savory side dish for turkey lovers. I used to serve a dramatic-looking, rice-stuffed pumpkin, but now I make this casserole, based on a Provençal favorite. Large pumpkins, while great-looking, have the least flavor, and there is a very fine line between the pumpkin being tender and falling apart. Keep this dish in mind for a supper or brunch main course when it isn't Thanksgiving.

Makes 8 to 12 servings

Make Ahead: The squash and sautéed vegetables can be prepared up to 1 day ahead.

3 pounds butternut squash
¼ cup extra virgin olive oil
1 large onion, chopped
1 large red bell pepper, cored, seeded, and chopped
2 garlic cloves, minced
1½ cups long-grain rice
6 large eggs
1½ cups (6 ounces) shredded Gruyère cheese
4 teaspoons chopped fresh sage or 2 teaspoons dried sage
¾ teaspoon salt
½ teaspoon freshly ground black pepper
½ cup fresh bread crumbs, preferably from day-old crusty bread
½ cup freshly grated Parmesan cheese

1. Using a sturdy vegetable peeler, peel the squash. Cut off the neck where it meets the bulb and reserve. Quarter the bulb. Scoop out and discard the fibers and seeds. Cut the squash neck and bulb into pieces about ½ inch thick and 1 inch long. You will have a variety of

shapes, but as long as they are relatively the same size, it doesn't matter.

2. Bring a large pot of lightly salted water to a boil over high heat and add the squash. Cook until barely tender when pierced with the tip of a sharp knife, 10 to 15 minutes. Drain and rinse under cold running water. Set aside. (The squash can be prepared up to 1 day ahead, cooled, stored in self-sealing plastic bags, and refrigerated.)

3. In a large skillet, heat 3 tablespoons of the oil over medium-high heat. Add the onion and red bell pepper and cook, stirring often, until the onion is golden, about 5 minutes. Add the garlic and stir until fragrant, about 1 minute. (The vegetables can be prepared up to 1 day ahead, cooled, stored in self-sealing plastic bags, and refrigerated.) Cool the vegetables until tepid, about 10 minutes.

4. Bring another pot of lightly salted water to a boil over high heat. Add the rice and cook until just tender, about 15 minutes. Drain, rinse under cold running water, and set aside.

5. Preheat the oven to 350°F. Lightly oil a 10 × 15-inch baking dish.

6. In a large bowl, beat the eggs. Add the rice, squash, sautéed vegetables, Gruyère, sage, salt, and pepper. Spread in the prepared dish. Mix the bread crumbs and Parmesan, and sprinkle over the top. Drizzle with the remaining 1 tablespoon oil.

7. Bake until the center feels set when pressed lightly, about 45 minutes. Serve hot, warm, or at room temperature.

Stuffings and Dressings

The Stuff That Dressings Are Made Of . . .

If you live north of the Mason-Dixon line, you probably call the savory side dish baked inside of a turkey "stuffing." If you are a Southerner, you probably know it as "dressing." (In classic cooking, such a mixture is called "forcemeat.") Until Victorian times, it was just called "stuffing." All of a sudden, stuffing seemed a bit improper, and dressing took over, especially in the South, where morals in society were well defined.

Stuffings are most commonly made with bread. While white sandwich bread is probably the favorite choice, other breads or starches can be turned into stuffing, depending on where the cook lives. On the West Coast, whole wheat or sourdough breads are often used, and the Amish can use rye bread (often with potatoes). Of course, in the South, few native cooks would dream of making their dressing from anything other than corn bread. Cooked grains make great stuffings, and again, the regional preferences come into play. Rice stuffing is a favorite in Louisiana and Texas, both big rice-producing states. Wild rice is used in the Great Lakes region, where it is abundant.

There is nothing wrong with packaged bread stuffing mix. In fact, the crisp texture of a mix ensures a moist, but not soggy, stuffing. If you want to use fresh bread (and I almost always do), it must be air-dried overnight. Use a firm sandwich bread like Pepperidge Farm or a high-quality, unsweetened bakery loaf. Crusty French or Italian breads make fine stuffing, too. With any bread, there is no need to cut off the crust. Don't use fluffy sandwich bread, which soaks up too much broth and makes soggy stuffing. Using a serrated knife, cut the bread into ½-inch cubes (or slightly larger for crusty breads.) If using corn bread, just crumble it. Let the cubes stand at room temperature overnight, uncovered, to dry out.

If you don't have the time to air-dry the bread, or you simply forget (which has happened to me more than once), bake the bread cubes to lightly toast and firm them. Spread the cubes on a baking sheet or two (they should not be crowded). Bake them in a preheated 350°F oven, stirring occasionally, until they are dry and beginning to crisp, 20 to 30 minutes. They do not have to color—they will crisp slightly upon cooling.

The amount of stock needed for the stuffing is variable, depending on the dryness of the bread. Be flexible, and stir in just enough stock to make a moist, but not wet, mixture. What is important here is the use of homemade turkey stock, and not canned chicken broth, for the stuffing. You want the stuffing to taste like turkey, not chicken. Even the most harried cook has the time to make the Small-Batch Turkey Stock (page 35) from the neck and giblets of the bird.

Allow about 3/4 cup stuffing for every pound of raw turkey (and for each serving). Never pack the stuffing into the bird, as it will expand when heated, and I have heard of birds cracking wide open because they were overstuffed. You do not have to sew up the openings. For the neck cavity, just pin the neck skin to the back with a thin metal or wooden skewer to enclose the stuffing. For the body cavity, cover the exposed stuffing with a small piece of aluminum foil.

You will rarely be able to stuff all of the dressing into the bird. Place the leftover stuffing in a buttered shallow baking dish and cover. Refrigerate the stuffing until ready to bake, up to 8 hours. To reheat, sprinkle the stuffing with about 1/2 cup turkey stock and bake in a preheated 350°F oven until heated to at least 160°F. The exact baking time, of course, depends on the amount of stuffing, but it generally takes about 30 minutes.

Bread Stuffing 101

Use this classic recipe, familiar in the best sense of the word, as the springboard for many equally classic variations. You can make your own variations by mixing and matching the different embellishments.

- **Most cooks use packaged cubed stuffing, which will give your stuffing a "just like Mom's" flavor. If you prefer crumb-texture prepared stuffing, use it. Skillet bread stuffings just aren't special enough for holiday meals.**
- **The directions on most stuffing bags recommend using two sticks of butter, which is too rich for me. If you wish, melt the extra stick of butter, and stir it into the stuffing with the broth.**
- **Even though stuffing cubes are often label "seasoned," they can be bland. If you think it needs it, add poultry seasoning.**
- **Homemade turkey stock makes the best stuffing, so make an effort to use it. In a pinch, you can use canned reduced-sodium chicken broth. The amount of stock needed will vary, depending on the dryness of the bread cubes and the moisture provided by the other ingredients.**

Makes about 10 cups stuffing

Make Ahead: See suggestions on page 81.

8 tablespoons (1 stick) unsalted butter
1 large onion, chopped
3 medium celery ribs with leaves, chopped
One 15-ounce bag cubed seasoned stuffing or 1 pound firm white sandwich bread, cut into 1/2-inch cubes (10 cups) and dried overnight or in the oven (see pages 77–78)
1/4 cup chopped fresh parsley

- 3 cups Homemade Turkey Stock 101 (page 34) or canned reduced-sodium chicken broth, as needed
- 2 teaspoons poultry seasoning, preferably homemade (recipe follows)
- Salt and freshly ground black pepper

1. In a large skillet, melt the butter over medium heat. Add the onion and celery, and cover. Cook, stirring often, until the onion is golden, about 10 minutes.

2. Scrape the vegetables and butter into a large bowl. Add the stuffing and parsley. Stir in enough of the broth to moisten the stuffing, about 2½ cups. Season with the poultry seasoning. Use to stuff the turkey, or place in a buttered baking dish, drizzle with an additional ½ cup broth, cover, and bake as a side dish.

Homemade Poultry Seasoning: Combine 1 teaspoon *each* crumbled dried rosemary, crumbled dried sage, dried thyme, dried marjoram, and celery salt with ¼ teaspoon freshly ground black pepper. Crush together with a mortar and pestle or in a mini-food processor or spice grinder.

Giblet Stuffing: Use the giblets from your turkey. With a heavy cleaver or large knife, chop the turkey neck into 2- to 3-inch pieces. Trim the liver and refrigerate (if added to the broth too soon, the liver will overcook and make the broth bitter). In a large saucepan, heat 1 tablespoon vegetable oil over medium-high heat. Add the neck, heart, and gizzard, and brown on all sides, about 10 minutes. Add 1 quartered small onion and 1 coarsely chopped small carrot. Add one 13¾-ounce can reduced-sodium chicken broth and enough cold water to cover the giblets by 1 inch. Bring to a simmer, skimming off the foam that rises to the surface. Add ¼ teaspoon dried thyme, ¼ teaspoon salt, and 8 peppercorns. Reduce the heat to low and simmer, partially covered, until the giblets are very tender, about 2 hours. During the last 15 minutes, add the turkey liver and simmer until cooked through. Strain, reserving the stock, if desired. Cool the giblets. Pull the meat off the neck. Chop the neck meat, heart, gizzard, and liver. Stir into Bread Stuffing 101 along with the bread cubes.

Sausage and Apple Stuffing: In a large nonstick skillet over medium heat, cook 1 pound bulk pork sausage, breaking up the meat with a spoon, until cooked through, about 10 minutes. Add to Bread Stuffing 101 with 1 cup (about 3 ounces) chopped dried apples.

Oyster Stuffing: Drain two 8-ounce containers of oysters and reserve the juices. (Or shuck 24 oysters, opening them over a fine wire sieve placed over a bowl to catch the juices.) If the oysters are large, cut them into 2 or 3 pieces. Add to Bread Stuffing 101 along with the bread cubes. Add enough turkey broth to the reserved oyster juices to make 2½ cups and use to moisten the stuffing.

Mushroom Stuffing: In a large skillet, melt an additional 3 tablespoons unsalted butter over medium heat. Add 1 pound cremini or button mushrooms, cut into quarters. Cook, stirring often, until the mushrooms are lightly browned, about 8 minutes. Transfer to a bowl and set aside. Stir into Bread Stuffing 101 along with the bread cubes.

Chestnut Stuffing: Preheat the oven to 400°F. Using a small, sharp knife, cut a deep "X" in the flatter side of each chestnut. Place in a single layer on a baking sheet and bake until the outer skin is split and crisp, about 30 minutes. The chestnuts never seem to be done at the same time, so work with the ones that are ready and continue roasting the others. Place the roasted chestnuts in a kitchen towel to keep them warm. Using a small, sharp knife, peel off both the tough outer and thin inner skins. To loosen the peels on stubborn, hard-to-peel chestnuts, return to the oven for an additional 5 to 10 minutes, or microwave on High for 30 seconds to 1 minute. You can also use one 15-ounce jar vacuum-packed chestnuts, available at specialty food stores. (Avoid canned chestnuts, which don't have much flavor.) Stir the coarsely chopped chestnuts into Bread Stuffing 101 along with the bread cubes. If desired, substitute 1/4 cup Cognac or brandy for an equal amount of the turkey stock.

Italian Stuffing with Sausage and Parmesan

When I asked a few of my Italian-American neighbors how they make their stuffing, they all shared what was essentially the same recipe. There's nothing subtle about this stuffing—Italian sausage, red bell pepper, Parmesan cheese, and lots of herbs give a zesty Mediterranean flavor. Some cooks add 1 cup toasted pine nuts or 1 cup coarsely chopped black Mediterranean olives to pump up the flavor even more.

Makes about 10 cups

Make Ahead: See suggestions on page 81.

2 tablespoons extra virgin olive oil
1 medium onion, chopped
2 medium celery ribs with leaves, chopped
2 medium red bell peppers, cored, seeded, and chopped
2 garlic cloves, minced
1 pound sweet or hot Italian sausage, casings removed
1 teaspoon dried basil
1 teaspoon dried oregano
1/2 teaspoon salt
1/2 teaspoon crushed hot red pepper flakes
12 ounces day-old crusty Italian bread, cut into 1-inch cubes (about 7 cups)
1 cup freshly grated Parmesan cheese
8 tablespoons (1 stick) unsalted butter, melted
1/2 cup dry white wine
1 1/2 cups Homemade Turkey Stock 101 (page 34) or canned reduced-sodium chicken broth, as needed

1. In a large skillet, heat the oil over medium heat. Add the onion, celery, red bell peppers, and garlic. Cook, stirring often, until softened, about 5 minutes. Add the sausage and cook, breaking up the sausage with a spoon, until it loses its pink color, 8 to 10 minutes. Stir in the basil, oregano, salt, and hot red pepper flakes. Transfer to a large bowl.

2. Add the bread and Parmesan and mix well. Stir in the butter, wine, and enough of the stock to moisten the dressing, about 1 cup. Use as a stuffing. Or place in a buttered baking dish, drizzle with an additional 1/2 cup of stock, cover, and bake as a side dish.

Playing It Safe with Stuffing

For years, roast turkey meant stuffed turkey. Then, health concerns arose about whether or not stuffed birds were safe. While these concerns are real, they shouldn't affect sensible cooks who are familiar with common food safety practice. Just follow these simple rules:

- Stuffing should always be cooked to at least 160°F in order to kill any potentially harmful bacteria. When the turkey is done, insert the meat thermometer deep into the center of the body cavity to check the temperature of the stuffing. If it isn't at least 160°F, scoop the stuffing out of the cavity and transfer it to a casserole. Cover and bake at 350°F until the stuffing reaches 160°F.
- Always prepare your stuffing just before filling and roasting the bird. Never stuff a bird the night before roasting, as the turkey cavity provides the warm, moist environment that encourages bacterial growth. To save time on Thanksgiving morning, prepare the stuffing ingredients the night before—chop the vegetables, toast the nuts, and so on—and store them in self-sealing plastic bags in the refrigerator. If you are really pressed for time, you can cook, cool, and refrigerate the seasoning meat and vegetables the night before. But reheat them thoroughly in a large nonstick skillet before adding to the bread or grains.
- The stuffing should be warm when placed in the turkey. It may sound contradictory to recommend stuffing an ice-cold turkey with warm stuffing, but chilled stuffing in a refrigerated bird may not cook to 160°F by the time the turkey is roasted.
- Never mix raw meat or vegetables into a stuffing. Raw onions and celery in particular will give the stuffing a very strong vegetable taste, and uncooked meat poses a health problem. All meat and vegetables should be thoroughly cooked.
- Before serving the stuffing, remove it from the turkey and place it in a serving bowl. Do not allow the turkey or stuffing to stand at room temperature for longer than 2 hours. Refrigerate any leftovers separate from the turkey and use within 2 days. Reheat leftover stuffing thoroughly before serving.

Savory Sausage and Mushroom Bread Pudding

If you aren't serving a stuffed turkey, this moist savory bread pudding will fill the bill. Seven cups of cubed seasoned bread stuffing can be substituted for the stale bread cubes.

Makes 8 to 10 servings

Make Ahead: The mushrooms and sausage can be prepared up to 1 day ahead.

2 tablespoons unsalted butter
10 ounces fresh mushrooms, sliced
1 medium onion, chopped
1 medium celery rib with leaves, chopped
1 pound bulk sausage
12 ounces firm-textured white sandwich bread, cut into ½-inch cubes (about 7 cups) and dried overnight or in the oven (see pages 77–78)
6 large eggs
3 cups milk
3 tablespoons chopped fresh parsley
2 teaspoons poultry seasoning, preferably homemade (see page 79)
½ teaspoon salt
¼ teaspoon freshly ground black pepper

1. Position a rack in the center of the oven and preheat the oven to 350°F. Lightly butter a 9 × 13-inch baking dish.

2. In a large skillet, melt the butter over medium heat. Add the mushrooms and cook, stirring occasionally, until they give off their juices, about 3 minutes. Add the onion and celery and cook, stirring occasionally, until the mushroom juices evaporate and the onion softens, about 10 minutes. Transfer to a large bowl.

3. In the same skillet, cook the sausage over medium-high heat, breaking it up with a spoon, until it loses its pink color, about 10 minutes. Transfer to the bowl of vegetables. (The vegetables and sausage can be prepared up to 1 day ahead, cooled, stored in self-sealing plastic bags, and refrigerated.) Stir in the bread cubes. In another bowl, whisk the eggs until combined. Gradually whisk in the milk, then the parsley, poultry seasoning, salt, and pepper. Stir into the bread cube mixture. Pour into the prepared dish.

4. Bake until the top is browned and a knife inserted in the center comes out clean, about 1 hour. Serve immediately.

"Tamale" Stuffing with Pork, Chiles, and Raisins

Many Texan cooks have told me that a tamale-stuffed roast turkey is right up there with the herb and bread–stuffed kind—I followed their advice, and they were right. In the Lone Star State, it is easy to purchase a dozen or so slender, 6-inch long, handmade pork tamales, mildly seasoned with chiles and dotted with dark raisins, to complement the pork's sweetness. But snagging tamales of high quality isn't so simple outside of the Southwest. So, I devised my own easy version that keeps all the flavor of the original without making individual tamales.

Makes 8 cups

Make Ahead: The cornmeal cubes can be prepared up to 1 day ahead.

1 teaspoon salt
2 cups white or yellow cornmeal, preferably stone-ground
1 tablespoon olive oil

- 1 large onion, chopped
- 1 small hot fresh green chile pepper (such as jalapeño), seeded and minced
- 2 garlic cloves, minced
- 1 pound ground pork
- ½ cup raisins
- 2 tablespoons chili powder
- 1 teaspoon salt
- 2 tablespoons tomato paste, dissolved in ¼ cup water
- 8 ounces stale crusty French or Italian bread, cut into ½-inch cubes (4 cups)
- 2 cups Homemade Turkey Stock 101 (page 34) or canned reduced-sodium chicken broth, as needed

1. Lightly oil a baking sheet. In a medium, heavy-bottomed saucepan, bring 4 cups water and the salt to a boil over high heat. Whisking constantly, add the cornmeal in a stream. Reduce the heat to low and cook, whisking often, until very thick and smooth. Using an oiled metal spatula, spread the hot cornmeal into a ½-inch thick slab. Let stand until cool and firm, about 1 hour. Cut into ½-inch cubes and set aside. (The cornmeal cubes can be prepared up to 1 day ahead.)

2. In a large skillet, heat the oil over medium heat. Add the onion, chile, and garlic. Cook, stirring often, until softened, about 3 minutes. Add the ground pork and raisins. Cook, stirring often to break up the meat with a spoon, until the pork is cooked through, about 10 minutes. Drain off any fat. Stir in the chili powder and salt, and cook for 30 seconds. Add the dissolved tomato paste and stir until it is absorbed by the meat, about 1 minute.

3. In a large bowl, toss the bread cubes and polenta cubes with the pork mixture, gradually adding enough of the stock to moisten, about 1½ cups. Use to stuff the turkey or place in a buttered casserole, drizzle with the remaining ½ cup stock, cover, and bake as a side dish.

Mason-Dixon Corn Bread Dressing 101

Moist, golden-brown corn bread dressing has as many variations as there are Southern cooks. This basic corn bread dressing recipe uses two equally popular Southern ingredients, ham and pecans.

- **This dressing is best made with homemade corn bread. Southern Corn Bread (page 128) has the proper firm texture. While corn bread stuffing mix is an acceptable substitute, don't use corn bread baked from packaged mixes—they are usually very sweet and make okay muffins but lousy dressing. The same warning goes for bakery corn bread, which tends to be very sweet. A sugary corn bread will ruin a savory dressing.**

- **Bake the corn bread a day or two ahead and let it stand at room temperature to dry out. The corn bread can also be dried in an oven. Crumble the corn bread onto baking sheets and bake in a preheated 350°F oven, stirring occasionally, until dried out but not toasted, 20 to 30 minutes.**

- **Because of the crumbly texture of corn bread, eggs help to hold the dressing together.**

- **As with Bread Stuffing 101, use homemade turkey stock for the best flavor, and be flexible about the amount of stock used to moisten the stuffing. Be sure the stock is cold (or at least cooled to lukewarm), as hot stock could scramble the eggs. Eggs are used here to help the crumbs hold together and make the dressing easier to serve. You can leave them out, if you prefer.**

Makes about 10 cups

Make Ahead: See suggestions on page 81.

8 tablespoons (1 stick) unsalted butter
8 ounces smoked ham, cut into ½-inch cubes
2 medium celery ribs with leaves, chopped
1 cup chopped scallions (white and green parts)
10 cups coarsely crumbled Southern Corn Bread (see page 128), dried overnight or in the oven
1 cup toasted and coarsely chopped pecans
2 large eggs, beaten
1 teaspoon poultry seasoning, preferably homemade (see page 79)
½ teaspoon salt
¼ teaspoon freshly ground black pepper
2½ cups Homemade Turkey Stock 101 (page 34) or canned reduced-sodium chicken broth, as needed

1. In a large skillet, melt the butter over medium heat. Add the ham and celery and cook until the celery softens, about 5 minutes. Add the scallions and cook until wilted, about 3 minutes.

2. Scrape the ham, vegetables, and butter into a large bowl. Stir in the corn bread, pecans, eggs, poultry seasoning, salt, and pepper. Stir in enough of the broth to moisten the stuffing, about 2 cups. Use to stuff the turkey, or place in a buttered casserole, drizzle with the remaining ½ cup stock, cover, and bake as a side dish.

Dried Cranberry and Walnut Corn Bread Dressing: Substitute 1 cup toasted and chopped walnuts for the pecans. Soak 1 cup (4 ounces) dried cranberries in hot water until plump, about 20 minutes; drain. Stir into the Mason-Dixon Corn Bread Dressing 101.

Sausage Gumbo Dressing: Substitute 1 pound andouille sausage or pork kielbasa, cut into ½-inch cubes, for the ham. Cook 1 medium red bell pepper, cored, seeded, and chopped, with the ham and celery. Add 2 garlic cloves, minced, to the mixture with the scallions. Substitute 1 tablespoon Cajun Seasoning (page 14) for the poultry seasoning. If desired, stir one 9-ounce box chopped frozen okra, thawed, into the dressing.

Southwestern Chorizo Dressing: Bake the Southwestern Chili and Cheese Corn Bread on page 129, and allow to dry out. Substitute 1 pound smoked chorizo sausage links, cut into ½-inch cubes, for the ham. Cook 1 medium red bell pepper, cored, seeded, and chopped, with the chorizo. Add 2 garlic cloves, minced, to the mixture with the scallions. Stir 1½ cups frozen corn kernels, thawed, and ½ cup chopped fresh cilantro into the dressing.

Corn Bread Stuffing with Ham, Fresh Fennel, Chestnuts, and Sage

I served this one year when friends from Italy were visiting, and they agreed that it was just the kind of dressing they would put in their own turkey back home. (In fact, I got an e-mail that Christmas, saying they had done that very thing, albeit with white bread.) Fresh fennel does not taste like licorice and adds a wonderful fragrance and flavor to this stuffing. If you balk at using fennel, substitute 5 celery ribs, cut into ½-inch dice. See the headnote in Mason-Dixon Corn Bread Dressing 101 on page 83 for some pointers about corn bread stuffings.

Makes about 12 cups

Make Ahead: See suggestions on page 83.

8 tablespoons (1 stick) unsalted butter, divided
1 ham slice (1 pound), bone discarded, meat cut into ½-inch dice

1 head fennel, fronds removed, cut into ½-inch dice
1 large onion, chopped
10 cups crumbled Southern Corn Bread (page 128), dried overnight or in the oven
One 15-ounce jar vacuum-packed chestnuts, coarsely chopped
⅓ cup chopped fresh parsley
2 tablespoons chopped fresh sage
2½ cups Homemade Turkey Stock 101 (page 34) or canned reduced-sodium chicken broth, as needed

1. Melt 2 tablespoons of the butter in a large skillet over medium-high heat. Add the ham and cook until lightly browned, about 5 minutes. Transfer to a large bowl.

2. Melt the remaining 6 tablespoons butter in the skillet. Add the fennel and onion. Cover and cook until tender, about 10 minutes. Stir into the ham. Add the corn bread, chestnuts, parsley, and sage, and mix. Stir in enough of the broth to moisten the stuffing, about 2 cups. Use to stuff the turkey, or place in a buttered casserole, drizzle with the remaining ½ cup stock, cover, and bake as a side dish.

Louisiana "Dirty" Giblet and Rice Dressing

Louisiana is a leading rice-farming state, so there are lots of recipes there for rice dressings. One of the most common is based on "dirty" rice, which is colored brown by a ground chicken, liver, and sausage mixture. Spicy andouille sausage, available at specialty food stores and many supermarkets and butchers, is the most authentic sausage, but pork kielbasa can be substituted, enlivened with a jolt of Cajun Seasoning (page 14). It isn't the prettiest dressing in the Bayou, but it sure is good, with lots of flavor supplied by the meats, vegetables, herbs, and spices.

Makes about 16 cups

Make Ahead: Although this dressing is best prepared just before using, it can be prepared up to 1 day ahead.

5 tablespoons vegetable oil
2 medium onions, chopped
3 celery ribs with leaves, chopped
1 large green or red bell pepper, cored, seeded, and chopped
2 garlic cloves, minced
1 pound chicken livers (include the turkey liver, too, if you wish), rinsed and trimmed
8 ounces andouille sausage or pork kielbasa, cut into ½-inch slices
1 tablespoon Cajun Seasoning (page 14), optional if using kielbasa
3 cups long-grain rice
6 cups Homemade Turkey Stock 101 (page 34) or canned reduced-sodium chicken broth
1 teaspoon salt
½ teaspoon ground black pepper, optional, if using kielbasa

1. In a large skillet, heat 3 tablespoons of the oil over medium heat. Add the onions, celery, bell pepper, and garlic, and cover. Cook, stirring occasionally, until the vegetables soften, about 6 minutes.

2. In a food processor, process the chicken livers and andouille until very finely chopped, almost a puree. Pour into the skillet and cook, stirring occasionally, until the meats are completely cooked and show no sign of pink, about 10 minutes. Stir in the Cajun Seasoning, if using. Remove from the heat and set aside.

3. In a large Dutch oven, heat the remaining 2 tablespoons oil over medium heat. Add the rice and cook, stirring almost constantly, until most of the rice turns opaque, 2 to 3 minutes.

Stir in the sausage mixture, stock, salt, and the pepper, if using. Bring to a boil over high heat. Reduce the heat to low and cover tightly. Cook until the rice is barely tender and absorbs the stock, about 17 minutes. Remove from the heat and let stand for 5 minutes. Stir well. (The dressing can be prepared up to 1 day ahead, cooled, covered, and refrigerated. Reheat in a large Dutch oven until warmed before using.)

4. Use to stuff the turkey. Place any remaining dressing in a buttered baking dish, cool, cover, and refrigerate. Drizzle with about 1/4 cup water or additional stock before reheating in a preheated 350°F oven for about 20 minutes.

Wild Rice, Dried Cherries, and Almond Stuffing

The deep, earthy flavors of this stuffing work especially well with wild turkey. Wild rice is really a grass and not rice at all. Cooking times depend on the type of wild rice. The most expensive is hand-harvested from canoes, and takes the longest time to cook. Machine-harvested brands, often from California, cook more quickly.

Makes about 10 cups

Make Ahead: The stuffing can be made up to 1 day ahead.

1 cup (4 ounces) dried cherries
2/3 cup tawny or ruby port
2 cups (11 ounces) wild rice, rinsed
2 tablespoons unsalted butter plus 3 tablespoons more if making ahead
3 medium celery ribs, finely chopped
1/2 cup minced shallots
1/3 cup finely chopped celery leaves
1 cup (4 ounces) slivered almonds, toasted
1 tablespoon plus 1 teaspoon chopped fresh sage or 2 teaspoons dried sage
3/4 teaspoon salt
1/2 teaspoon freshly ground black pepper
1/4 cup Homemade Turkey Stock 101 (page 34) or canned reduced-sodium chicken broth, for reheating

1. In a small bowl, mix the dried cherries and port, and let stand while preparing the stuffing.

2. Bring a large pot of lightly salted water to a boil over high heat. Add the wild rice and reduce the heat to medium. Cook until the wild rice is tender and most of the grains have burst, 45 to 60 minutes. Drain well and rinse under cold running water. Place the rice in a large bowl.

3. In a large skillet, melt the butter over medium heat. Add the celery and cook until crisp-tender, about 5 minutes. Add the shallots and celery leaves, and cook until softened, about 2 minutes. Add the cherries and their soaking liquid. Boil until the port has almost completely evaporated, about 3 minutes. Stir the mixture into the wild rice, with the almonds, sage, salt, and pepper. (The stuffing can be made up to 1 day ahead, cooled, covered, and refrigerated. To reheat the stuffing, melt 3 tablespoons butter over medium heat in a large Dutch oven. Add the stuffing and cook, stirring often, until warmed.)

4. Use to stuff the turkey or place the dressing in a buttered casserole, cover, and refrigerate. Drizzle with about 1/4 cup stock before reheating in a preheated 350°F oven for about 20 minutes.

Side Dishes

And the Award for the Best Supporting Side Dish Goes to . . .

As hard as I try to buck the concept of excess at the Thanksgiving table, I am as guilty as the next person when it comes to side dishes. How am I supposed to choose between mashed potatoes and sweet potatoes? Why not make both? Green beans or glazed carrots? Heck, green beans *and* glazed carrots! Most of the time, my menu is limited only by the amount of help I have in the kitchen and how many dishes I can fit on the table. There is no other holiday meal where side dishes are as important as the main course itself. No cranberry sauce? Unthinkable! Hold the gravy? I don't think so. . . .

Thanksgiving side dishes are not known for their subtlety. They can usually be described in one word: rich. When putting together a menu, balance it with some simply prepared sides like Green Beans with Portobello Mushrooms and Bacon (page 95). And try to include a brightly colored dish like Not-Your-Grandmother's Succotash (page 93).

Admittedly, there are a lot of cranberry sauces in this chapter. I just couldn't decide on which one to leave out, since every single one of them has been dubbed "the best one I ever had" by different friends and students over the years. I hope you have fun deciding which one to make.

In the midst of all the cream and marshmallows, I sometimes long for the clean flavors of simply prepared vegetables. Often my side dishes are no more than sautéed vegetables sprinkled with nuts, seeds, or herbs. The vegetables are parcooked in boiling salted water just until crisp-tender. Drain and rinse under cold water, and drain again. Pat them completely dry with paper towels and store, wrapped loosely in more paper towels, in self-sealing plastic bags. When you're ready to serve, it's just a matter of sautéing in butter or olive oil until heated through. These don't need full recipes, just a few words to point you in the right direction, and inspire you to come up with your own combinations.

Broccoli and Cauliflower with Almonds: In a large skillet, sauté parboiled broccoli and cauliflower florets in extra virgin olive oil. Sprinkle with toasted, chopped almonds. Season with salt and crushed hot red pepper flakes.

Carrots with Tarragon: Cut carrots into ½ × 3-inch sticks; parboil (and store) as directed above. In a large skillet, cook chopped shallots in butter until softened. Add the carrots and cook until heated through. Toss with chopped fresh tarragon. Season with salt and pepper.

Carrots with Sesame Seeds: Sauté the carrots in butter and sprinkle with sesame seeds.

Green Beans with Hazelnuts: In a large skillet, cook chopped shallots in butter until softened. Add the parboiled green beans and cook until heated through. Sprinkle with toasted, skinned and chopped hazelnuts. Season with salt and pepper.

To be sure that your side dishes are served at their piping-hot best, follow these tips:

- Unless you plan accordingly, you could easily have a traffic jam in the oven trying to reheat all those sides. Be sure that at least one dish is prepared on top of the stove to lessen the load in the oven.
- Many side dishes can be prepared and stored in the refrigerator until ready to serve. Increase the baking times by 10 to 15 minutes if the dishes are chilled.
- Allow at least 20 minutes for the food to heat through in the oven. Cover the dishes with their lids or aluminum foil.
- Warm the serving dishes (in a preheated 200°F oven for a few minutes, or by filling them with hot water) before adding the food.
- Have the serving utensils ready.
- If a hot dish is going to be served in the casserole or baking dish it was heated in, have clean pot holders and trivets at the table to make serving easier.

Broccoli with Roasted Garlic Butter

Roasted garlic has become a classic American flavor—future cooks may regard it in the same way we do the Pilgrims' pumpkin! Roasted garlic butter, tossed with good old broccoli, turns that familiar vegetable into a side dish that will have everyone asking for seconds. The garlic butter can be made well ahead—it's a simple matter to cook the broccoli, drain, and mix with the butter just before serving.

Makes 8 to 10 servings

Make Ahead: The roasted garlic butter can be made up to 3 days ahead, covered tightly, and refrigerated. Bring the garlic butter to room temperature before using. The broccoli can be cut up 1 day ahead, stored in plastic bags, and refrigerated. Boil the broccoli just before serving.

ROASTED GARLIC BUTTER

2 large, plump heads garlic (about 3½ ounces each)
2 teaspoons extra virgin olive oil
Salt and freshly ground black pepper
8 tablespoons (1 stick) unsalted butter, at room temperature

2 large heads broccoli (3 pounds)

1. To make the roasted garlic butter, position the rack in the center of the oven and preheat to 400°F.

2. Cut each garlic head in half crosswise. Drizzle the cut surfaces with the oil, then season with a sprinkle of salt and pepper. Put the halves back together to re-form into heads. Wrap each head in aluminum foil and place on a baking sheet. Bake until the garlic is tender when squeezed and the cut surfaces are deep beige (open up the foil to check), about 35 minutes. Cool completely.

3. Squeeze the soft garlic flesh out the hulls into a small bowl. Add the butter, ½ teaspoon salt, and ½ teaspoon pepper. Using a rubber spatula, mash the garlic and butter until well combined. Cover tightly and refrigerate until ready to use. (The garlic butter can be prepared up to 3 days ahead.) Bring to room temperature before using.

4. To prepare the broccoli, cut off the tops and separate into florets. Using a sharp paring knife, trim the thick skin off the stems. Cut the pared stems crosswise into ¼-inch rounds. (The broccoli can be prepared up to 1 day ahead, stored in plastic bags, and refrigerated.)

5. Bring a large saucepan of lightly salted water to a boil over high heat. Add the broccoli stems and cook for 2 minutes. Add the florets and cook until the broccoli is crisp-tender, about 2 more minutes. Drain quickly and return to the warm cooking pot. Do not drain the broccoli completely dry—leave some water clinging to the broccoli.

6. Add the softened garlic butter to the broccoli and mix gently, allowing the butter to melt and combine with the small amount of water in the pot to form a light sauce. Transfer to a warmed serving bowl and serve immediately.

Brussels Sprouts in Sherry Cream Sauce

My friend Diane Kniss contributed this recipe, which is a regular item on her annual Thanksgiving menu. And as Diane rarely serves less than two dozen particular folks who expect nothing but the best from her, she is very careful about what dishes make the cut. Try to buy the firmest, smallest sprouts, as they have the most delicate nutty flavor.

Makes 8 to 12 servings

Make Ahead: The Brussels sprouts can be made up to 1 day ahead, cooled, covered, and refrigerated.

4 tablespoons (½ stick) unsalted butter
4 garlic cloves, minced
1 pound Brussels sprouts, bottom stems trimmed, cut crosswise into ½-inch slices
2 tablespoons all-purpose flour
¼ cup dry sherry, such as Manzanilla
1 cup heavy cream
½ cup freshly grated Parmesan cheese
½ teaspoon salt
⅛ teaspoon freshly ground black pepper
A few gratings of fresh nutmeg

1. Preheat the oven to 350°F. In a large skillet, melt 2 tablespoons of the butter over medium heat. Add half of the garlic and stir until fragrant, about 1 minute. Add half of the Brussels sprouts. Cook, stirring occasionally, until heated through, about 2 minutes. Tossing the sprouts, sprinkle with 1 tablespoon of the flour, and stir for 1 minute without letting the flour brown. Stir in 2 tablespoons of the sherry, then ½ cup of the heavy cream. Bring to a simmer. Cook, stirring often, until the sauce thickens and the Brussels sprouts are just tender, about 3 minutes. Transfer to a large bowl. Repeat the procedure with the remaining butter, garlic, Brussels sprouts, flour, and cream. Stir in ¼ cup of the cheese. Season with the salt, pepper, and nutmeg. Spread in a buttered 9 × 13-inch baking dish. Sprinkle with the remaining ¼ cup cheese. (The Brussels sprouts can be prepared up to 1 day ahead, cooled, covered, and refrigerated.)

2. Bake until the sauce is bubbling, about 25 minutes. Serve hot.

Brussels Sprouts and Chestnuts, Italian Style

In many households, a mixture of Brussels sprouts and chestnuts is considered to be the quintessential turkey side dish. These two ingredients are very full flavored, so serve this dish in small portions.

Makes 8 to 12 servings

Make Ahead: The chestnuts can be peeled and roasted up to 2 days ahead; the Brussels sprouts can be parcooked up to 1 day ahead.

1½ pounds Brussels sprouts, trimmed
2 tablespoons extra virgin olive oil
⅓ cup finely chopped (¼-inch dice) prosciutto
1 pound chestnuts, roasted and peeled (see page 79), coarsely chopped, or one 15-ounce jar vacuum-packed chestnuts
⅓ cup Homemade Turkey Stock 101 or Homemade Chicken Stock (pages 34 and 35) or canned reduced-sodium chicken broth
¼ teaspoon salt
¼ teaspoon freshly ground black pepper

1. Using a small, sharp knife, cut a small, deep "X" into the bottom stem of each sprout. Bring a large pot of lightly salted water to a boil over high heat. Add the sprouts and cook until barely tender, about 8 minutes. Drain and rinse well under cold running water. Pat dry with paper towels, and cut the larger sprouts into halves or quarters. (The sprouts can be prepared up to 1 day ahead, wrapped in paper towels, stored in self-sealing plastic bags, and refrigerated.)

2. In a large skillet, heat the oil over medium heat. Add the prosciutto and cook until very lightly browned, about 3 minutes. Add the Brussels sprouts, chestnuts, and stock, and bring to a boil over high heat. Cook, stirring often, until the stock has evaporated, about 5 minutes. Season with the salt and pepper. Transfer to a warmed serving dish and serve hot.

Maple-Glazed Baby Carrots with Pecans

"Baby-cut" carrots are as convenient as they are ubiquitous and a real time-saver when serving a holiday crowd. Skillet size is especially important in this recipe, as a smaller skillet will not hold the large amount of carrots and liquid. If necessary, divide the recipe in half and cook in a 9-inch skillet.

Makes 8 to 12 servings

Make Ahead: The carrots can be made up to 2 hours ahead of serving, kept at room temperature.

2 tablespoon unsalted butter
2 pounds "baby-cut" carrots
1¾ cups beef broth, preferably homemade or canned reduced-sodium broth
½ cup maple syrup, preferably Grade B (see Note)
¼ teaspoon salt
¼ teaspoon freshly ground black pepper
½ cup toasted, coarsely chopped pecans (see page 38)

1. In a 12-inch skillet, preferably nonstick, heat the butter over medium heat. Add the carrots and stir to coat with the butter. Add the broth, maple syrup, salt, and pepper; increase the heat to high and bring to a boil. Cover tightly and cook for 6 minutes.

2. Uncover and cook, stirring often, until the carrots are tender and the liquid reduces to a glaze, 12 to 15 minutes. (The carrots can be prepared up to 2 hours ahead, kept at room temperature. To reheat, add ¼ cup water and cook over medium heat, stirring occasionally, until the carrots are hot and the water evaporates, about 5 minutes.) Stir in the pecans. Transfer to a warmed serving dish and serve immediately.

Port-Glazed Carrots: Substitute ⅓ cup tawny or ruby port for the maple syrup. Add ⅓ cup packed light brown sugar to the skillet.

Note: Grade B maple syrup, available at most natural food stores, has a robust maple flavor and works well in this recipe. The maple flavor in Grade A syrup is subtle, but you can use it, if you wish. Maple-flavored pancake syrup, which is not true maple syrup but artificially flavored corn syrup, is too sweet for this recipe.

Tender Corn Pudding

Dried corn played a large part in the Pilgrim (and Indian) diet. They would probably appreciate that this comforting dish is made with frozen corn, our modern method of food preservation. This is a mildly seasoned version, but it is easy to add Southwestern flavors to make a spicy variation.

Makes 8 to 12 servings

Make Ahead: Corn pudding is best prepared just before serving.

2 tablespoons unsalted butter
1 large green bell pepper, cored, seeded, and finely chopped
3 scallions, white and green parts, finely chopped
2 garlic cloves, minced
Three 10-ounce packages frozen corn kernels (see Note, page 93)
¾ cup heavy cream
1½ cups milk
5 large eggs, beaten
1 teaspoon salt
½ teaspoon freshly ground white pepper

1. Position a rack in the center of the oven and preheat the oven to 350°F. Lightly butter a 10 × 15-inch baking dish.

2. In a large skillet, melt the butter over medium heat. Add the bell pepper, scallions, and garlic. Cook, stirring often, until the bell pepper softens, about 4 minutes. Remove from the heat and set aside.

3. In a blender, process 3 cups of the corn with the heavy cream until smooth. Transfer to a large bowl. Add the remaining 3 cups corn, milk, eggs, salt, and pepper, and whisk well to combine the milk and eggs. Stir in the vegetables. Transfer to the prepared dish.

4. Place the dish in a large roasting pan on the oven rack. Pour in enough nearly boiling water to come ½ inch up the outside of the baking dish. Bake until a knife inserted in the center comes out clean, about 1 hour. Remove the dish from the roasting pan and let stand for 5 minutes before serving.

Southwestern Corn Pudding: Substitute 1 red bell pepper for the green bell pepper. Sauté 2 jalapeños, seeded and minced, with the vegetables.

Maque-Choux

This Cajun side dish has so much going for it, I hardly know where to begin. First of all, it adds a welcome splash of color to the Thanksgiving menu, which frankly can be somewhat bland-looking. Also, its spiciness complements, rather than overwhelms, the other dishes. Next, it can be made well ahead and reheated. Finally, it has bacon in it, which adds an old-fashioned flavor that my guests love. In fact, this simple dish has been the sleeper hit at many of my Thanksgiving spreads.

While *choux* means "cabbage" in French, there is no literal translation of "maque-choux" in either French or Cajun patois. The word (and the basis for the recipe) probably comes from the native Indians who lived in the Bayou. In other words, it is the Cajun version of succotash, the corn-and-bean dish that the northeastern Indians taught the Pilgrims.

Makes 8 servings

Make Ahead: The maque-choux, without the tomatoes, can be prepared up to 1 day ahead.

6 strips thick-sliced bacon
1 medium onion, chopped
1 medium red bell pepper, cored, seeded, and chopped

2 medium celery ribs, chopped
4 cups thawed frozen corn kernels (see Note)
2 garlic cloves, minced
1½ teaspoons Cajun Seasoning (page 14)
2 large ripe tomatoes, seeded and chopped
Salt

1. Cook the bacon in a 12-inch skillet over medium heat, turning occasionally, until crisp and brown, about 5 minutes. Using a slotted spatula, transfer to paper towels to drain.

2. Pour out all but 3 tablespoons of the bacon fat from the pan. Add the onion, bell pepper, and celery to the pan, and cook until the onion is golden brown, about 10 minutes. Add the corn, garlic, and Cajun Seasoning, and cook, stirring frequently, until the corn is heated through, about 5 minutes. (The maque-choux can be prepared up to this point 1 day ahead, cooled, covered, and refrigerated. Reheat gently in the skillet over low heat, stirring often.)

3. Stir in the tomatoes and cook, stirring occasionally, until they are heated through, about 5 minutes. Chop the bacon and stir it into the maque-choux. Season with the salt. Serve immediately.

Note: Even if you can get fresh corn in November, I don't recommend it at that time of year. It would probably be a supersweet hybrid, and too sugary. Thawed frozen corn kernels are processed from a less sweet variety, and are a better choice in autumn.

Not-Your-Grandmother's Succotash

Succotash was one of the mainstays of the Native American diet. Originally, it consisted of corn and beans cooked with bear fat. The original word was from the Narraganset Indian word *misickquatash*, which meant both "stewpot" and "ear of corn." Many versions of succotash are uninspiring, to say the least. This updated version has its roots in tradition, but is flavor packed to match today's tastes.

Makes 8 servings

Make Ahead: The succotash, without the cherry tomatoes, can be prepared up to 1 day ahead.

5 ounces salt pork or slab bacon, rind removed, cut into ½-inch cubes (see Note)
1 large onion, chopped
1½ cups Homemade Turkey Stock 101 or Homemade Chicken Stock (pages 34 and 35) or canned reduced-sodium chicken broth
3 cups frozen corn kernels, thawed (see Note in previous recipe)
Two 10-ounce packages thawed frozen lima beans
2 teaspoons chopped fresh thyme or 1 teaspoon dried thyme
1 pint cherry tomatoes, halved
¼ teaspoon freshly ground black pepper
Salt

1. Cook the salt pork in a large nonstick skillet over medium-high heat, stirring often, until golden brown, about 5 minutes. Add the onion and cook, stirring often, until golden, about 5 minutes. Add the stock and bring to a boil. Cook until the stock is reduced to about ¼ cup, 12 to 15 minutes.

2. Add the corn, lima beans, and thyme. Cook, stirring often, until heated through,

about 5 minutes. (The succotash can be prepared up to this point up to 1 day ahead, cooled, covered, and refrigerated. Reheat gently in a large skillet over low heat, stirring occasionally, until hot.)

3. Add the cherry tomatoes and cook, stirring often, until they are heated through but not collapsing, about 2 minutes. Season with the pepper and add salt to taste (be careful, as the salt pork may have seasoned the succotash enough). Transfer to a heated serving dish and serve hot.

Note: Choose a meaty piece of salt pork. Don't confuse salt pork with salt fatback, which is entirely fat. Slab bacon is a good substitute. If you can't find either, use pancetta or even sliced bacon.

CLASSIC RECIPE

Green Bean Bake

Here it is, one of America's favorite recipes. It is served every year at the Rodgers family Thanksgiving, prepared by my brother Greg, who calls it "Greg's Casserole," although history says that he was not the originator. It was invented in 1955 by a Campbell Soup Company home economist, Dorcas Reilly. Here are some amazing Green Bean Bake statistics:

- **Campbell Soup Company estimates that over 20 million Green Bean Bakes are served during the holiday season.**
- **A recent survey showed that over 50 percent of all Americans have tasted Green Bean Bake. Over 38 percent said that the best time to serve it is at Thanksgiving or during the holidays, but 35 percent serve it all year.**
- **Over 325 million cans of Campbell's Cream of Mushroom Soup are sold annually. Over 80 percent of the soup is used as an ingredient in recipes.**

Makes 6 to 8 servings

Make Ahead: The bake, without the onion topping, can be prepared up to 1 day ahead.

One 10¾-ounce can Campbell's Cream of Mushroom Soup
½ cup milk
1 teaspoon soy sauce
Dash of freshly ground black pepper
One 20-ounce bag frozen cut green beans, thawed (see Note)
One 2.8 ounce can French-fried onions

1. Preheat the oven to 350°F. In a 1½-quart casserole, combine the soup, milk, soy sauce, and pepper. Stir in the green beans and half of the onions. (The casserole can be prepared up to 1 day ahead, covered, and refrigerated.)

2. Bake until bubbling, about 25 minutes. Top with the remaining onions and bake for 5 more minutes. Serve hot.

Note: Instead of the frozen green beans, use two 15½-ounce cans green beans, drained. Or cook 1½ pounds fresh green beans in lightly salted water until tender, about 5 minutes, and drain.

Green Beans with Portobello Mushrooms and Bacon

Green beans and bacon go together like, well, turkey and gravy. Portobello mushrooms, full of meaty flavor, are a fine addition to the classic dish. However, sautéed portobellos often give off a lot of dark liquid, which some cooks feel ruins the look of a dish. Scraping the dark gills out of each cap with a spoon solves the problem.

Makes 8 servings

Make Ahead: The green beans can be blanched up to 1 day ahead. The mushrooms and bacon can be prepared up to 2 hours ahead.

1½ pounds green beans, trimmed and cut into 2-inch lengths
4 large portobello mushrooms (about 1 pound)
3 tablespoons vegetable oil
¼ cup finely chopped shallots
4 ounces sliced smoked bacon (usually 1 slice equals 1 ounce)
½ teaspoon salt
¼ teaspoon freshly ground black pepper

1. Bring a large pot of lightly salted water to a boil over high heat. Add the green beans and return to the boil. Cook until crisp-tender, about 3 minutes. Drain and rinse under cold running water. (The green beans can be prepared to this point up to 1 day ahead. Pat the green beans dry with paper towels. Roll them up in a double thickness of paper towels and place in a large self-sealing plastic bag and refrigerate.)

2. Cut off the stem from each mushroom, and slice crosswise into ½-inch rounds. Using a teaspoon, scrape out the tender, dark brown gills from the underside of each mushroom cap and cut into ¼-inch-thick strips.

3. In a 12-inch nonstick skillet, heat 2 tablespoons of the oil over medium heat. Add the mushroom stems and caps, and cook, stirring often, until lightly browned and tender, about 5 minutes. Add the shallots and cook, stirring often, until the shallots soften, about 2 minutes. Transfer to a plate and set aside. (The mushrooms can be prepared up to 2 hours ahead, loosely covered, and kept at room temperature.)

4. In the same skillet, place the remaining 1 tablespoon oil and tilt to coat the skillet. Add the bacon and place over medium heat. Cook, occasionally turning the bacon, until the bacon is crisp and brown, about 5 minutes. Using a slotted spatula, transfer to paper towels to drain. Keep the bacon drippings in the skillet. Cool the bacon, chop coarsely, and set aside. (The bacon and its drippings can be prepared up to 2 hours ahead, covered, and kept at room temperature.)

5. Place the skillet over medium heat and heat until the bacon drippings sizzle. Add the green beans and mushrooms, and cover. Cook, stirring occasionally, until heated through, about 5 minutes. Stir in the bacon and season with the salt and pepper. Transfer to a warmed serving dish and serve immediately.

Green Bean and Cremini Mushroom Gratin

I swore that I would never attempt a fresh version of the beloved Green Bean Bake (page 94) because it seemed redundant to alter a recipe that is all about convenience. And then I got a request to create one from my students, and now it threatens to usurp the original. Of course, it is more trouble to make than its ancestor, but this recipe is all about fresh ingredients.

Makes 8 to 10 servings

Make Ahead: The gratin can be made 1 day ahead.

1½ pounds green beans, trimmed and cut into 1½-inch lengths
5 tablespoons (½ stick plus 1 tablespoon) unsalted butter
12 ounces cremini (baby portobello) mushrooms, thinly sliced
3 tablespoons chopped shallots
¼ cup all-purpose flour
1⅓ cup half-and-half
1⅓ cup Homemade Chicken Stock (page 35) or canned reduced-sodium chicken broth
1½ teaspoons soy sauce
Salt and freshly ground black pepper to taste
⅓ cup freshly grated Parmesan cheese

1. Cook the green beans in a large pot of lightly salted water until crisp-tender, about 4 minutes. Do not overcook, as they will bake in the oven. Drain, rinse under cold water, and drain again. Pat the green beans dry with paper towels.

2. Heat 4 tablespoons of the butter in a large saucepan over medium-high heat. Add the mushrooms and cook, stirring occasionally, until the mushrooms are tender and the liquid has almost evaporated, about 12 minutes. Add the shallots and cook, stirring often, until softened, about 1 minute. Sprinkle with the flour and stir well.

3. Whisk in the half-and-half, broth, and soy sauce, and bring to a simmer. Reduce the heat to medium-low. Simmer until slightly reduced, about 5 minutes. Add the green beans and mix well. Spread in a buttered 2-quart baking dish. (The gratin can be prepared up to this point 1 day ahead. Press plastic wrap directly on the surface of the sauce, pierce a few holes in the wrap to allow the steam to escape, then cool to tepid and refrigerate. Remove the wrap before reheating.)

4. Position a rack in the center of the oven and preheat to 350°F.

5. Sprinkle the Parmesan over the gratin. Cut the remaining 1 tablespoon butter into tiny cubes and dot the top of the gratin with butter. Bake until the sauce is bubbling and the top is browned, 25 to 35 minutes. Serve hot.

Vegetable Casserole with Smoked Cheddar Crust

This is another dish that leads a double life—it can be a fine side dish or act as a vegetarian main course. It leaves plenty of room for the cook's personal stamp, as you could substitute leeks for the onion, add parcooked cubes of butternut squash, or bolster it with sautéed mushrooms.

Makes 8 servings

Make Ahead: The casserole can be made 1 day ahead.

1½ pounds yellow squash, cut into ½-inch rounds
1½ pounds zucchini, cut into ½-inch rounds
2 tablespoons olive oil

5 tablespoons (½ stick plus 1 tablespoon) unsalted butter
1 large onion, chopped
1 medium red bell pepper, ribs and seeds discarded, cut into ½-inch dice
2 garlic cloves, minced
1½ cups fresh or frozen defrosted corn kernels
2 teaspoons chopped fresh rosemary

CHEDDAR CRUMBS

1 cup fresh bread crumbs (made from French or Italian bread, including crust)
1 cup shredded smoked Cheddar cheese

1. To prepare the vegetables, position a rack in the center of the oven and preheat the oven to 425°F. Lightly oil a 10 × 15-inch baking dish.

2. Place the yellow squash and zucchini in the dish, and toss with the oil. Bake, stirring occasionally, until tender, about 30 minutes.

3. Meanwhile, melt 2 tablespoons of the butter in a large skillet over medium heat. Add the onion, red bell pepper, and garlic. Cook, stirring occasionally, until tender, about 8 minutes. Stir in the corn and rosemary. Stir the onion mixture into the vegetables. (The casserole can be prepared up to this point 1 day ahead, cooled, covered, and refrigerated. Bake the chilled casserole, uncovered, in a preheated 400°F oven until the vegetables are heated through, about 20 minutes.)

4. To make the crumbs, reduce the oven temperature to 400°F. Mix the bread crumbs and cheese in a medium bowl. Melt the remaining 3 tablespoons butter, stir into the crumbs, and mix with your hands until they are thoroughly combined. Sprinkle the crumbs evenly over the vegetables. Bake until the crumbs are crisp and golden brown, about 20 minutes. Serve hot.

Creamed Onions 101

When I serve creamed onions, I make Cheddar-Scalloped Baby Onions (page 98), which I love so much I sometimes worry that I might eat the whole dish by myself. Yet for many Americans it just isn't Thanksgiving without a blindingly white (and bland, to my taste) bowl of creamed onions on the table. Once I made a huge bowl at the request of my friend Rose Curry. When I proudly presented them to her, she took exactly two onions. "I didn't say I liked them," she said quietly. "I just said it wouldn't be Thanksgiving without them!!"

- **My version uses milk and broth for a deeper flavor—the sauce turns out light beige, but the flavor makes the compromise worthwhile. If you want Mom's white-sauce-on-white-onions version, use all milk.**

- **Practical cooks use frozen baby onions (which are an excellent product) with no apology. If you want to use fresh pearl onions, they must be peeled and cooked. There are three kinds of pearl onions available. White pearl onions are the most common. Many specialty produce markets carry yellow and red pearl onions, too, and a bowl of creamed onions is especially attractive and tasty if you use all three colors. You may also use small white boiling onions (16 to 20 onions to a pound). Two pounds of fresh pearl or white boiling onions equals 2 pounds of frozen.**

- **To cook fresh baby onions, bring a large pot of water to a boil over high heat. Add the onions and cook pearl onions for 1 minute and boiling onions for 2 minutes (the water may not return to a boil). Drain well and rinse under cold running water. Using a small, sharp knife, trim off the tops and bottoms of the onions, and pierce the side of each onion with the tip of the knife**

(this helps the onions keep their shape during cooking). Place the onions in a 12-inch skillet and add 2 cups chicken stock, preferably homemade, or use reduced-sodium chicken broth and enough water to barely cover the onions. Bring to a boil over high heat. Cover and reduce the heat to medium. Cook until the onions are tender when pierced with the tip of a small, sharp knife, about 8 minutes for pearl onions or 12 minutes for boiling onions. Drain well, reserving the broth to make the creamed onion sauce, if desired. The fresh onions can be cooked up to 1 day ahead, cooled, stored in self-sealing plastic bags, and refrigerated.

- **When I serve plain creamed onions, I usually make them on the stove to avoid having one more baking dish in the oven. However, if you wish, mix the onions and sauce and place in a lightly buttered 9 × 13-inch baking dish, and dot with 2 tablespoons unsalted butter, cut into small cubes. The dish can be made 1 day ahead, cooled, covered with a piece of plastic wrap pressed directly on the surface of the sauce, and refrigerated. Bake, uncovered, in a preheated 350°F oven until the sauce is bubbling, about 30 minutes.**

Makes 8 to 12 servings

Make Ahead: The creamed onions can be made up to 1 hour ahead.

1 cup milk
1 cup Homemade Turkey Stock 101 or Homemade Chicken Stock (pages 34 and 35) or reduced-sodium canned chicken broth
1 bay leaf
4 tablespoons (½ stick) unsalted butter
¼ cup all-purpose flour
¼ teaspoon salt
¼ teaspoon freshly ground white pepper
2 (1-pound) bags thawed frozen baby onions, or 2 pounds pearl or white boiling onions, peeled and cooked (see above)

1. In a small saucepan over medium-low heat, heat the milk, broth, and bay leaf until tiny bubbles appear around the edges of the milk, about 5 minutes. Remove from the heat and set aside for 5 minutes. Discard the bay leaf.

2. In a medium saucepan, melt the butter over low heat. Whisk in the flour and let bubble without browning for 1 minute. Whisk in the hot milk mixture and bring to a simmer. Cook, stirring often, until the sauce thickens and no taste of raw flour remains, 2 to 3 minutes. Season with the salt and white pepper. Remove from the heat. Set the sauce aside. Press a piece of plastic wrap directly onto the surface of the sauce, and pierce a few times with the tip of sharp knife to release the steam. Set the sauce aside. (The sauce can be prepared up to 2 hours ahead and kept at room temperature. Reheat gently over low heat, stirring often, until hot.)

3. Meanwhile, bring a large pot of lightly salted water to a boil over high heat. Add the onions and return to the boil. Cook, stirring occasionally, until the onions are tender, about 3 minutes. Drain very well. Return to the warm cooking pot. Add the warm sauce and mix well. Transfer to a warmed serving dish and serve immediately. (The creamed onions can be prepared up to 1 hour ahead, stored at room temperature. Reheat in a large saucepan over low heat, stirring often, until heated through.)

Cheddar-Scalloped Baby Onions: Preheat the oven to 350°F. Prepare Creamed Onions, preferably with 2 pounds of fresh white, yellow, and red pearl onions. Stir 1½ cups extra-sharp Cheddar cheese into the hot creamed onions until melted. Transfer to a lightly buttered 9 × 13-inch baking dish. Mix ⅔ cup freshly prepared bread crumbs (preferably from day-old crusty bread) and ⅓ cup freshly grated Parmesan cheese and sprinkle over the onions. Dot with 2 tablespoons unsalted butter, cut into small cubes. The onions can be prepared up to this point, cooled, covered, and refrigerated, for up to 1 day. Bake, uncovered, until the sauce is bubbling and the top is golden brown, about 30 minutes.

Old-fashioned Mashed Potatoes 101

Mashed potatoes are as American as Thanksgiving itself. Variations range from wasabi to lobster chunks. But at Thanksgiving, nothing beats a well-made bowl of classic mashed potatoes. As with many other deceptively simple dishes, there are reasons why sometimes you have good mashed potatoes, and other times you have *great* mashed potatoes. Here are my secrets to make those great ones, served piping hot, ready for that big ladle of gravy:

- **Potatoes with a high starch content (the kind used for baking) provide the traditional flavor and texture. The same starch that gives a baked potato its fluffy interior also contributes to perfect mashed potatoes. Yellow-fleshed varieties like Yukon golds or yellow Finns are excellent as well, but they turn out the same color as mashed turnips, which can be disconcerting to potato purists. If you live near a farmers' market, take the potato farmers' advice on local favorites—they may suggest an interesting heirloom variety that will become your favorite, too.**

- **If possible, buy your potatoes about a week ahead of time and age them in a cool, dark place (not the refrigerator)—mature potatoes are drier and mash up lighter. Don't let them sprout eyes, though.**

- **Always make mashed potatoes just before serving. Warmed-over mashed potatoes leave me cold, although the Make-Ahead Mashed Potato Casserole, on page 101, can be made well ahead and is delicious.**

- **Don't overcook the potatoes—they should just yield to a sharp knife when pierced. If the drained potatoes seem soggy, return them to the pot and cook over low heat, stirring constantly, until they begin to stick to the bottom of the pot, about 2 minutes. This step forces the excess steam out of the potatoes and dries them out.**

- **Mash the drained potatoes in the still-warm cooking pot with *hot* milk—a cold bowl and cold milk make for lumpy, lukewarm potatoes. The exact amount of milk is a matter of taste, so use more or less to reach your desired consistency.**

- **Use an efficient mashing utensil. Some cooks swear by a potato ricer, which does make the smoothest potatoes, as long as you enlist another pair of hands to make the job go quickly. I use an electric hand mixer. If you want to use a low-tech, old-fashioned hand potato masher, go to a restaurant supply store and get a large one, or the chore will take forever, with the potatoes cooling off by the second. Never mash potatoes in a food processor, which will give you gummy mashed potatoes.**

- **Season the mashed potatoes well with salt and pepper. I have suggested amounts, but use your taste. White pepper (which is**

actually spicier than black) will give you pristine mashed potatoes, but certainly use black if you wish.

Makes 8 to 12 servings

Make Ahead: The potatoes can be peeled and cut ahead, placed in the cooking pot, covered with cold water, and stored in a cool place for up to 4 hours.

5 pounds baking potatoes (such as russet, Idaho, Burbank, or Eastern)
Salt
4 tablespoons (½ stick) unsalted butter
¾ cup milk, heated, as needed
½ teaspoon freshly ground white pepper

1. Fill a large (5 quarts or larger) pot halfway with cold water. Peel the potatoes and cut into chunks about 1½ inch square, and drop them into the pot. Add more cold water to completely cover the potatoes by 1 to 2 inches. (The potatoes can be prepared up to this point for 4 hours, stored at cool room temperature.)

2. Stir in enough salt so that the water tastes mildly salted. Cover tightly and bring to a full boil over high heat, which should take at least 20 minutes, so allow sufficient time.

3. Reduce the heat to medium-low and set the lid askew. Cook at a moderate boil until the potatoes are tender when pierced with the tip of a small, sharp knife, about 25 minutes. Add more boiling water, if needed, to keep the potatoes covered.

4. Drain the potatoes well and return to the warm cooking pot. Add the butter. Using an electric hand mixer, mash the potatoes, gradually adding enough milk to reach your desired consistency. Season with 1 teaspoon salt and the pepper. Transfer to a warmed serving dish and serve immediately.

Garlic-Mascarpone Mashed Potatoes with Leeks

You simply won't find a more sinful, more awe-inspiring mashed potato recipe on the planet. At first I balked at putting them on my Thanksgiving menu, which is hardly lacking in flavors or calories. But I knew I did the right thing when one guest remarked, "No offense, but next year, let's serve these potatoes as the main course and serve the turkey on the side." Because these are at their best when served immediately after making, have everything ready to roll so there's no last-minute confusion.

Makes 8 servings

Make Ahead: The leeks can be prepared 1 day ahead, cooked, covered, and refrigerated.

LEEKS

4 tablespoons (½ stick) unsalted butter
6 large leeks, white and pale green parts only, coarsely chopped and well washed (4 cups)
Salt and freshly ground black pepper

GARLIC MASHED POTATOES

4 pounds baking potatoes (such as russet, Idaho, Burbank, or Eastern)
Salt
½ cup milk, heated
12 garlic cloves, coarsely chopped
One 8-ounce container mascarpone, at room temperature
6 tablespoons (¾ stick) unsalted butter, at room temperature

1. To prepare the leeks, melt the butter in a large skillet over medium heat. Add the leeks and cover. Cook, stirring occasionally, until the leeks are golden brown, about 20 minutes.

Season with salt and pepper. Remove from the heat. (The leeks can be prepared 1 day ahead, cooled, covered, and refrigerated. Reheat in a skillet over medium heat.)

2. To make the potatoes, peel the potatoes and cut them into 1-inch chunks. Place the potatoes in a large pot of lightly salted water and cover. Bring to a boil over high heat. Reduce the heat to medium and cook until the potatoes are tender, about 25 minutes. Drain well.

3. Meanwhile, slowly heat the milk and garlic in a small saucepan over low heat until bubbles form around the edges of the milk. Remove from the heat and cover. Let stand to infuse the milk with the garlic, 15 to 30 minutes.

4. Mash the drained potatoes with a potato masher or handheld electric mixer. Add the mascarpone and butter. Mix, adding enough of the garlic-milk mixture to reach the desired consistency. Season with salt and pepper. Transfer to a serving bowl and top with the leeks. Serve immediately.

Make-Ahead Mashed Potato Casserole

I was a mashed potato snob who held tight to the belief that mashed potatoes are only worth eating when they are freshly made, until my friend, caterer/food stylist/restaurateur Katy Keck, set me straight. Katy, who is in the habit of cooking Thanksgiving dinner for over two dozen people, would never dream of trying to mash that many potatoes in one batch. She gave me this recipe for a delicious make-ahead casserole, with lots of dairy ingredients to keep the spuds moist.

Makes 8 to 12 servings

Make Ahead: The casserole can be prepared up to 1 day ahead.

5 pounds baking potatoes (such as russet, Idaho, Burbank, or Eastern)
Salt
8 ounces cream cheese, cut into chunks, at room temperature
6 tablespoons (¾ stick) unsalted butter, at room temperature
1 cup sour cream, at room temperature
½ cup milk, heated
½ teaspoon freshly ground white pepper
Chopped chives or parsley, for garnish (optional)

1. Fill a large pot (at least 5 quarts) halfway with cold water. Peel the potatoes and cut into chunks about 1½ inch square, and drop them into the pot. Add more cold water to cover the potatoes by 1 to 2 inches.

2. Stir in enough salt so that the water tastes mildly salted. Cover tightly and bring to a full boil over high heat, allowing at least 20 minutes. Reduce the heat to medium-low and set the lid askew. Cook at a moderate boil until the potatoes are tender when pierced with the tip of a small, sharp knife, about 20 minutes. Do not overcook the potatoes.

3. Drain the potatoes well and return to the warm pot. Add the cream cheese and butter. Using a handheld electric mixer, mash the potatoes until the cream cheese and butter melt. Beat in the sour cream and milk. Season with 1 teaspoon salt and the pepper. Transfer to a buttered 9 × 13-inch baking dish. Cool completely. (The potatoes can be prepared up 4 hours ahead, covered loosely with plastic wrap, and stored at cool room temperature; or cool, cover tightly with plastic wrap, and refrigerate for up to 1 day.)

4. Preheat the oven to 375°F. Bake until the potatoes are heated through, 30 to 40 minutes. Serve hot, sprinkled with the chives, if using.

Candied Yam and Marshmallow Casserole 101

I wonder how many sweet potato and marshmallow casseroles are trotted out every Thanksgiving? This dish is so entrenched in the American psyche that it seems centuries old—surely sweet potatoes were served at the first Thanksgiving. Although candied yams had been popular for years, in the 1920s cooks began to top them with marshmallows. Personally, I prefer yams that aren't so sweet, but I know I'm in the minority.

- **Many cooks use canned yams in syrup to make their casseroles. If you prefer a less sweet version, use freshly cooked yams. Cook 3½ pounds (about 5 medium) yams in lightly salted water just until barely tender, 20 to 25 minutes. Do not overcook them—they will cook further in the oven. Drain well, rinse under cold water until easy to handle, then peel and cut into 1-inch chunks.**

- **It is best to *broil* the marshmallow topping onto the yams just before serving. If the weather is humid and the casserole is allowed to stand, the browned marshmallows can melt into syrup. If you put the marshmallows on the casserole and accidentally overbake it (which can happen in the flurry of kitchen activity), the marshmallows can also dissolve. I learned this firsthand the time I popped my sister-in-law's sweet potato casserole into the oven, and when I came back, found that the marshmallows had disappeared! Even though we jokingly served it as "yams with marshmallow sauce," Linda never let me near her yams again.**

Makes 8 to 12 servings

Make Ahead: The yams can be prepared up to 8 hours ahead.

Two 40-ounce cans yam (sweet potato) chunks in light syrup, drained
⅓ cup packed light brown sugar
5 tablespoons (½ stick plus 1 tablespoon) unsalted butter, cut into pieces
¼ cup water
2½ cups miniature marshmallows (about 5 ounces)

1. Preheat the oven to 350°F. Lightly butter a 9 × 13-inch baking dish.
2. Spread the yams in the prepared dish. Sprinkle with the brown sugar, then dot with the butter and drizzle with the water. (The yams can be prepared up to 8 hours ahead, stored in a cool place.)
3. Bake, stirring occasionally, until syrupy and bubbling, about 45 minutes. Remove from the oven. Position the broiler rack 6 inches from the source of heat and preheat the broiler.
4. Spread the marshmallows on top of the yams. Broil until the marshmallows are lightly toasted, 1 to 2 minutes. Serve immediately.

Rum-Baked Yams and Apples

Rows of yams, with apples interspersed throughout, make this an especially good-looking side dish. If you don't want to serve rum to the kids, substitute more cider.

Makes 8 to 12 servings

Make Ahead: The casserole can be prepared up to 8 hours ahead.

2 Golden Delicious apples
1 tablespoon fresh lemon juice
3 medium orange-fleshed yams (about 2 pounds), peeled and cut into ½-inch slices
8 tablespoons (1 stick) unsalted butter
1½ cups apple cider
¾ cup packed light brown sugar
3 tablespoons dark rum
2 tablespoons cornstarch

1. Peel the apples and cut into quarters. Cut out the cores, then cut each apple quarter crosswise into ½-inch thick wedges. Place in a medium bowl and toss with the lemon juice; set aside.

2. Bring a large pot of lightly salted water to a boil over high heat. Add the yams and cook just until crisp-tender, 3 to 5 minutes. Do not overcook. They should hold their shape when drained. Drain and rinse under cold running water.

3. Preheat the oven to 350°F. Lightly butter a 9 × 13-inch baking dish. Overlapping in vertical rows, arrange the yams in the prepared dish, slipping the apple wedges between the yams, letting the curved edges of the apples peek out.

4. In a medium saucepan, melt the butter over medium heat. Add the cider, brown sugar, and rum. Bring to a boil. In a small bowl, sprinkle the cornstarch over 2 tablespoons cold water and mix until dissolved. Stir into the boiling cider mixture and return to the boil; the mixture will be very thick, but it will thin during baking. Pour over the yams and apples. (The dish can be prepared up to 8 hours ahead, cooled, covered tightly with plastic wrap, and refrigerated.)

5. Bake, basting occasionally, until the yams are tender and the cooking liquid is syrupy, about 45 minutes. Serve hot.

It Wouldn't Be Thanksgiving Without . . . Marshmallows

The roots of the marshmallow plant (*Althaea officinalis*) were used to make a homemade confection that took the plant's name. When confectioners developed a mass-produced version around the turn of the century, they switched to corn syrup and egg whites to create the bouncy consistency of the original. It didn't take long for marshmallows to establish themselves as a truly American food, spawning such offspring as Marshmallow Fluff and a range of marshmallow-filled, chocolate-coated cookies. While their sweetness is appropriate in dessert icons like Rice Krispies Treats and S'Mores, their presence in gelatin salads, fruit salads, and sweet potato casseroles is truly a testament to the tenacity of the American sweet tooth.

Scalloped Yams with Praline Topping

This is one of my favorite dishes to demonstrate how yams don't have to be cloyingly sweet to be good. Whenever I make it, it never fails that someone remarks, "I don't even like yams, but I could eat a whole dish of these!"

Makes 8 to 12 servings

Make Ahead: The yams can be parboiled and placed in their baking dish up to 8 hours before baking; the praline topping can be prepared up to 8 hours ahead.

½ cup all-purpose flour
¼ cup packed light brown sugar
4 tablespoons (½ stick) unsalted butter, at room temperature
⅓ cup (about 2 ounces) finely chopped pecans
6 medium orange-fleshed yams, peeled and cut into ½-inch rounds (about 3 pounds)
1½ cups heavy cream, heated

1. In a small bowl, using your fingers, work the flour, brown sugar, and butter together until well combined, then work in the pecans. Set aside. (The praline topping can be prepared up to 8 hours ahead, stored at room temperature.)

2. Bring a large pot of lightly salted water to a boil over high heat. Add the yams and cook just until crisp-tender, about 5 minutes. Do not overcook. They should be able to hold their shape when drained. Drain and rinse under cold running water.

3. Preheat the oven to 375°F. Lightly butter a 9 × 13-inch baking dish.

4. Overlapping in vertical rows, place the yams in the prepared dish. (The yams can be parboiled and placed in their baking dish up to 8 hours before baking, covered tightly with plastic wrap, and refrigerated.)

5. Pour the heavy cream over the yams. Bake for 20 minutes. Crumble the pecan mixture over the yams and continue baking until the yams are tender and the topping is browned, 20 to 30 more minutes. Serve hot.

It Wouldn't Be Thanksgiving Without . . . Sweet Potatoes (Yams)

Life used to be so simple. When Thanksgiving rolled around, there was only one kind of sweet potato to be found. It had a light brown skin, and was orange on the inside. Sometimes it was called a yam. No one but botanists knew the difference between the true sweet potato and the orange-fleshed yam, and no one cared.

Times change. One year, during my annual Thanksgiving cooking class marathon at ten schools from Seattle down to Long Beach, I wrote, "10 pounds sweet potatoes" on the

shopping list that was sent ahead to each school. When I arrived, every grocer provided sweet potatoes, all right—but they were the true sweet potato, sometimes called *batata* or *boniato*, beloved by Latino and Japanese cooks. I guess I should have asked for yams.

Let's straighten out the situation, as best as possible. When Columbus arrived in the Caribbean, he found the natives eating a yellow-fleshed tuber, the *batata*. It was brought back to Europe, where it gained some popularity as a "potato." Even Shakespeare mentions the potato, but he was talking about the *batata*. When a white-fleshed tuber, originally from Ecuador or Peru, was introduced to the Old World in the 1500s, its resemblance to the yellow sweet potato was so strong that people began to call it a potato, too. As we know, the white potato became a staple of the European diet. It wasn't until 1775 that "sweet potato" was entered into the *Oxford English Dictionary*, distinguishing it permanently from the white one. The potato established itself on tables throughout the world, while the farmers in the American South remained faithful to the sweet potato.

Yet another tuber was eaten by the Caribbean natives. The *igname* (ig-NYAM-eh) had a dark brown, almost black skin, pale flesh with streaks of gray-purple, and a bland flavor not unlike the white potato. Eventually, the *igname* found its way to Africa, where it was cultivated. When the African slaves were brought to America, they found the sweet potato, which they dubbed *igname*, as the two tubers resembled each other. Eventually, *igname* contracted to *yam*. In today's Latino markets, you will find the *igname*, the "true" yam, labeled *name* or Colombian yam.

What most Americans call a yam is really a sugary sweet potato. True sweet potatoes are not very sweet at all. They cannot be substituted for the orange yam in our traditional Thanksgiving dishes, as they take too long to bake and taste quite starchy, like regular potatoes. The Louisiana yam, developed by the farmers of that state to be especially sweet, is the most familiar variety. Well-stocked produce markets also sell beautiful Garnet or Jewel yams with purple skins and deep orange flesh, which make wonderful substitutes for the tried-and-true Louisiana version. Yams should be stored in a cool, dark place, even the refrigerator, for no longer than 1 week. Even though they look like potatoes, they don't have the same long-keeping qualities.

I doubt if you'll ever send someone to the store to get yams, only to have them return with a bag full of *ignames*. On the other hand, it was only a few years ago that few Americans knew what cilantro was. In my multiethnic neighborhood, the supermarket carries Louisiana yams, sweet potatoes, true yams, and Jewels or Garnets during the holidays. Even supermarket produce sections mislabel sweet potatoes and yams. If you have any doubts, scratch the skin with your fingernail to check the color. You won't easily mistake a *name* for the other two tubers, because it looks so different.

Cider-Mashed Yams

These yams take the mashed route, and deliciously. They also are one of the best low-fat side dishes around (welcome at a meal typically high in calories and fat grams), and the one to serve if you're not a fan of overly sweet yams. In order to intensify the apple flavor, the cider is reduced by half, but you could use ⅓ cup thawed frozen apple juice concentrate. If you wish, this dish is easy to marshallowize.

Makes 8 to 10 servings

Make Ahead: The yams can be made up to 8 hours ahead.

⅔ cup apple cider
5 large orange-fleshed yams (about 4½ pounds), scrubbed but unpeeled
4 tablespoons (½ stick) unsalted butter
2 tablespoons light brown sugar
½ teaspoon salt

1. In a small saucepan, boil the cider over high heat until reduced by half, about 7 minutes. Set aside.

2. Bring a large pot of lightly salted water to a boil over high heat. Add the yams and cook until tender, 30 to 40 minutes, depending on the size of the yams. Drain well. Using a kitchen towel to protect your hands, peel the yams and return to the warm pot. Add the reduced cider, butter, brown sugar, and salt. Mash until well blended. (The mashed yams can be prepared up to 8 hours ahead, cooled, covered tightly with plastic wrap, and refrigerated. To reheat, spread in a buttered 9 × 13-inch baking dish. Cover loosely with aluminum foil, and bake in a preheated 350°F oven until heated through, about 30 minutes. Serve from the baking dish.) Serve hot.

Mashed Yams with Marshmallows: Spread half of the hot yams in a buttered 9 × 13-inch casserole. Sprinkle with 1½ cups miniature marshmallows. Top with the remaining yams. Bake in a preheated 350°F oven for 20 minutes. Sprinkle the top with another 1½ cups marshmallows. Broil in a preheated broiler, about 4 inches away from the source of heat, until the marshmallows are lightly browned, about 1 minute. Serve immediately. (This casserole can be prepared up to 8 hours ahead, made with cooled mashed yams, following the reheating instructions in the main recipe, and broiling the marshmallow topping just before serving.)

Maple-Glazed Roasted Yams

My motto could be "the simpler, the better." Here's a perfect example—all you do is roast some cubed sweet potatoes, then toss them with maple syrup and butter to glaze them at the end. That's it, and you will still collect plenty of compliments. The only trick is being sure that your oven is free for the hour or so they take to roast to sweet, tender perfection.

Makes 8 to 10 servings

Make Ahead: The yams can be cut 8 hours ahead, stored at room temperature. The yams are best roasted just before serving.

4 pounds orange-fleshed yams, peeled and cut into ¾-inch chunks
2 tablespoons vegetable oil
½ cup Grade B maple syrup
3 tablespoons unsalted butter, thinly sliced

1. Position a rack in the center of the oven and preheat the oven to 400°F. Lightly oil an 18 × 13-inch rimmed baking sheet. Spread the yams on the sheet in a single layer. Add the oil and toss to coat the yams.

2. Bake, turning occasionally with a metal spatula, until the yams are almost tender, about 40 minutes. Drizzle the yams with the maple syrup and mix well to coat. Bake until the syrup has evaporated into a glaze and the yams are tender, about 15 minutes more. Remove the pan from the oven.

3. Scatter the butter over the yams, and let stand to melt the butter. Season lightly with salt and pepper. Transfer to a serving bowl and serve hot.

Parmesan-Mashed Yellow Turnips

Like succotash, mashed yellow turnips (also called wax turnips, rutabagas, or Swedes) are another Thanksgiving must-have for many people on the East Coast. They are usually served just mashed with milk and butter like potatoes, but they take to this fillip with garlic, onion, and freshly grated Parmesan cheese. Use a sharp, sturdy knife for cutting up the turnips—they can be very hard.

Makes 8 servings

Make Ahead: The turnips can be pared up to 8 hours ahead.

2 medium yellow turnips (about 3¼ pounds total)
1 large, plump head garlic, peeled
1 large onion, chopped
½ cup freshly grated Parmesan cheese
4 tablespoons (½ stick) unsalted butter, at room temperature
1 teaspoon salt
½ teaspoon freshly ground black pepper
Approximately 1 cup milk, heated

1. Using a sturdy vegetable peeler, remove the thick skin from the turnips. Using a large knife, cut the turnips into pieces about 1½ inches square. Place the turnips and garlic in a large pot and add enough lightly salted water to cover. Cover tightly with the lid, and bring to a boil over high heat. Uncover and reduce the heat to medium-low. Boil gently for 20 minutes.

2. Add the onion and continue cooking until the turnips are tender when pierced with the tip of a small, sharp knife, 15 to 20 more minutes. Drain well, then return to the warm cooking pot.

3. Add the Parmesan, butter, salt, and pepper. Using a large masher or an electric hand mixer, mash the turnips, gradually adding enough milk to reach the desired consistency. Transfer to a warmed serving dish. (The mashed turnips can be kept warm in a 170°F oven, loosely covered with aluminum foil, for up to 20 minutes.) Serve hot.

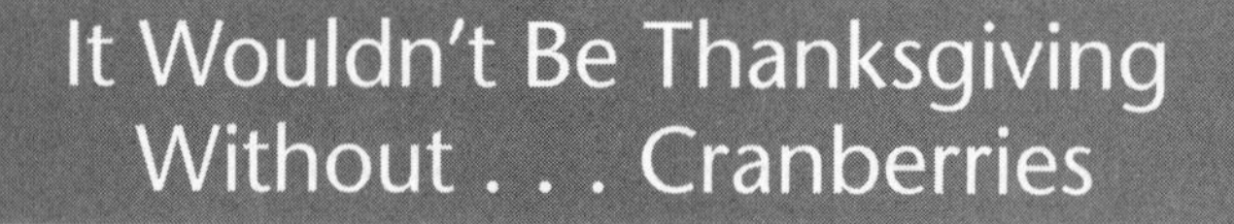

It Wouldn't Be Thanksgiving Without . . . Cranberries

No one is sure that cranberries were served at the first Thanksgiving. The cranberry was an important food to the Pawtuxet Indians, so historians assume they offered it as a contribution to the feast. Instinct must have taught the Indians that the berries were an excellent source of vitamin C, because they used them in many dishes. They ate them raw and boiled with maple syrup, but perhaps the most common use was in *pemmican*, a kind of low-tech energy bar made with berries, dried venison meat, and melted animal fat. Pemmican kept well, and went along with the Indians as food on long journeys. It couldn't be much worse than some of the instant modern food I've had on camping trips.

The Pilgrims probably referred to cranberries as "fenberries," a common fruit in old England that they resembled. However, the cranberry gets its modern name from the Dutch and German settlers, who called it a "crane berry." When the cranberry vines bloom, the blossom looks like the head and bill of a crane. Eventually, the name became cranberry. Colonial Americans called them "bounce berries," referring to their bounciness. Bouncing berries are an indication of freshness—bruised, old berries don't bounce.

A recipe for cranberry sauce is included in the very first printed American cookbook, Amelia Simmons's *American Cookery*, in 1796. Canned cranberry sauce first hit the shelves in 1912, a product of the Cape Cod Cannery Company, which eventually became the Ocean Spray Preserving Company. The president of the company is a Boston lawyer, Marcus L. Urann. In 1930, Urann organized a merger between his company and two other cranberry canneries to form the Cranberry Canners, Inc., a cranberry farming cooperative. The cooperative, which eventually acquired Urann's former company's name after a few months of squabbling, now provides over 70 percent of the world's cranberries. The world's supply of cranberries are grown on only about 42,000 acres, which is an area equal to the size of Manhattan. If you've ever wondered how many cranberries are in a 12-ounce bag, the number is 360 (give or take a few berries).

The high amount of vitamin C in cranberries makes homemade cranberry sauce a long keeper (and the sugar helps, too). It can be refrigerated for at least one week before serving. To prepare cranberries for cooking, simply rinse them off and sort through them to discard any bruised or soft ones. Cranberries are one of the best fruits for freezing. Just rinse them off and store them in self-sealing plastic bags. Don't thaw the frozen berries before using. Rinse them before freezing, as it is difficult to rinse off frozen berries.

Acidic cranberries can react when they come in contact with aluminum and pick up the metal's taste. Be sure to cook them in pots with nonreactive metal surfaces, such as stainless steel or nonstick coating.

CLASSIC RECIPE

Spiced Cranberry–Orange Mold

One of Jell-O's most requested recipes, it graces countless Thanksgiving tables every year.

Makes 10 servings

Make Ahead: The mold can be made up to 3 days ahead.

1½ cups boiling water
Two 3-ounce packages Jell-O Brand Cherry Flavor Gelatin Dessert
One 16-ounce can whole berry cranberry sauce
1 tablespoon fresh lemon juice
¼ teaspoon ground cinnamon
⅛ teaspoon ground cloves
1 orange, peeled, sectioned, and cut into ½-inch cubes
½ cup chopped walnuts

1. In a medium bowl, stir the boiling water into the gelatin, and stir until completely dissolved, about 2 minutes. Stir in the cranberry sauce, 1 cup cold water, lemon juice, cinnamon, and cloves. Refrigerate until thickened and almost set (a spoon drawn through the mixture will leave a definite impression), about 1½ hours.
2. Stir in the orange and walnuts. Spoon into a 5-cup mold. Cover and refrigerate until firm, at least 4 hours or overnight. (The mold can be made up to 3 days ahead.)
3. To unmold, dip into a large bowl of hot water and hold for 5 seconds. Dry the outside of the mold and invert onto a serving dish.

CLASSIC RECIPE

Jell-O–Cream Cheese Mold

This two-toned mold combines two Thanksgiving favorites, Jell-O and cream cheese. I love it.

Makes 12 servings

Make Ahead: The mold can be made up to 3 days ahead.

1½ cups boiling water
Two 3-ounce packages Jell-O Brand Cranberry Flavor Gelatin Dessert (or any other flavor red gelatin)
½ teaspoon ground cinnamon
1 medium apple, chopped
1 cup whole-berry cranberry sauce, optional
One 8-ounce package Philadelphia cream cheese, well softened

1. In a medium bowl, pour the boiling water over the gelatin and stir until completely dissolved, at least 2 minutes. Stir in 1½ cups cold water and the cinnamon. Reserve 1 cup of the gelatin at room temperature. Refrigerate the remaining gelatin until thickened and partially set (a spoon drawn through the gelatin leaves a definite impression), about 1½ hours.
2. Stir the apple and the cranberry sauce, if using, into the thickened gelatin. Spoon into a 6-cup mold. Refrigerate until set but not firm (it will stick to your finger when touched, and a small spoonful will mound on a plate), about 30 minutes.
3. In a medium bowl, gradually whisk the reserved gelatin into the cream cheese until smooth. Pour over the gelatin in the mold.
4. Cover and refrigerate until firm, at least 4 hours or overnight. To unmold, dip into a large bowl of hot water and hold for 5 seconds. Dry the outside of the mold and invert onto a serving dish.

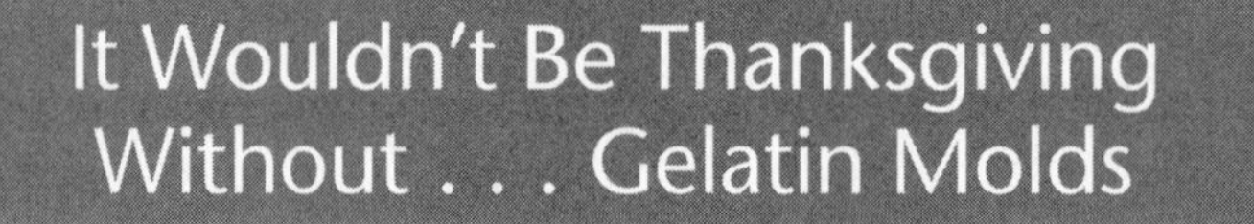

It Wouldn't Be Thanksgiving Without . . . Gelatin Molds

In the nineteenth century, cold, jellied aspics and desserts were the height of fashion. They also relied on the talents of a dedicated cook. Most thickeners, such as isinglass (the dried air bladder of sturgeon), agar-agar (a seaweed), and various mosses, weren't readily available to the home cook. As a last resort, gelatin had to be painstakingly extracted from veal bones or calves' feet. This was absolute drudgery, and the long simmering, skimming, and clarification procedure took hours and hours.

By the 1880s, technology had advanced enough that gelatin was available in sheets, a version that is still preferred by some professional pastry chefs. But it had to be soaked before use, and it still took a certain amount of guesswork to figure out how much to use to jell the food. In 1890, Charles B. Knox bought a gelatin company in Johnstown, New York. At first, it was business as usual, and the Knox Gelatin Company sold gelatin sheets. Fatefully, Knox met a true innovator in American cooking, Sarah Tyson Rorer, principal of the Philadelphia Cooking School. Mrs. Rorer suggested that Knox granulate the gelatin so it would dissolve easily without soaking. This brainstorm was enhanced with the idea to sell the powdered gelatin in individual premeasured packets. This was the beginning of America's love affair with the bouncy, jiggly, transparent gelatin salad.

The affair heated up in 1897, when a cough medicine manufacturer in Leroy, New York, Mr. Pearle B. White, introduced Jell-O. The name was created by his wife, Mary. White improved the product from a recipe developed in 1845. Initially, his sweetened gelatin product failed as miserably as his predecessor's, but as Knox Gelatin became popular, Jell-O did, too. By 1906, it was approaching $1,000,000 in annual sales—back when a million bucks meant something.

Fruits and vegetables were not very popular with cooks of the early twentieth century, and were often cooked to disguise their identity. And as refined sugar became cheaper and more available, our nation quickly became hooked on sweets. It was perfectly acceptable to mix savory vegetables in sweet Jell-O. By 1905, when Knox conducted a national salad contest, the third-place winner was Mrs. John Cooke's "Perfection Salad." It didn't contain Jell-O, but it could have, being a sweet-and-sour gelatin salad with shredded cabbage, celery, green pepper, and pimientos. Knox printed the recipe in its popular recipe booklets, and one of the contest judges, Fannie Farmer, put it in the next edition of her cookbook. From this American classic, cooks created endless variations on a theme, and their popularity lives on, especially at Thanksgiving.

Cranberry, Ginger, and Lemon Chutney

This is my most requested cranberry sauce recipe. As a matter of fact, many friends and students now make quarts of this chutney at Christmas time for gift-giving. Crystallized ginger can be purchased inexpensively in bulk at Asian and natural food markets. It can also be found at many supermarkets and specialty food stores, where it gets pricey.

Makes about 3 cups, 12 servings

Make Ahead: The chutney can be made up to 2 weeks ahead, cooled, covered, and refrigerated.

1 medium lemon
One 12-ounce bag cranberries
2 cups sugar
½ cup diced (¼-inch) crystallized ginger (about 2½ ounces)
⅓ cup finely chopped onion
1 garlic clove, minced
1 jalapeño, seeded and minced
1 cinnamon stick
½ teaspoon dry mustard
½ teaspoon salt

1. Using a grater, remove the yellow zest from the lemon. Using a small, sharp paring knife, cut away and discard the thick white pith. Cut the lemon in half horizontally and pick out the seeds with the tip of the knife. Dice the lemon into ¼-inch pieces.

2. In a medium, nonreactive saucepan, combine the cranberries, diced lemon and zest, sugar, ginger, onion, garlic, jalapeño, cinnamon stick, mustard, and salt. Bring to a boil over medium heat, stirring often to help dissolve the sugar. Reduce the heat to low and simmer until the sauce is thick and the cranberries have burst, 10 to 15 minutes. Cool completely. (The chutney can be prepared up to 2 weeks ahead, covered tightly, and refrigerated.) Remove the cinnamon stick just before serving. Serve at room temperature.

Cranberry-Orange Chutney: Substitute 2 navel oranges for the lemon. Grate the zest from the oranges, then cut off and discard the thick white pith. Carefully cut between the membranes to release the orange sections. Use the orange zest in segments in place of the lemon zest and pieces. Stir 3 tablespoons orange-flavored liqueur into the chutney just as it is removed from the stove.

Cranberry-Tomato Chutney

Here's another contender for the cranberry chutney crown. Cranberries and tomatoes may sound like a odd combination, but when you consider that tomatoes are a fruit and take well to sugar and spice, the pairing makes sense. Not only is this a terrific condiment for turkey, I often offer it as an appetizer, spooned over cream cheese and served with crackers.

Makes about 4 cups, 12 to 16 servings

Make Ahead: The chutney can be made up to 2 weeks ahead.

One 12-ounce bag cranberries
One 28-ounce can tomatoes in juice, drained
1 cup packed light brown sugar
½ cup raisins
1 medium onion, chopped
1 tablespoon shredded fresh ginger (use the large holes on a box grater)
1 jalapeño, seeded and minced
1 teaspoon yellow mustard seeds
1 cinnamon stick
1 garlic clove, minced

In a medium, heavy-bottomed saucepan over medium heat, bring all of the ingredients to a simmer, stirring often to dissolve the brown sugar. Reduce the heat to low and simmer until thickened, about 10 minutes. Cool completely. Remove the cinnamon stick. (The chutney can be made up to 2 weeks ahead, covered, and refrigerated.) Serve at room temperature.

Spiked Cranberry–Orange Sauce

Oranges and cranberries are old friends, and but it is the orange liqueur that makes this sauce extraordinary. Use a dark-hued orange liqueur, which indicates that it is made with brandy and has more flavor than the clear varieties.

Makes about 3 cups, 12 servings

Make Ahead: The cranberry sauce can be made up to 1 week ahead.

2 large navel oranges
One 12-ounce bag cranberries
1½ cups sugar
2 tablespoons orange-flavored liqueur, such as Grand Marnier or Grand Gala

1. Grate 2 teaspoons zest from the oranges and set aside. Using a sharp knife, cut off and discard the thick white pith. Carefully cut between the membranes to release the orange sections. Set the orange sections aside.

2. In a medium, heavy-bottomed saucepan, combine the cranberries, sugar, 1 cup water, and the zest. Bring to a boil over medium heat, stirring often to help dissolve the sugar. Reduce the heat to low and simmer until the sauce is thick and the cranberries have burst, 10 to 15 minutes. During the last few minutes, stir in the orange sections. Remove from the heat and stir in the Grand Marnier. Cool completely. (The cranberry sauce can be made up to 1 week ahead, covered, and refrigerated.) Serve at room temperature.

CLASSIC RECIPES

Homemade Cranberry Sauce

There are really three "classic" cranberry sauce recipes. The first two, whole berry and jellied, are cooked. Cranberry-orange relish is prepared from raw berries. Which of these three is your idea of classic just depends on which one you grew up on. Thanks to Ocean Spray Cranberries for providing the following archetypal versions of these timeless classics.

Fresh Cranberry Sauce

Makes 2¼ cups, 8 to 10 servings

Make Ahead: The sauce can be made up to 1 week ahead.

1 cup sugar
One 12-ounce bag Ocean Spray Cranberries

In a medium saucepan, bring 1 cup water and the sugar to a boil over high heat, stirring to dissolve the sugar. Stir in the cranberries and return to a boil. Reduce the heat to low and boil gently, stirring occasionally, until the cranberries have all popped and the sauce is thick, about 10 minutes. The sauce will thicken upon standing. Transfer to a small bowl and cool completely. Cover tightly with plastic wrap and refrigerate until ready to serve. (The sauce can be made up to 1 week ahead.) Serve chilled or at room temperature.

Homemade Jellied Cranberry Sauce

Makes 1 cup, 4 to 6 servings

Make Ahead: The sauce can be made up to 1 week ahead.

1 cup sugar
One 12-ounce bag Ocean Spray Cranberries

1. In a medium saucepan, bring 1 cup water and the sugar to a boil over high heat, stirring to dissolve the sugar. Stir in the cranberries and return to a boil. Reduce the heat to low and boil gently, stirring occasionally, for 10 minutes.
2. Place a wire sieve over a medium mixing bowl. Pour the sauce into the sieve. Mash the sauce with the back of a large spoon, frequently scraping the outside of the strainer, until there is no pulp left in the sieve. Stir well and transfer to a small bowl. Cool completely. Cover tightly with plastic wrap and refrigerate until ready to serve. (The sauce can be made up to 1 week ahead.) Serve chilled or at room temperature.

Fresh Cranberry–Orange Relish

Makes 3 cups, 12 servings

Make Ahead: The relish can be made up to 1 day ahead.

1 medium orange
One 12-ounce bag Ocean Spray Cranberries
¾ to 1 cup sugar

Cut the unpeeled orange into eighths, and pick out any seeds. Place half of the orange pieces and half of the cranberries in the work bowl of a food processor. Process until the mixture is evenly chopped. Transfer to a bowl.

Repeat with the remaining orange and cranberries. Stir in sugar to taste. (The relish can be made up to 1 day ahead, covered tightly with plastic wrap, and refrigerated.) Serve chilled or at room temperature.

Rick's Cranberry–Double Orange Relish: Substitute 1 cup orange marmalade for the sugar, adding ½ cup to each batch in the food processor.

Rick's Cranberry-Kumquat Relish: Substitute 1½ cups (about 5 ounces) sliced fresh kumquats for the orange.

Cranberry-Pineapple Salsa

The fresh, crisp texture of this sweet-and-tangy salsa is very refreshing, and just the foil for Southwestern flavors like smoked turkey. The ingredients are all mixed together in a food processor, but it is best to coarsely chop some of the ingredients before they go into the bowl or they won't attain the proper consistency. Don't make this salsa too far ahead of time, as the scallions and garlic will overwhelm the fruit.

Makes about 3½ cups, 12 servings

The Cranberry Sauce Incident

Of course, many people consider canned cranberry sauce more classic than any homemade version. While I always serve some kind of homemade cranberry sauce (or chutney or salsa), I have learned that I'd better have a backup of canned sauce, too.

One Thanksgiving, I was visiting my family in California, and I was designated head chef (Mom was taking a break that year). As I was pulling food out of the refrigerator, my brothers noticed something different.

"Where's the cranberry sauce?!" they demanded.

"This *is* cranberry sauce," I calmly replied, presenting the Cranberry, Ginger, and Lemon Chutney (page 111) that my New York friends eat by the barrel.

They looked at me as if I had gone crazy. "No, not that fancy stuff. The kind we always put on Grandma's glass plate!"

"Well, just give this a try . . ."

But they would have none of it. They hopped into the car and drove to the convenience store down the road, and returned, minutes (or was it seconds?) later, with their prize—a can of cranberry sauce.

They carefully unmolded the quivering tube of canned sauce onto Grandma's cut-glass oblong serving dish (which, to my knowledge, has not been used to serve anything else in over fifty years). Cutting into the sauce was ritualistic, each serving carefully designated by the rings on the tube—again proving that nostalgia is one of the most important ingredients served up at Thanksgiving.

Make Ahead: The salsa is best made no longer than 2 hours before serving.

One 12-ounce bag cranberries
½ medium pineapple, pared, cored, and coarsely chopped (about 2 packed cups)
¼ cup sugar
1 scallion (white and green parts), coarsely chopped
2 tablespoons chopped fresh mint or cilantro
1 jalapeño, seeded and minced
1 garlic clove, minced
¼ teaspoon salt

Place all of the ingredients in a food processor fitted with the metal chopping blade. Pulse until the cranberries are coarsely chopped. Transfer to a serving dish and cover tightly with plastic wrap. Refrigerate for at least 30 minutes but no longer than 2 hours. Serve chilled.

Cranberry and Fig Sauce

I developed this recipe to go with my Italian-style Thanksgiving menu. It is inspired by *mostarda di Cremona* (candied fruits in a mustard syrup), a wonderful Italian condiment for turkey and ham. Make it at least 1 day ahead to allow the mustard flavor to blossom.

Makes about 3 cups, 10 to 12 servings

Make Ahead: The cranberry sauce must be made 1 day before serving; it can also be made up to 1 week ahead, covered, and refrigerated.

One 12-ounce bag fresh cranberries
2 cups sugar
7 ounces Calimyrna figs, cut into ¼-inch cubes (about 1½ cups)
2 teaspoons yellow mustard seeds
¼ teaspoon crushed hot red pepper flakes
1 tablespoon dry English mustard

1. In a medium saucepan, combine all of the ingredients except the dry mustard. Bring to a boil over medium heat, stirring often to help dissolve the sugar. Reduce the heat to low and simmer until the sauce is thick and the cranberries have burst, 10 to 15 minutes.

2. Dissolve the dry mustard in 1 tablespoon cold water. Stir into the cranberry sauce. Cool completely. Cover tightly with plastic wrap and refrigerate overnight. (The cranberry sauce can be made up to 1 week ahead.) Serve chilled or at room temperature.

Mulled Wine Cranberry Sauce

The vibrant flavor of this homemade condiment will banish memories of mundane cranberry sauce. The spices are mild enough not to be overwhelming, but sufficiently assertive to make their presence known.

Makes about 4 cups, 8 to 12 servings

Make Ahead: The sauce can be made up to 1 week ahead.

2 large navel oranges
One 12-ounce bag fresh or frozen cranberries
1½ cups hearty red wine, preferably a Cabernet-Shiraz blend
½ cup packed light brown sugar
¼ cup chopped crystallized ginger
½ teaspoon ground cinnamon
⅛ teaspoon ground cloves
⅛ teaspoon ground nutmeg

1. Grate the zest from 1 orange and set aside. Peel both of the oranges. Working over bowl to catch the juices, cut between the membranes to release the segments. Set the orange segments and juices aside.

2. Mix the cranberries, orange zest, red wine, brown sugar, ginger, cinnamon, cloves, and nutmeg in a medium, heavy-bottomed saucepan over medium heat. Strain the orange juice into the saucepan. Bring to a boil over medium heat, stirring often. Reduce the heat to medium-low and simmer uncovered, stirring often, until the berries are completely popped and the juices thicken, about 20 minutes. Remove from the heat and stir in the orange segments. Cool to room temperature. (The cranberry sauce can be prepared up to 1 week ahead, cooled, covered, and refrigerated.)

Four Gravies to Go

When I first moved to Manhattan, my kitchen was the size of an average-sized bedroom bureau. The best thing about the apartment was the neighborhood—the Upper West Side. I lived near the block where Macy's blew up the balloons for the parade. Every Thanksgiving Eve, my friends and I would leave our restaurant jobs and meet at about 1 a.m. to watch the amazing sight of those enormous rubber sculptures being inflated. Of course, we'd get to bed around 3:30 a.m., only to get up a couple of hours later to reserve our spaces along the parade route. Then, we would stagger back to my place and start Thanksgiving dinner. (Once, we were so behind schedule, we sped up the turkey by splitting it lengthwise and roasting the halves. It worked.)

There was a door in the apartment that led into the service staircase, down to the street. Everyone was in the living room, and I was making gravy. While I was balancing the pan on the minuscule stove, something terrible happened . . . the pan fell to the floor, spilling the gravy with a loud crash.

My friends tried to run into the kitchen and see what went wrong, but I diverted them. "Everything's fine. Have another drink. I'll be right out." I ran down the back stairs and straight into the twenty-four-hour coffee shop on the corner. (Yes, it was just like the one on *Seinfeld*.) Luckily, the friendliest waiter on the staff was working.

"Nick! Happy Thanksgiving! Do you have any turkey gravy?"

"Sure. How much do you need?"

"Enough for eight people."

So he filled up four coffee cups with canned turkey gravy (what else?) and put them in a bag. I ran upstairs, poured them into a pot, and stirred in a slug of bourbon. Without telling a soul of my trials, I poured the gravy into a sauceboat and calmly served it.

Everyone told me it was the best gravy I ever made. And I have put bourbon in my gravy ever since.

Pan Gravy 101

You'll find details for making an appropriate gravy or sauce for each of the turkey recipes, but here are separate instructions to use as an overview. There are a lot of ways to make gravy—thickening with a flour-water paste or cornstarch, using a saucepan or a roasting pan. But here's how to make the most delicious, greasefree, lumpless, dark mahogany brown gravy in the world.

- Treat gravy as a classic French roux-based sauce, which has exact proportions of fat, flour, and liquid. Many cooks just stir enough flour into the pan drippings to make a paste and add water to make gravy. The problem here is that one never knows how much fat will be released during roasting, and if the proportions are off, the paste gets lumpy or greasy. And in the flour-water paste method, where the paste is whisked into the simmering drippings, the flour does not combine properly with the fat, so the gravy still turns out greasy. My recipe uses a measured amount of the fat skimmed from the drippings and turkey stock to give a rich turkey flavor. I prefer a flour-based gravy to a cornstarch-thickened one, as the latter turns out glossy rather than opaque and is more a sauce than a gravy.
- Homemade turkey stock makes the best gravy. You want brown, not pale beige, gravy that tastes like turkey, and stock's color and depth of flavor help achieve this. If you don't want to make the full large-batch recipe (page 34), at least make the small-batch version (page 35) with the neck and giblets (without the liver). Some upscale butchers make turkey stock during the holiday season, and that is another alternative. Canned or aseptically packaged turkey broth is becoming easier to find, but I prefer to simmer the browned neck and giblets in the canned broth for an hour or so to freshen the flavor. Canned chicken broth will only do if you are under the most dire time restrictions. I know that may sound a bit heavy-handed, but after making countless batches of gravy, I am not talking through my hat.
- The proportions for gravy are 1½ tablespoons each fat and all-purpose flour to each cup of liquid, part of which should be the pan drippings. Use these proportions for any size turkey and any amount of gravy. For example, to yield slightly less than 4 cups of gravy (some of the liquid will evaporate during simmering), use 6 tablespoons each fat and flour, and 4 cups liquid. If your family likes thicker gravy, increase the fat and flour to 2 tablespoons—you can always thin it down with more stock. Because you want to measure the ingredients accurately, you will need both a small (1- or 2-cup) and large (1-quart) glass measuring cup, as well as a set of measuring spoons.
- The secret to dark, rich gravy? Dark, rich pan drippings. Let the drippings evaporate into a dark brown glaze during roasting, but don't let them burn. Whenever the pan looks dry, moisten the drippings with more turkey stock or water so they don't scorch. The darker and heavier your roasting pan, the darker and richer the drippings. Disposable aluminum roasters make wimpy drippings.
- Always degrease the drippings and stock before making gravy, reserving the skimmed fat. Pour the pan drippings into a large glass bowl or gravy separator. Gravy separators are great, but they are not all created equal. Be sure to use a large 4-cup model, as the smaller 2-cup ones are really for chicken and cannot accommodate the copious amounts of

drippings that a huge turkey can produce. The separator should have a wide spout—some of them have narrow spouts that clog so easily they are more of a nuisance than a help. Models with perforated tops to strain the drippings as they enter the cup are well worth having.

- **Let the drippings stand for 5 minutes so the clear yellow fat can rise to the top of the drippings. If the fat is in a bowl, use a large spoon to skim off the fat and transfer to a 1- to 2-cup glass measuring cup. If using a gravy separator, pour off the fat into the cup. If you don't have enough fat to make the amount of gravy needed, add melted butter.**

- **The degreased drippings add color and flavor to the gravy. Combine them with the turkey stock or chicken broth to get the desired amount of liquid. You'll never resort to commercial gravy coloring again.**

- **Use a whisk to avoid lumpy gravy. A flat, paddle-shaped whisk works better than a balloon whisk to reach into the corners of the pan. If you have a nonstick roasting pan, use a heatproof plastic whisk, available at kitchenware stores. My flat, plastic whisk has become an indispensable tool.**

- **Allow ⅓ cup gravy per person, more if you want leftovers for sandwiches.**

Makes about 3½ cups

Pan drippings from roast turkey
About 3½ cups Homemade Turkey Stock 101 (page 34)
6 tablespoons all-purpose flour
Salt
Freshly ground black pepper

1. When the turkey is done, transfer it to a serving platter and set aside. Pour the pan drippings into a medium glass bowl or gravy separator, leaving any browned bits in the bottom of the roasting pan. Let stand for 5 minutes. If the drippings are in a bowl, use a large metal spoon to skim and transfer clear yellow fat that rises to the surface to a 1- to 2-cup measuring cup and reserve the fat. For a gravy separator, pour the drippings into a 1-quart measuring cup, leaving the fat in the separator.

2. Assess the color of the drippings. If they don't seem dark enough, pour half back into the roasting pan and set over two burners. Bring to a boil over high heat, and cook until the drippings reduce and darken, occasionally adding the remaining drippings until the liquid in the pan is as dark as you want. The amount of drippings will decrease, but the finished gravy will be darker and taste better without having to resort to bottled gravy coloring. Return the drippings to the large measuring cup, and add enough stock to the drippings to measure 4 cups total cooking liquid.

3. Set the roasting pan on top of the stove over two burners on moderately low heat. Add 6 tablespoons of the reserved fat to the pan. Sprinkle the flour into the pan, whisking constantly. Let the mixture bubble, whisking constantly, until it turns light beige, 1 to 2 minutes. It is important to let the mixture cook for a minute or two to allow the flour to lose its raw taste, but adjust the heat as needed to keep it from burning. If the flour is overcooked, it will lose its thickening power. Whisk in the stock/drippings mixture, scraping up the browned bits on the bottom of the pan. Simmer for 2 to 3 minutes, whisking occasionally. If the gravy seems too thin, increase the heat to medium and boil until it is as thick as you wish. If the gravy seems too thick, thin with additional stock. Season with salt and pepper. If you wish, strain the gravy through a wire sieve to remove any extraneous browned bits.

Giblet Gravy: If you have made Homemade Turkey Stock 101, finely chop the cooked giblets and neck meat. Or simmer the giblets and neck with 3½ cups canned reduced-sodium chicken broth; 2½ cups water; 1 small onion, sliced; and 1 small carrot, coarsely chopped, until tender, about 2 hours. Cool and chop the meat. Strain the mixture and use in place of the turkey stock.

Roast Garlic Gravy: For every 4 cups finished gravy, stir in 1 head garlic, roasted and pureed (see page 89).

Wine Gravy: Substitute up to one-quarter the cooking liquid with dry white wine. For example, for about 4 cups gravy, use 3 cups cooking liquid and 1 cup wine. Red wine makes a murky gravy, so stick to white.

Spiked Gravy: For every 1 cup cooking liquid, add 1 to 2 tablespoons dry sherry; ruby or tawny port; Madeira, brandy, or Cognac; or bourbon. Do not overdo the alcohol, or the gravy will taste too strong.

Herbed Gravy: For every 4 cups finished gravy, stir in up to 2 tablespoons minced fresh herbs, such as thyme, sage, rosemary, parsley, or tarragon, or a combination.

Head Start Gravy

When you have a crowd coming, you may want to get a head start on the gravy before the troops arrive. Here's my strategy: A couple of days ahead, make a turkey gravy base with butter instead of turkey fat. On Thanksgiving, color and enrich the base by stirring it into the degreased drippings from the roasted bird. Voila! It's not exactly "instant" gravy, but pretty close.

Follow the proportions for Pan Gravy 101 (page 117), substituting unsalted butter for the skimmed turkey fat. Melt the butter in a large, heavy-bottomed saucepan over medium heat. Whisk in the flour and let bubble until very lightly browned, 2 to 3 minutes. Whisk in the stock and bring to a simmer. Reduce the heat to medium-low and cook until lightly thickened, about 10 minutes. The gravy base will be pale and thin-bodied. Cool the gravy base completely, cover, and refrigerate for up to 2 days. Don't worry about a skin forming, as it will melt away when the gravy is reheated.

After the Thanksgiving turkey has roasted, pour out the drippings into a gravy separator or glass bowl and let stand for 5 minutes. Pour or skim off and discard the turkey fat that rises to the surface. Pour the degreased brown drippings back into the pan and place over two burners on medium heat. Whisk in the gravy base and bring to a boil, stirring up the browned bits in the pan, which will color the gravy base. Cook, stirring often, until the gravy reduces and thickens, about 10 minutes. Season with salt and pepper. (If you have too much gravy base to fit into the pan, whisk in 1 quart of the base and pour this mixture back into the remaining gravy base. Transfer to a large pot and reheat over medium heat, stirring often.) Skim, if needed, and serve hot.

This "head start gravy" can also be served with turkeys that don't produce drippings, such as Bayou Deep-fried Turkey (page 64). It also acts as an insurance policy against recipes that might not produce perfect drippings, like Oven-Blasted Turkey (page 57) or Herb-Brined Roast Turkey (page 59).

Bloody Marys (page 22), Glittering Spiced Walnuts (page 13), Savory Cheddar and Jalapeño Jelly Cookies (page 18)

Above: Baby Spinach and Fuyu Persimmon Salad with Ginger Vinaigrette (page 36)
Opposite: Sweet Potato and Peanut Soup (page 32)

Following pages: Perfect Roast Turkey (page 56), Sausage Gumbo Dressing (page 84), Scalloped Yams with Praline Topping (page 104), Broccoli and Cauliflower with Almonds (page 88), Cranberry, Ginger, and Lemon Chutney (page 111)

Opposite: Rosemary and Cracked Pepper Corn Sticks (page 129), Fluffy Angel Biscuits (page 124), Spiced Yam and Pecan Muffins (page 130). *Above:* Pumpkin-Hazelnut Pie (page 142)

Turkey and Black Bean Tamale Pie (page 169)

Yeast and Quick Breads

Rising to the Occasion

If there is one day of the year when home-baked breads should be served, it's Thanksgiving. To me, the ritual of passing a basket of hot rolls is as important as that of carving the turkey. Baking bread is one of the most satisfying things a cook can do, and it doesn't have to be complicated. All of the recipes in this chapter are designed for beginning bakers, although practiced bread makers will appreciate their old-fashioned flavor. Only two recipes use yeast, and only one of them requires kneading. In other words, you'll have scant excuse for not serving fragrant, warm, home-baked bread at your meal. Here is a guide to some ingredients in this chapter:

Flour: For most yeast doughs, use unbleached or bread flour. Organic unbleached flour, available at natural food stores, gives the bread an incredible flavor and a chewy texture. Quick breads, leavened with baking powder or baking soda, are best made with all-purpose flour, either bleached or unbleached.

Cornmeal: Stone-ground cornmeal has a coarser texture than mass-processed cornmeal, which translates into fuller flavor. Stone-ground cornmeal is available in natural food stores and many supermarkets. Some cooks feel that white cornmeal is sweeter than yellow cornmeal, and has a fuller corn flavor. All cornmeal is fairly perishable and should be stored in the refrigerator. However, the stone-ground variety is even more delicate, as it contains more oils that can turn rancid than its overprocessed kin, and should be stored in a plastic bag in the freezer. Let the frozen cornmeal stand at room temperature for about 30 minutes to warm up before using.

Yeast: I use active dry yeast because it is commonly available. However, some of my local supermarkets have only been carrying quick-rising instant yeast, also called "yeast for bread machines." This yeast is formulated differently from active dry yeast, and reduces the rising time. That's all well and good, but good bakers know that dough needs time to rise to develop flavor. Rather than follow the instructions on the label, which reduce the rising time by about half, I prefer to use slightly less instant yeast to give the traditional rising time. These recipes give measurements for both active dry and instant yeast. Don't worry about using the hot liquids recommended in the instant yeast's instructions, and just dissolve the yeast in warm water as required for the active dry yeast. If you want to speed the rising, substitute equal amounts of instant yeast for active dry yeast, following the instructions on the package of the former. Store yeast in the refrigerator and use by the expiration date on the package. Freezing yeast does not extend its shelf life.

Yeast is a living thing, and hot water will kill it. Just use warm water that feels slightly warmer than body temperature, which means a range of 105° to 115°F. If you are nervous about the correct temperature, test the water with an instant-read thermometer.

Buttermilk: Buttermilk makes bread with a deliciously tender crumb. The acids in the tangy buttermilk tenderize the gluten proteins in the flour. (I know that not everyone loves to drink buttermilk, but it is inexpensive, so if you have leftovers that you have to throw out, you won't go broke.) Dried buttermilk powder, which can be reconstituted with water and is available at some supermarkets and natural food stores, is all right, but the viscosity doesn't match that of fresh buttermilk. I prefer substituting ⅔ cup plain yogurt whisked with ⅓ cup low-fat or whole milk for each cup of buttermilk.

Dinner Rolls 101

Fresh-baked rolls, right out of the oven . . . I bet your mouth is watering just reading those words. Here is my favorite dinner roll recipe—chewy, with a thin crust and unsurpassable homemade flavor. Once you have the basic dough, you can form it into balls, cloverleaf rolls, or knots. I am partial to the knots, because even though they are easy to make, they look like you bought them at a bakery. Leave the rolls plain, or take a couple of seconds to sprinkle them with poppy or sesame seeds. You can make the dough by hand, in the food processor, or in a heavy-duty electric mixer. There are a bunch of make-ahead options, but I prefer to time the rolls to come out of the oven just before serving.

- **The dough can be made the night before baking, using only 1½ teaspoons yeast. Divide the dough in half, and close each half in a self-sealing plastic bag. Refrigerate overnight. The next morning, punch down the dough and refrigerate again until ready to shape the rolls. Punch down the dough, shape the rolls as desired, and cover loosely with plastic wrap. Allow the shaped rolls to stand at warm room temperature for about 2 hours to come to room temperature and rise until doubled. Bake as directed. Some bakers freeze the dough, but it takes so long for the dough to defrost and warm up enough to rise, it is not worth the hassle.**

- **The baked rolls can be made up to 1 month ahead, cooled completely, stored in self-sealing plastic bags, and frozen. Allow the rolls to defrost for 1 hour at room temperature before reheating. To reheat, wrap the rolls in aluminum foil, 6 rolls to a package. Bake in a preheated 350°F oven until heated through, 10 to 15 minutes.**

- **To bake and serve the rolls the same day, bake them up to 8 hours before serving. Cool completely. Wrap the rolls in aluminum foil packages and reheat as directed above.**

Makes 1½ dozen

Make Ahead: See the suggestions at left.

One ¼-ounce package active dry yeast or 1¾ teaspoons instant yeast
1½ cups buttermilk
6 tablespoons unsalted butter, melted, plus additional for brushing the rolls
2 large eggs
3 tablespoons sugar
¾ teaspoon baking soda
1½ teaspoons salt
5 cups unbleached flour, as needed
About 2½ teaspoons poppy seeds or sesame seeds, for sprinkling (optional)

1. In a small bowl, sprinkle the yeast over ¼ cup warm (105° to 115°F) water and let stand until creamy, 5 to 10 minutes. Stir to dissolve the yeast.

2. In a medium saucepan, heat the buttermilk, stirring constantly, just until warm (about 100°F). Or place the buttermilk in a 1-quart glass measuring cup and microwave on High for 1 minute, stirring occasionally, until warm. Transfer the buttermilk to a bowl and stir in the dissolved yeast mixture, melted butter, eggs, sugar, baking soda, and salt.

3. *To make the dough by hand*, transfer the liquid ingredients to a large bowl. Gradually stir in enough of the flour to form a shaggy dough. Turn out onto a lightly floured work surface. Knead the dough, adding more flour as needed, until the dough is smooth and elastic, 8 to 10 minutes. Form the dough into a ball.

To make the dough in a heavy-duty standing mixer, pour the liquid ingredients in the mixer bowl, and attach the paddle blade. With the machine on low speed, gradually add enough of the flour to make a stiff dough that collects around the blade. Change to the dough hook. Knead the dough in the machine, adding more flour as needed to make an elastic dough, about 8 minutes. Transfer to a lightly floured work surface and knead by hand until smooth, about 2 minutes. Form the dough into a ball.

To make the dough in a food processor, fit an 11-cup (or larger)-capacity machine with the metal blade. Make the dough in two batches. Place 2½ cups of the flour in the machine and pulse to combine. With the machine running, pour about half of the liquid ingredients through the feed tube to form a soft ball of dough that rides on top of the blade. Process for 45 seconds to knead the dough. Transfer the dough to a lightly floured work surface and cover with plastic wrap. Repeat with the remaining ingredients. Knead the two portions of dough together by hand until smooth and combined. Form the dough into a ball.

4. Place the dough in a large, buttered bowl. Turn the dough to coat with the butter, and turn the dough smooth side up. Cover tightly with plastic wrap and let stand in a warm place until doubled in volume (if you poke the dough with your finger, an impression will remain), about 1¼ hours.

5. Lightly butter two 9-inch round cake pans. Punch down the dough and knead briefly on an unfloured work surface. Cut the dough into 18 equal pieces. (This is easiest to do by cutting the dough into thirds, then each third in half, and each half into 3 pieces.) Cover the cut pieces of dough with a piece of plastic wrap. Place a piece of dough on the work surface. Using the sides of your hands, tuck the dough underneath itself, turning the dough as you tuck, stretching the top surface and eventually forming a taut ball. Transfer the roll to a

prepared pan. Repeat with the remaining piece of dough, allowing 9 balls per pan. Cover loosely with plastic wrap and let stand in a warm place until almost doubled in volume, about 40 minutes.

6. Preheat the oven to 375°F. Brush the tops of the rolls lightly with melted butter and sprinkle with the seeds, if using. Bake until golden brown, 20 to 25 minutes. Remove from the pans and serve warm.

Knot Rolls: Lightly butter two baking sheets. Work with one piece of dough at a time, keeping the others covered with plastic wrap. Roll the dough between your palms into a thick rope. Place the rope on an unfloured work surface. Put your hands on top of the dough and roll it back and forth, stretching the dough into a 9-inch-long rope. Tie the dough into an overhand knot, with the knot positioned in the center of the rope. Place the knots 2 inches apart on the prepared baking sheets. Cover loosely with plastic wrap and let rise until almost doubled in size. Bake as directed above.

Cloverleaf Rolls: Lightly butter 18 muffin cups. Cut each piece of dough into thirds and form each piece into a small, taut ball. Place 3 balls, smooth sides up, in each muffin tin. Cover loosely with plastic wrap and let rise until almost doubled. Bake as directed.

Fluffy Angel Biscuits

These are a variation on the biscuit theme, with a bit of yeast to add fluffiness. Not only does the recipe make sensational biscuits, the dough can be mixed a couple of days ahead of baking. While Buttermilk Biscuits 101 (page 125) uses a homemade baking powder, use a store-bought one in this recipe, as the homemade version will lose its leavening power if the dough stands for too long. Even though this dough contains yeast, all-purpose flour will yield the tenderest biscuits.

This recipe makes a lot of biscuits, perfect for a crowd. When I am not having a big guest list, I still make the entire batch and freeze the leftover biscuits, individually wrapped in aluminum foil. To reheat, bake the unwrapped frozen biscuits in a preheated 400°F oven until heated through, about 10 minutes.

Makes about thirty 2-inch biscuits

Make Ahead: The dough can be prepared up to 2 days ahead; the biscuits are best freshly baked, but they can be baked up to 8 hours ahead.

1 teaspoon active dry yeast or ¾ teaspoon instant yeast
5 cups all-purpose flour
¼ cup sugar
1 tablespoon baking powder, preferably an aluminum-free brand, such as Rumford's
1 teaspoon baking soda
1½ teaspoons salt
1 cup solid vegetable shortening, chilled, cut into pieces
2 cups buttermilk

1. In a small bowl, sprinkle the yeast over 2 tablespoons warm (105° to 115°F) water in a small bowl and let stand until creamy, about 5 minutes. Stir until dissolved and set aside.

2. In a large bowl, mix the flour, sugar, baking powder, baking soda, and salt. Using a pastry blender, cut in the shortening until the mixture resembles coarse crumbs. If the shortening sticks to the pastry blender, just scrape it off. Add the dissolved yeast and the buttermilk, and stir to make a shaggy dough. Knead in the bowl for about a minute to form a soft, sticky dough. Divide the dough between two self-sealing plastic bags, close, and refrigerate at least 3 hours or up to 2 days. If refrigerating for longer than 3 hours, punch down the dough from time to time, but no less than twice every 24 hours.

3. Position racks in the center and top third of the oven, and preheat the oven to 400°F. Turn out the dough onto a lightly floured surface and knead briefly. On a lightly floured surface, pat out the dough with lightly floured hands (or dust the top of the dough with flour and roll out) until ½ inch thick. Using a 2½-inch round biscuit or cookie cutter, cut out biscuits and place them 1 inch apart on ungreased baking sheets. Gather up dough scraps and knead briefly to combine, and repeat the procedure as needed to make about 30 biscuits.

4. Bake, switching the positions of the baking sheets from top to bottom halfway during baking, until the biscuits are barely golden, 15 to 20 minutes. Serve immediately.

Buttermilk Biscuits 101

Here they are, the most tender, most delicious, most buttery old-fashioned biscuits in the land. For the classic biscuit shape and texture, roll out the dough and cut into rounds or squares. Or add some whole milk to mix a softer dough that can be dropped from a spoon to create biscuits with a crispy surface. Either way, you will be serving an American classic.

- **Ask any Southern cook for the secret to making tender biscuits, and the answer is usually the flour. Southern flour (like White Lily brand) is milled from soft wheat and has a low gluten content, whereas the rest of the country uses a combination of hard and soft flours with a higher gluten. To approximate soft wheat flour, mix cake flour (made from very soft wheat) with all-purpose flour. Of course, if you live in the South, just use White Lily.**

- **Many biscuits use baking powder as a leavening, which starts with a simple combination of acid (cream of tartar) and alkali (baking soda). When moistened, the mixture forms carbon dioxide gases that make the biscuits rise. Most commercial baking powders include aluminum derivatives, too, that can give your baked goods a metallic taste. (An exception is my favorite brand, Rumford's, which is available at natural food stores and many supermarkets. If you wish, you can substitute 4½ teaspoons Rumford's baking powder for the cream of tartar and baking soda combination here.) This recipe calls for a homemade baking powder made from the cream of tartar and baking soda, which are probably already in the kitchen cabinet.**

- **Handle the biscuit dough as little as possible to keep the gluten in the flour from**

toughening. (See Perfect Piecrust 101 on page 135 for a more detailed discussion of gluten.)

- **Use a ruler to measure the dough's thickness. If the dough is rolled too thin, the biscuits will be skimpy.**
- **To cut out round biscuits, use a 2½-inch round biscuit or cookie cutter. Juice glasses don't make a clean cut, and are a barely acceptable substitute for a cutter. With round biscuits, you will always have scraps. Taking care not to overhandle the dough, gently knead the scraps together and roll out again. Although the subsequent batches will not be quite as tender as the first, most people won't be able to tell the difference.**
- **To make square biscuits (which avoid the scrap problem altogether), roll or pat the dough into a ¾-inch square, and cut into 12 squares.**
- **To make drop biscuits, mix in an additional ¼ cup *whole* milk, not buttermilk, to make a loose, sticky dough. Drop the dough by heaping tablespoons onto ungreased baking sheets, spacing them 1 inch apart.**

Makes 1 dozen

Make Ahead: The biscuits can be prepared up to 8 hours ahead.

1½ cups cake flour (not self-rising)
1½ cups all-purpose flour
1 tablespoon cream of tartar
1½ teaspoons baking soda
¾ teaspoon salt
12 tablespoons (1½ sticks) unsalted butter, cut into ½-inch cubes
1 cup plus 2 tablespoons buttermilk

1. Position a rack in the top third of the oven and preheat the oven to 400°F.

2. In a large bowl, sift together the cake flour, all-purpose flour, cream of tartar, baking soda, and salt. Using a pastry blender, cut in the butter until it resembles coarse meal. Mix in the buttermilk until combined. Knead lightly in the bowl to make a soft dough. Do not overwork the dough.

3. On a lightly floured work surface, pat out the dough with floured hands to a ¾-inch thickness. (Or lightly dust the top of the dough with flour and roll it out.) Using a 2½-inch round cookie cutter, cut out biscuits and place on an ungreased baking sheet. Gather up the scraps, knead gently to combine, pat out again, and repeat the procedure to get a total of 12 biscuits.

4. Bake until the biscuits are risen and golden brown, about 15 minutes. (The biscuits can be baked up to 8 hours ahead, cooled, and stored at room temperature. To reheat, wrap the biscuits, 6 to a package, in aluminum foil. Bake in a preheated 350°F oven for about 15 minutes.) Serve hot or warm.

Anadama Rolls

Legend says that these cornmeal mush–molasses rolls are named for a New England fisherman's curse on his wife: "Anna, damn her!" Regardless of what she may have done to upset her spouse, she was a great baker. These rolls are mildly sweet, with a satisfyingly substantial crumb.

Makes 18 rolls

Make Ahead: The rolls can be made the night before serving.

1 cup milk
2 teaspoons salt
½ cup yellow cornmeal
⅓ cup unsulfured (light) molasses
2 tablespoons (¼ stick) butter
½ cup warm water (105° to 115°F)
1 envelope dry yeast
5½ cups unbleached flour, as needed
2 tablespoons (¼ stick) butter, melted, plus additional softened butter for the bowl and pans
2 teaspoons sesame seeds or poppy seeds

1. Bring 1 cup water, the milk, and salt to a boil in a medium saucepan over medium heat. In a steady stream, whisk in the cornmeal and return to the boil. Cook, whisking constantly, until the cornmeal is thick, about 1 minute. Remove from the heat and whisk in the molasses and butter. Transfer to a large bowl (or the bowl of a standing heavy-duty mixer). Let cool to lukewarm (105°F or below), whisking often.

2. Meanwhile, pour the warm water into a small bowl and sprinkle in the yeast. Let stand until the yeast looks creamy, about 10 minutes.

3. Whisk the dissolved yeast mixture into the lukewarm cornmeal mixture. Gradually mix in enough flour to form a soft dough that pulls away from the sides of the bowl. Knead the dough on a floured work surface, adding more flour as needed (the dough will remain slightly sticky) to keep the dough from clinging to your hands and the work surface. Knead until the dough is smooth and elastic, about 10 minutes.

To make the dough in a heavy-duty mixer, attach the bowl with the cornmeal-yeast mixture to the mixer. Attach the paddle blade and turn the speed to low. Gradually add enough of the flour to make a soft dough that barely pulls away from the sides of the bowl, being careful not to add too much flour (the dough will remain slightly sticky). Transfer to the dough hook and knead until the dough is smooth and elastic, about 8 minutes.

4. Form the dough into a ball. Butter a large bowl well. Add the dough, turning the dough to coat. Cover the bowl with plastic wrap. Let the dough rise in a warm draft-free area until doubled, about 1¼ hours.

5. Butter two 9-inch-diameter cake pans. Punch down the dough. Cover the dough with plastic wrap and let stand 10 minutes. Divide the dough in half. Roll each piece of dough into a 9-inch log and cut each log into 9 equal pieces. Form each dough piece into a taut ball, and place 9 rolls in each pan smooth side up. Cover each pan with plastic wrap. Let stand until almost doubled, about 30 minutes.

6. Position a rack in the center of the oven and preheat the oven to 400°F. Brush the tops of the rolls with the melted butter and sprinkle with the seeds. Place the pans of rolls in the oven, and immediately reduce the oven temperature to 350°F. Bake until the rolls are golden brown, about 25 minutes. Serve warm. (The rolls can be prepared the night before serving. Completely cool the rolls. Store airtight at room temperature. Rewarm the rolls wrapped in foil in a 350°F oven, about 10 minutes before serving.)

Southern Corn Bread

More solid and crumbly than Yankee Corn Bread (at right), this is the one to use for dressing, or if your tastes run to firm corn bread. Use white or yellow cornmeal, according to what your Granny taught you.

Makes 12 servings, or 10 cups crumbled corn bread for stuffing

Make Ahead: Corn bread is best freshly baked, but it can be made up to 8 hours ahead.

2½ cups white or yellow cornmeal, preferably stone-ground
1½ cups all-purpose flour
1 tablespoon plus 1 teaspoon baking powder
1 teaspoon salt
2 cups milk
6 tablespoons (½ stick plus 2 tablespoons) unsalted butter, melted
2 large eggs, beaten

1. Position a rack in the center of the oven and preheat the oven to 375°F. Lightly butter a 9 × 13-inch baking pan.

2. In a large bowl, whisk the cornmeal, flour, baking powder, and salt well to combine. Make a well in the center, and pour in the milk, melted butter, and eggs. Stir just until combined. Pour into the prepared pan and smooth the top.

3. Bake until golden brown and a toothpick inserted in the center comes out clean, 25 to 30 minutes. Cool for 5 minutes. (The corn bread can be baked up to 8 hours ahead. To reheat, cool and cut it into serving pieces. Wrap in aluminum foil, about 6 pieces to a package, and bake in a preheated 350°F oven for about 15 minutes.)

4. Cut the corn bread into serving pieces, and remove from the pan with a spatula. Serve warm.

Note: Corn bread for stuffing can be baked up to 1 month ahead, cooled, wrapped tightly in plastic wrap and an overwrap of aluminum foil, and frozen. Or bake up to 2 days ahead and store at room temperature.

To use for stuffing, crumble the corn bread onto baking sheets. Let stand overnight at room temperature to dry out. Or bake in a preheated 350°F oven, stirring occasionally, until slightly dried out but not toasted, about 20 minutes.

Yankee Corn Bread

Northerners like their corn bread on the sweet side. Some bakers increase the sugar to ¼ cup in this recipe, but I prefer to use a lighter hand. With the minimum of sugar, you can make two excellent variations: one with chiles and cheese, the other with bacon.

Makes 12 servings

Make Ahead: Corn bread is best freshly baked, but it can be made up to 8 hours ahead.

1⅓ cups yellow cornmeal, preferably stone-ground
1⅓ cups all-purpose flour
2 tablespoons sugar
1 teaspoon salt
1 teaspoon baking soda
2 cups buttermilk
8 tablespoons (1 stick) unsalted butter, melted
2 large eggs, beaten

1. Position a rack in the center of the oven and preheat the oven to 375°F.

2. In a large bowl, whisk the cornmeal, flour, sugar, salt, and baking soda well to combine. Make a well in the center. Pour in the buttermilk, 4 tablespoons of the melted butter,

and the eggs. Stir just until smooth. Do not overbeat.

3. Pour the remaining 4 tablespoons butter in a 9 × 13-inch baking dish and place in the oven. Heat until the butter is very hot but not browned, about 2 minutes. Pour the batter into the hot pan. Bake until the top is golden and a toothpick inserted in the center comes out clean, 25 to 30 minutes. Cool for 5 minutes. (The bread can be baked up to 8 hours ahead. To reheat, cool and cut the corn bread into serving pieces. Wrap in aluminum foil, about 6 pieces to a package, and bake in a preheated 350°F oven for about 15 minutes.)

4. Cut the corn bread into serving pieces, and remove from the pan with a spatula. Serve warm or at room temperature.

Southwestern Chile and Cheese Corn Bread: Stir 1½ cups (6 ounces) extra-sharp Cheddar cheese and 2 jalapeño peppers, seeded and minced, into the batter.

Old-fashioned Bacon Corn Bread: In a large skillet over medium heat, cook 6 strips of bacon until crisp. Reserving the bacon drippings, transfer the bacon to paper towels; cool and chop the bacon. Combine ¼ cup of the bacon drippings with ¼ cup melted butter and substitute for the 8 tablespoons melted butter in the batter. Fold the chopped bacon into the finished batter; do not overmix.

Rosemary and Cracked Pepper Corn Sticks

Savory with rosemary and cracked peppercorns, this is corn bread with a delicious difference. You'll need cast-iron corn-stick molds to make these. Before any cast-iron utensil is used for the first time, it needs to be "seasoned" according to the manufacturer's instructions to build up a patina of oil on the cooking surface. And after baking, never wash the molds with soap and water or you'll wash off the seasoning and have to season them again. If you don't have corn-stick molds, the batter can also be baked as muffins, according to the instructions following this recipe.

Makes 12 corn sticks

Make Ahead: The corn sticks can be baked up to 8 hours ahead.

1¼ cups all-purpose flour
1 cup yellow or white cornmeal, preferably stone-ground
2 teaspoons chopped fresh rosemary or 1 teaspoon crumbled dried rosemary
1 teaspoon baking powder
1 teaspoon salt
¾ teaspoon coarsely cracked black peppercorns (use a mortar and pestle or crush under a heavy skillet or saucepan)
1½ cups milk
4 tablespoons unsalted butter (½ stick), melted
1 large egg
Nonstick vegetable oil spray

SPECIAL EQUIPMENT

Two 6-stick corn stick molds

1. Position a rack in the top third of the oven and place the corn-stick molds in the oven to heat while the oven is preheating. Preheat the oven to 425°F.

2. In a medium bowl, whisk the flour, cornmeal, rosemary, baking powder, salt, and pepper to combine. Make a well in the center. Pour in the milk, melted butter, and egg. Beat the egg to break it up, then stir the wet ingredients into the dry, just until combined. Do not overbeat.

3. Carefully remove the hot molds from the oven and spray with the oil. Spoon the batter into the molds (they will almost fill the molds completely). Return the molds to the oven. Bake until golden brown and the corn sticks pull away from the sides of the molds, about 15 minutes. Let cool in the pan for 2 minutes, then unmold. (The corn sticks can be baked up to 8 hours before serving. Cool completely, then wrap in aluminum foil, 6 corn sticks to a package. To reheat, bake in a preheated 350°F oven until heated through, 10 to 15 minutes.) Serve immediately.

Old-fashioned Corn Sticks: Delete the rosemary and cracked peppercorns. Add 1 tablespoon sugar to the batter.

Rosemary and Cracked Pepper Muffins: Spoon the batter into 9 buttered muffin tins. So the muffins will bake evenly, add about 2 tablespoons water to each empty tin. Bake until a toothpick inserted in the center comes out clean, about 20 minutes.

Spiced Yam and Pecan Muffins

Yams (call them sweet potatoes, if you wish) add their distinctive taste and color to these not-too-sweet muffins. When preparing mashed yams to use in batters and doughs, yams that have been baked are better than those that have been boiled or steamed. Baked yams have more flavor and are drier than boiled ones, which can get waterlogged and throw off the liquid measurements. Even so, the moisture in these muffins makes them bake longer than typical recipes. Use nonstick muffin cups or paper muffin liners, so muffins unmold easily.

Makes 1 dozen muffins

Make Ahead: The muffins can be baked up to 8 hours before serving.

3 medium orange-fleshed yams (1¼ pounds), scrubbed but unpeeled
½ cup packed light brown sugar
1 cup milk
4 tablespoons (½ stick) unsalted butter, melted
2 large eggs
2 cups all-purpose flour
2 teaspoons baking powder
1 teaspoon ground cinnamon
½ teaspoon ground nutmeg
½ teaspoon salt
½ cup coarsely chopped pecans plus 12 pecan halves

1. Preheat the oven to 400°F. Lightly butter 12 nonstick muffin cups (butter them even though they are nonstick) or line with muffin cups.

2. Pierce each yam a few times with a fork. Place on a baking sheet and bake until tender, about 1 hour. Cool until easy to handle. Remove the skins and discard. Rub the yams

through a wire sieve into a small bowl. Cool completely.

3. Transfer 1 cup of the baked yam puree to a medium bowl. Rub the brown sugar through a dry wire sieve into the bowl (this removes any lumps and allows the brown sugar to dissolve easily in the batter) and mix well. Add the milk, melted butter, and eggs, and mix well. Sift together the flour, baking powder, cinnamon, nutmeg, and salt. Stir into the wet ingredients, just until combined. Fold in the chopped pecans. Do not overmix. Spoon equal amounts of the batter into the muffin cups. Top each muffin with a pecan half.

4. Bake until the muffins are lightly browned and a toothpick inserted in the center comes out clean, about 40 minutes. Cool slightly, then unmold. (The muffins can be baked up to 8 hours before serving. Cool completely, then wrap in aluminum foil, 6 muffins to a package. Bake in a preheated 350°F oven until heated through, 10 to 15 minutes.) Serve warm.

Desserts

How Many Ways Can You Say "Pumpkin"?

The turkey dinner may have been wonderful, but afterwards comes another indelible symbol of the Thanksgiving feast: pie. It doesn't have to be pumpkin pie—it could be chocolate, apple, or pecan. You can serve other desserts, too, but don't try to get away with leaving out the pie.

Desserts are chemistry that tastes good. More than other kinds of cooking, which can be instinctive, dessert making calls for a careful balance of the right ingredients. Use a quarter teaspoon too much baking soda (something that is very easy to do if you measure improperly), and the shortcake could be crumbly and flat instead of rising to tender, golden heights.

I don't say this to intimidate you, but to let you in on a few not-so-secret secrets. The happiest bakers follow two basic rules:

1. Measure all ingredients properly. When I cook at friends' homes, I am surprised to see that many people only have one glass measuring cup to do all their measuring chores. These are the same people that are afraid of baking because they have had a few failures. Perhaps if they had measured properly, they would have had successes.

2. Use the right ingredients for the job. This means butter (not margarine), the correct type of flour, and the right size eggs.

Here are some tips on techniques and ingredients to help you make blue-ribbon desserts every time:

- **Measuring:** To measure accurately, use metal measuring cups for dry ingredients, glass measures for liquids, and measuring spoons for small amounts. You can never correctly measure a half-cup of milk in a metal cup, because to get the full measure, the milk would probably overflow. Conversely, you can never get a level cup of flour in a glass measure.

I use the dip-and-sweep method to measure flour. Even though there are other ways to measure, I prefer dip-and-sweep because I am convinced it is the one that most home cooks use. Just dip the measuring cup or measuring spoon into the bag of flour or sugar to completely fill the cup without packing the ingredient. Using the flat side of a knife, sweep the excess from the top of the cup to get a level measurement. When following a recipe in other cookbooks, read the introductory remarks to see what dry-measuring method that cook prefers. Some bakers insist that you spoon the flour into the cup and level it off, but that makes a mess. Others like to weigh the flour on a kitchen scale.

Measure liquid ingredients in glass measuring cups. Plastic cups can warp when filled with hot ingredients. If necessary, hold the cup at eye level to check the measurement.

- **Your Oven:** The position of the oven rack makes a difference. Foods cooked in the top third of the oven brown more efficiently. If you bake a pie in the lower third of a gas oven, nearest the heat source, the crust will crisp better. (For some of the savory recipes in the book, when you will no doubt be crowding many things into the oven to reheat them, I have left out the rack positions for practicality's sake.) Position the rack as directed before preheating the oven. Preheat the oven for at least 15 minutes for it to reach the correct temperature. To verify the oven temperature, use an oven thermometer—oven thermostats are notoriously inaccurate.

- **Mixers:** I use a handheld electric mixer in many of these recipes because it is what most cooks own. If you have a heavy-duty standing mixer, you can certainly use it, but remember that it has a stronger motor and the ingredients will mix in less time.

- **Flour:** Supermarkets carry many different types of flour. Each flour is meant to do a specific job, even if the mills like to use the word "all-purpose." Gluten is a substance found in wheat that gives a dough strength. The more gluten, the tougher the baked dough. Bakers call high-gluten flours "hard," and low-gluten flours "soft." If you are baking a yeast dough that will be kneaded, you want a strong, hard flour, like unbleached flour. If you are baking a pie with a tender crust, you want a moderately strong flour, like bleached "all-purpose," as the bleaching process reduces the gluten's strength (and removes some vitamins, too). Because the actual gluten content of unbleached all-purpose flour varies from brand to brand, many unbleached all-purpose flours aren't versatile at all, and should be reserved for yeast doughs. If you are averse to using bleached flour, you can use the unbleached, but expect slightly less tender results. In this book, "all-purpose flour" means the *bleached* kind. Cake flour is the softest of all to give a delicate crumb, but should not be used unless indicated in the recipe or your baked goods will be too tender.

- **Sugar Products:** *Granulated sugar* is a generic product, and you can use any brand. However, check the label to be sure it is cane sugar. *Brown sugar* comes in two varieties, light and dark. The dark sugar has a deeper flavor, but they are interchangeable. Brown sugar is always dry-measured in packed, level amounts. *Molasses* is a by-product of sugar refining. It is important to use the right kind, as the acidity changes in each of the three varieties and could react differently with the leavenings in the batter. I use unsulfured molasses, which has the most rounded flavor. The other two types are sulfured (sometimes labeled "robust") and blackstrap (which is very bitter and found at natural food stores), but I only mention them so you don't use them by accident. As with brown sugar, corn syrup comes in light and dark varieties, and can be switched according to taste. To measure molasses and corn syrup, use a glass cup sprayed lightly with nonstick vegetable oil so the liquid won't stick to the cup.

- **Butter:** Unsalted butter allows the baker to control the amount of salt in the recipe. Also, salting hides off flavors, so unsalted butter has a shorter shelf life and is therefore fresher. Do not substitute margarine for butter in any of these desserts. Margarine has a totally different consistency than butter, and the recipes, especially piecrusts, may not turn out well.

- **Eggs:** Use USDA Grade A "large" eggs. There is a big difference between small and jumbo eggs, and using the wrong size will lead to problems.

- **Decorating:** When it comes to decorating desserts, keep it simple. A few swirls of whipped cream or a dusting of confectioners' sugar are all most desserts need. However, with very little trouble, you can pipe the cream through a pastry bag and give the dessert a professional, finished look.

  Buy a moderately large-capacity pastry bag, so you only have to fill it once. A makeshift pastry bag can be created by clipping the corner from a heavy-duty plastic storage bag.

  I have only a handful of decorating tips for almost all garnishing jobs. Large open-star tips, about ½ inch wide, are the most versatile, and their size allows you to cover a lot of surface quickly. With a small twist of the wrist, you can produce rosettes, stars, and curls. I don't feel I even need to give instructions, because when you give it a try, your imagination will take over. Pastry bags and large decorating tips are available at restaurant supply outlets and most kitchenware stores.

- **Cooking Desserts for a Crowd:** If you want to bake two or more cakes, you should make them one at a time, and don't double the recipe. If the batter includes baking soda or baking powder, the leavening needs to change with the volume of batter. Pie fillings, cheesecakes, and other desserts are much more forgiving and can be multiplied as needed.

Perfect Piecrust 101

Granted, many Thanksgiving cooks rely on frozen or refrigerated piecrusts. But homemade piecrust tastes immeasurably better. Knowing how to make a good piecrust is one of those kitchen skills that make a cook's reputation.

Leave behind any doubts you may have about making piecrust. I have taught hundreds of people how to make this dough. It has all of the qualities that make a perfect crust—it's flaky yet crisp, tender, and golden. The recipe is lengthy, not because it's difficult, but because the key to making good piecrust is understanding the details.

- Cold temperatures help a piecrust maintain its flakiness and shape. The fats should be chilled (in warm kitchens the flour can be chilled, as well) and the water ice-cold (but with ice cubes removed). The idea is to work the fat into the flour to create small, flour-coated pellets. The dough is held together with ice water, which helps keep the fat distinct—warm water would soften the fat. When the dough is rolled out, the fat is flattened into flakes. When baked, the fat creates steam, which lifts the dough into flaky layers. As vegetable shortening shouldn't be stored in the refrigerator, place the cubes of shortening in the freezer for 10 to 15 minutes to chill thoroughly.

- Handle the dough as little as possible. As dough is mixed, the gluten is activated and starts to strengthen, so use a light hand. Mix the dough just until it is completely moistened and begins to clump and hold together without crumbling when pressed between your thumb and forefinger.

- Dough likes to relax, and there are two key rest periods in the pie-making process. After the dough is mixed, refrigerate it for at least 30 minutes to allow the activated gluten to relax (a cool place also keeps the fat flakes chilled and distinct). If the dough is rolled out too soon, the gluten contracts and the crust shrinks. The optimum chilling period is 2 hours, which is long enough for the dough to chill throughout without becoming too hard to actually roll out. However, it can be refrigerated for up to 2 days. After the piecrust is fitted into the pan, freeze it for about 20 minutes for another rest period, again to discourage shrinkage.

- The type of fat used in the dough is another important factor. Americans love flaky piecrust, which is made with vegetable shortening or lard. Butter makes a crisp crust with a texture that resembles crisp and crumbly French tart crust or shortbread. This recipe benefits by using both fats. For an excellent crust with an old-fashioned flavor that works beautifully with apple or mincemeat pie, substitute lard for the shortening and butter. Measure shortening in a dry measure in level amounts. Or use the new stick-wrapped shortening—a real boon to the piecrust maker.

- Some recipes use only ice water to bind the dough. I add an egg yolk (a fatty protein that adds richness and color) and vinegar (an acid that tenderizes the gluten). I also use a little sugar for tenderness and for browning. A bit of salt is imperative to enhance the flavors.

- A pastry blender (usually made of flexible wire, but some models have stiff metal blades) is the best tool for cutting the fat into the flour. An electric hand mixer also works well, set at low speed. Or use a food processor, but freeze the fats first—the friction from the spinning metal blade can melt the fat. If you mix the dough in the work bowl, pulse it just until it clumps together. If overprocessed into a ball, the dough will be tough. It's safer to pour the dry fat/flour mixture from the processor bowl into a mixing bowl, and stir in the chilled liquids by hand. The old-fashioned "two-knife" method is awkward and takes too much time.

- The amount of liquid will always vary because of the humidity when you mix the dough. Stir in just enough liquid to make the dough clump together. If you need more liquid, use additional ice water.
- A large, heavy rolling pin is better than a small, light one, because its weight makes it easier to roll out the dough. If you have a smaller (12-inch) rolling pin, be careful that the edges of the pin don't dig into the dough while rolling it out. Silicone rolling pins are especially useful because they discourage the dough from sticking to the pin.
- Allow enough space to roll out the dough—at least 2 feet square. When I had a small kitchen with no counter space, rolling out pie dough was a feat for a contortionist. I finally went out and bought a large wooden pastry board to set up on my dining room table and roll out the dough with some elbow room. My life as a baker was changed, and I have been happily baking pies ever since.
- The technique for rolling out the dough—starting at the center of the dough and moving it a quarter turn after each roll—gradually creates a well-shaped pastry round that doesn't stick to the work surface. Sprinkle some flour on top of the dough to act as a barrier between the dough and the rolling pin. Flouring the rolling pin doesn't do anything. To be sure it isn't sticking, occasionally slide a long metal spatula or knife under the dough. If needed, sprinkle more flour under and on top of the dough.
- Pyrex pie pans give the best results. Their transparency allows the baker to see how the bottom crust is browning, and their thickness allows the heat to be more evenly distributed than metal pans. My second choice is a solid aluminum metal pan.
- These recipes yield generous amounts of dough. When I was a beginning baker, nothing was more exasperating than making recipes that provided barely enough dough to line the pan. After the pan is lined, simply trim the excess dough from the edges.
- Dough scraps can be cut into decorative shapes to garnish the top of a double-crust pie. Gather up the scraps, knead briefly, and reroll to ⅛-inch thickness. Using cookie cutters or a cardboard template, cut out the desired shapes, such as leaves or stars. Arrange them on the glazed crust, then brush the shapes lightly with more glaze. Bake the pie as directed.
- To bake crisp bottom crusts, bake the pie on a preheated baking sheet. The pie will be sitting on a flat, hot surface, instead of the oven rack, and will crisp better.
- Baking an empty pie shell is called "baking blind." Sometimes an unfilled crust is only partially baked, which sets the shape and dries the surface, discouraging a soggy bottom crust from developing when it comes in contact with a wet filling. Other recipes call for the pie to be completely baked until golden brown, usually to hold a finished filling, like the Dark Chocolate Cream Pie on page 144. In either case, the raw piecrust would collapse in the oven if not supported with aluminum foil and some kind of weights until it bakes long enough to hold its shape. The amount of fat in the piecrust keeps the foil from sticking, so there's no need to grease it. Aluminum or ceramic pie weights are a very good investment, as they absorb the oven heat and help crisp the crust. They

aren't cheap, but they last for years. Dried beans and raw rice are inexpensive alternatives, and can be saved in a jar to use a few subsequent times. But they will eventually spoil, so if they have an off smell, toss them out and use fresh beans and rice. You don't have this problem with pie weights, which is why I think they are the better choice.

- **As stated above, the dough can be prepared up to 2 days ahead, wrapped in wax paper, and refrigerated. Let stand at room temperature for 10 to 20 minutes to soften slightly before rolling out or it may crack.**
- **The dough can be frozen, wrapped in wax paper and an overwrap of aluminum foil, for up to 1 month. Defrost in the refrigerator overnight.**
- **Unbaked piecrusts can be kept in the freezer in metal pie pans, covered tightly with a double covering of plastic wrap, for up to 2 weeks. (I don't recommend this for Pyrex pans, because even though they are supposed to be fine going from the freezer to the oven, I still think there is a risk of breakage.) Do not defrost before baking. Bake the frozen piecrusts as directed, allowing an extra 5 minutes. However, unless you have a big freezer, it may be more space-efficient to freeze the unrolled dough.**

Makes one 9- or 10-inch single piecrust, or one 9- to 10-inch double piecrust

Make Ahead: See the suggestions above.

SINGLE CRUST (FOR A 9- TO 10-INCH PIE)

1½ cups all-purpose flour
1 tablespoon sugar
¼ teaspoon salt
⅓ cup plus 1 tablespoon vegetable shortening, chilled, cut into ½-inch cubes
3 tablespoons unsalted butter, chilled, cut into ½-inch cubes
¼ cup ice-cold water
1 large egg yolk
½ teaspoon cider or wine vinegar

DOUBLE CRUST (FOR A 9- TO 10-INCH PIE)

2¼ cups all-purpose flour
1½ tablespoons sugar
½ teaspoon salt
½ cup plus 1 tablespoon vegetable shortening, chilled, cut into ½-inch cubes
5 tablespoons (½ stick plus 1 tablespoon) unsalted butter, chilled, cut into ½-inch cubes
⅓ cup plus 1 tablespoon ice-cold water
1 large egg yolk
¾ teaspoon cider or wine vinegar

1. In a large bowl, mix the flour, sugar, and salt until combined. Using a pastry blender, rapidly cut the shortening and butter into the flour mixture until it is the consistency of coarse bread crumbs with some pea-sized pieces. Do not blend to a fine cornmeal-like consistency. If the fats stick to the wires of the blender, scrape them off.

2. In a glass measuring cup, mix the ice water, egg yolk, and vinegar. Tossing the flour mixture with a fork, gradually add the ice-water mixture, sprinkling it all over the ingredients in the bowl. Be stingy with the water—you can always add more, but it is difficult to remedy pie dough that is too wet. Mix well, being sure to moisten the crumbs on the bottom of the bowl. Add just enough liquid that the dough clumps together. It does not have to come together into one big ball. To check the consistency, press the dough between your thumb and forefinger. The dough should be moist, but not wet and not crumbly. If necessary, gradually mix in more ice water, 1 teaspoon at a time, until you reach the correct consistency.

3. Gather up the dough into a thick disk and wrap in wax paper or plastic wrap. *If making a double-crust pie,* divide the dough into two disks, one slightly larger than the other. Refrigerate the dough for at least 30 minutes and up to 2 days. The optimum rest period is 2 hours, which allows the dough to relax and chill without becoming rock hard. If the dough is well chilled and hard, let it stand at room temperature for 10 to 15 minutes to soften slightly before rolling out.

4. To roll out a single crust, sprinkle the work surface (preferably a pastry or cutting board) lightly but completely with flour, then spread out the flour with the palm of your hand into a very thin layer. Place the dough on the work surface, then sprinkle the top of the dough with a little flour. Don't bother to sprinkle the rolling pin with flour—it just falls off. Starting at the center of the disk, roll the dough away from you. Do not roll back and forth. Think of stretching, not rolling, the dough into shape. (If the dough cracks while you are rolling out, it may be too cold. Let it stand for a few minutes to warm up slightly, then try again.) Turn the dough a quarter of a turn. Roll out again from the center of the dough. Continue rolling out the dough, always starting from the center of the dough and turning it a quarter turn after each roll, until the dough is about 13 inches in diameter and ⅛ inch thick. (If you aren't sure what ⅛ inch looks like, stand a ruler up next to the dough and check. This sounds elementary, but many bakers make the mistake of rolling out the dough too thin or too thick, and until you learn by practice, a ruler is the best insurance.) Be sure that the dough is the same thickness throughout, especially at the edges, which tend to be thicker than the center. Work as quickly as possible so the dough doesn't get too warm.

5. Carefully fold the dough in half. If you think the dough is too warm to fold without breaking, and you have rolled out the dough on a cutting board, transfer the entire board to a cool place—if it's a cold day, outside, on a windowsill, or in an unheated room is fine—for a few minutes to firm up. Transfer the dough to the pie pan, with the fold in the center of the pan. Unfold the dough, letting the excess dough hang over the sides of the pan. Gently press the dough snugly into the corners of the pan. If the dough cracks, just press the cracks together. Gaps can be patched with a scrap of dough, moistened lightly around the edges to adhere it to the crust. Using kitchen scissors or a sharp knife, trim the dough to extend only ½ inch beyond the edge of the pan.

6. *To flute the crust,* fold over the dough so the edge is flush with the edge of the pan. Use one hand to pinch the dough around the knuckle or fingertip of your other hand, moving around the crust at 1-inch intervals. Cover the dough with plastic wrap and freeze until ready to use, 20 to 30 minutes.

7. To roll out a double-crust pie, roll out the larger dough disk, place it in the pan, and trim the edges so they hang about ½ inch over the pan. Fill the pie with the cooled filling, if necessary. Immediately roll out the smaller disk of dough into a 10- to 11-inch round about ⅛ inch thick. Fold the dough in half, position over the filling, and unfold. Press the edges of the two crusts together to seal. Using kitchen scissors or a sharp knife, trim the dough to extend only ½ inch beyond the edge of the pan. Flute the dough as directed in step 6.

CLASSIC RECIPE

Famous Pumpkin Pie

This recipe has been on the can of Libby's Solid Pack Pumpkin for over thirty years—mildly spiced, smooth, and just about perfect. Not for nothing is it truly "famous." Libby's estimates that over 55 million pumpkin pies are made from their canned pumpkin every Thanksgiving. For classic results, mix the ingredients by hand in the order given. I have added some tips to the back-of-the can instructions, but the recipe remains unchanged.

There are a number of crust options, all with slightly different oven temperatures and cooking times. Homemade piecrust makes the best pie, so I start with those directions, giving variations for frozen deep-dish and regular piecrusts. To be sure the crust holds all of the filling, it is important to flute the piecrust to stand high around the edge of the pan. If you still have a little too much filling, just discard it.

A crack will appear where the pie was tested with the knife. To disguise it, just spread a thin layer of whipped cream over the top. With experience, you will be able to test the pie without cutting into it—when the pie is shaken, only the very center, a round area about the size of a quarter, of the pie will jiggle.

Makes 8 servings

Make Ahead: The pie can be baked up to 1 day ahead.

Perfect Piecrust 101 for a single-crust pie (page 135)
2 large eggs, slightly beaten
One 15-ounce can Libby's Solid Pack Pumpkin (1¾ cups)
¾ cup sugar
½ teaspoon salt
1 teaspoon ground cinnamon
½ teaspoon ground ginger
¼ teaspoon ground cloves
One 12-ounce can evaporated milk or 1½ cups half-and-half
Sweetened Whipped Cream (page160)

1. Following the instructions on page 138, line a 9-inch (1-quart/1-liter capacity) pie pan with the pie dough. Flute the dough so the edge stands about ½ inch above the rim. (Libby's does not suggest doing this, but to reduce crust shrinkage, loosely cover the shell with plastic wrap and freeze for 20 minutes.)

2. Position a rack in the bottom third of the oven and place a baking sheet on the rack. Preheat the oven to 425°F.

3. In the order given, place the ingredients in a large bowl and mix well. Place the pie shell on the hot baking sheet and pour in the pumpkin filling. Place on the baking sheet. Bake for 15 minutes. Reduce the temperature to 350°F, and bake until a knife inserted near the center comes out clean, 40 to 50 minutes. Cool completely on a wire cake rack. Cover with plastic wrap and refrigerate until ready to serve. (The pie can be baked up to 1 day ahead.) Serve chilled with whipped cream.

Deep-Dish Pumpkin Pie (made with frozen crust): Substitute one 9-inch (4-cup capacity) deep-dish frozen pie shell for the homemade crust. Preheat the oven and baking sheet to 375°F. While the oven preheats, allow the crust to thaw until the dough is chilled but malleable, about 20 minutes. Recrimp the pie shell so the edge stands ½ inch above the rim. Pour the filling into the crust and bake until the pie tests done with a knife as in step 3, about 70 minutes.

Double-Batch Pumpkin Pie (made with frozen crusts): The pumpkin mixture will also fill two regular (not deep-dish) piecrusts. Let the crusts thaw slightly while mixing the filling. Preheat the oven and filling to 375°F. Pour the filling into the crusts and bake until the pies test done as in step 3, about 45 minutes.

Berkshire Pumpkin Pie

For many years, we spent Thanksgiving with our friend Ron Dier in the picture-perfect Berkshire Mountains, on the border between New York and Massachusetts. Ron always made this pumpkin pie according to his mom Rita's recipe. Its light texture and generous spicing had everyone coming back for more. In fact, many times when there was pie left when we cleared the table, it would be gone the next morning because we had all snuck into the kitchen during the night and devoured it in the time-honored tradition of the Thanksgiving Midnight Snack. If you are looking for an extra-special pumpkin pie, look no further.

Makes 8 to 10 servings

Make Ahead: The pie can be baked up to 1 day ahead.

Perfect Piecrust 101 for a single-crust pie (page 135)
One 15-ounce can solid-pack pumpkin (1¾ cups)
1 cup heavy cream
⅔ cup granulated sugar
½ cup packed light brown sugar
2 tablespoons all-purpose flour
1½ teaspoons ground cinnamon
1 teaspoon ground ginger
1 teaspoon grated nutmeg
¼ teaspoon ground cloves
¼ teaspoon salt
3 large eggs, at room temperature
Sweetened Whipped Cream (page 160)

1. Following the instructions on page 138, line a 10-inch pie pan with the pie dough. Cover loosely with plastic wrap. Freeze for 20 minutes.

2. Position a rack in the top third of the oven. Place a baking sheet on the rack and preheat the oven to 400°F.

3. Line the pastry shell with aluminum foil, then fill it with pie weights, dried beans, or raw rice. Bake on the hot baking sheet until the pastry seems set, about 12 minutes. Remove the foil and weights. Leave the oven on.

4. In a medium bowl, whisk together all of the filling ingredients (except the eggs and whipped cream) until smooth. In another medium bowl, using a handheld electric mixer set at high speed, beat the eggs until very light and tripled in volume, about 3 minutes. Fold the eggs into the pumpkin mixture. Pour into the pie shell.

5. Place on the hot baking sheet and bake for 15 minutes. Reduce the heat to 350°F. Continue baking until a knife inserted into the filling 2 inches from the center comes out clean, 40 to 50 minutes. The center will seem slightly unset when shaken, but will firm upon standing. Let cool completely on a wire cake rack. Cover with plastic wrap and refrigerate until chilled, at least 2 hours or overnight. (The pie can be baked up to 1 day ahead.) Serve chilled or at room temperature with the whipped cream.

It Isn't Thanksgiving Without . . . Pumpkin Pie

Pumpkin pie was certainly not included in the first feast. The *Mayflower*'s stores of wheat had long been depleted, and the first planting had failed. No wheat, no piecrust. As with so many other foods, the Indians taught the Pilgrims about pumpkin. Along with beans and corn, it was one of the three major foods in the Native American diet throughout the continent. There is some argument over pumpkin's origin. Some botanists say it is a New World vegetable, and others claim it was known in Europe before the Exploration Age. It is likely that the "pumpkins" in the pre-Columbus era were really gourds, and that we can truly claim the pumpkin as an American original that deserves a place of honor at the Thanksgiving meal.

The Indians probably roasted pumpkin over an open fire or boiled it with maple syrup. Pumpkin pudding became one of the favorite dishes of the Puritan era. The pumpkin flesh was scooped out and mixed with milk, spices, and syrup, then returned to the pumpkin shell, where it was roasted for hours in hot ashes. It is easy to see where the basic recipe for pumpkin pie filling came from. Known to the settlers as *pompion* (the name given by French explorers in the late 1500s), it saved them from starvation in the lean early years of their colony.

One of the first recipes for pumpkin pie appeared in 1655 in a book called *Queens Closed Open*. This version represented the then-current taste for highly seasoned foods, and includes thyme, rosemary, cinnamon, nutmeg, pepper, cloves, and apple. In 1672, an English-American merchant named John Josselyn was already calling pompion stew "an Ancient New-England dish." He says to take diced, ripe squash and ". . . so fill a pot with them of two or three gallons, stew them upon a gentle fire a whole day, then as they sink . . . fill again with fresh pompions not putting any liquor to them and when it is stirred enough it will look like baked Apples, this Dish putting Butter to it and Vinegar and some Spice as Ginger which makes it tart like an Apple, and so serve it up to be eaten with fish or flesh." Josselyn's "stew" would be recognized today as the pumpkin butter put up by New England cooks. Amelia Simmons included "pompkin" pie in the first American cookbook, published in 1796.

The history of the modern pumpkin pie can be dated to 1929. In that year, Libby, McNeil and Libby bought the small pumpkin pie cannery Dickinson Canning Company. The little cannery's pride and joy was their special eating pumpkin, now called the "Dickinson" variety. Eating pumpkins, much different than the Jack-o'-lantern varieties grown just for size and appearance, are elongated and buff-colored, with thin walls. The Dickinson was noted for its bright orange color, creamy texture, and fresh taste. Libby's took years to develop its own strain, improving upon the Dickinson, now called "Libby's Select." Today, Libby's, a division of Nestlé, plants more than four thousand acres of pumpkin annually.

Pumpkin-Hazelnut Pie

Turn to this pumpkin pie when you want to stray from the beaten path of tradition. To tell the truth, this one isn't an enormous diversion, just enough to make your guests appreciate the undertone of ground hazelnuts. If you wish, sprinkle each portion with minced crystallized ginger and finely chopped, roasted and peeled hazelnuts.

Makes one 9-inch pie, 8 servings

Make Ahead: The pie can be made 1 day ahead.

Perfect Piecrust 101 for a single-crust pie (page 135)

FILLING

½ cup (2 ounces) hazelnuts, toasted and peeled (see Note)
½ cup packed light brown sugar
¼ cup granulated sugar
One 15-ounce can solid-pack pumpkin (1¾ cups)
1¼ cups half-and-half
2 large eggs, beaten
1 teaspoon ground cinnamon
½ teaspoon ground ginger
¼ teaspoon ground cloves
¼ teaspoon ground nutmeg

TOPPING

⅔ cup heavy cream
2 tablespoons confectioners' sugar
½ teaspoon vanilla extract

1. Following the instructions on page 138, line a 9-inch pie pan with the pie dough and flute the edges. Line the pastry shell with aluminum foil. Freeze for 20 minutes.

2. Position a rack in the lower third of the oven and place a baking sheet on the rack. Preheat the oven to 400°F.

3. Fill the foil with pie weights or dried beans. Place the pastry shell on a baking sheet. Bake until the edges of the crust look set, about 12 minutes. Remove from the oven and lift off the foil and beans.

4. Meanwhile, prepare the filling. Process the hazelnuts, brown sugar, and granulated sugar in a food processor with the metal chopping blade until the hazelnuts are powdery. Transfer to a medium bowl and add the pumpkin, half-and-half, eggs, cinnamon, ginger, cloves, and nutmeg. Whisk well.

5. Pour the filling into the hot crust and return to the oven. Bake for 15 minutes. Reduce the oven temperature to 350°F. Bake until the filling is puffed with a 1-inch diameter area in the center that remains unpuffed, about 45 minutes.

6. Transfer to a wire rack and cool completely. Cover the pie and refrigerate until chilled. (The pie can be prepared 1 day ahead.)

7. To prepare the topping, whip the heavy cream, confectioners' sugar, and vanilla until soft peaks form. Transfer the cream to a pastry bag fitted with a ½-inch fluted tip. Pipe 8 large rosettes around the edge of the pie. (Or spread the cream over the filling in a thin layer.) Serve chilled.

Note: Many markets now sell toasted and peeled hazelnuts. If you have hazelnuts with their skins, bake them on a baking sheet in a preheated 350°F oven, stirring occasionally, until the skins are cracked and the nut beneath the skin looks toasted, about 10 minutes. Wrap the nuts in a clean kitchen towel and let stand for 10 minutes. Using the towel, rub the nuts to remove the skins—do not be concerned if some of the peel remains on the nuts.

Down-Home Pecan and Bourbon Pie

Pecan pie is another one of those American desserts that seem to have been around forever. Pecans are a native nut, grown on the estates of Washington and Jefferson. But Jean Anderson, in her *American Century Cookbook*, says that she cannot find a cookbook reference to pecan pie until the 1940s. Food historian Meryle Evans believes the first instance of the modern version shows up in 1925, and thinks it may have been the invention of Karo syrup home economists. (Older recipes are made with brown sugar without corn syrup.) Karo was introduced in 1902, during the early-twentieth-century American food revolution, when canned and bottled products were replacing homemade goods with alarming speed. Consumers were anxious to try these new foods that promised to increase their leisure time. Product-sponsored cookbooks were all the rage, and when a new recipe showed up on the back of, for example, a corn syrup can, it could quickly gain fans.

This version is less sweet than most. A little bourbon works wonders, cutting through the richness and adding a gentle aroma. If you have kids around, you can leave out the bourbon, and still have a darned fine pie. There are two schools of thought about the pecans. One camp uses coarsely chopped pecans, so the pie is easier to slice. The opposition places the whole pecan halves in concentric circles in the piecrust before pouring in the filling, so the pie has a beautiful symmetrical design after baking. For the nuttiest filling, sprinkle chopped pecans on the crust, then top with the pecan halves. Just have a good sharp, thin-bladed knife handy for slicing.

Makes one 9-inch pie, 8 servings

Make Ahead: The pie can be baked up to 2 days ahead.

Perfect Piecrust 101 for a single-crust pie (page 135)
3 large eggs
1 cup light corn syrup
½ cup light brown sugar, rubbed through a sieve to remove lumps
4 tablespoons unsalted butter, melted
2 tablespoons bourbon
1 teaspoon vanilla extract
9 ounces pecan halves (2 heaping cups)
Sweetened Whipped Cream (page 160)

1. Following the directions on page 138, line a 9-inch pie pan with the pie dough. Cover loosely with plastic wrap. Freeze for 20 minutes.
2. Position a rack in the bottom third of the oven and place a baking sheet on the rack. Preheat the oven to 425°F.
3. In a medium bowl, whisk the eggs. Add the corn syrup, brown sugar, melted butter, bourbon, and vanilla, and whisk until well combined.
4. To gauge exactly how many pecan halves are needed to decorate the pie, arrange the pecan halves in concentric circles on a 9-inch round space on the work surface. Gather up the pecan halves and set aside. Finely chop the remaining pecan halves and sprinkle in the crust. Place the unchopped pecan halves on top. Carefully pour the filling into the crust.
5. Remove the hot baking sheet from the oven, and place the pie on the sheet. Return to the oven and bake for 15 minutes. Reduce the oven temperature to 350°F. Continue baking until the topping is almost completely puffed and a knife inserted 1 inch from the center comes out clean, 30 to 35 more minutes. Cool completely on a wire cake rack. (The pie can be baked up to 2 days ahead, covered tightly with plastic wrap, and refrigerated.) Serve at room temperature with the whipped cream.

Florida Sweet Potato Pie

Down South, sweet potato pie holds the place of honor in many homes as the favorite Thanksgiving dessert. But if candied yams were served at dinner, a sweet potato pie might be overkill, even south of the Mason-Dixon line. One year, I solved the problem by serving small slivers of this pie as a side dish, figuring that it's no sweeter than the usual recipes you often find next to the turkey on your plate, and my guests loved it. Oranges, in the form of marmalade, give this version a special fillip. After all, Florida is a Southern state.

Makes one 9-inch pie, 8 servings

Make Ahead: The pie can be baked up to 2 days ahead.

Perfect Piecrust 101 for a single-crust pie (page 135)
2 medium orange-fleshed yams (1 pound), unpeeled
2 tablespoons unsalted butter
½ cup orange marmalade
⅓ cup packed dark brown sugar
¼ teaspoon ground cinnamon
¼ teaspoon salt
2 large eggs plus 1 large yolk, beaten together
1 cup half-and-half
About 20 pecan halves
Sweetened Whipped Cream (page 160)

1. Following the directions on page 138, line a 10-inch pie plate with the pie dough. Cover loosely with plastic wrap, and freeze for 20 minutes.

2. Position racks in the center and bottom third of the oven and place a baking sheet on the bottom rack. Preheat the oven to 400°F.

3. Pierce the yams a few times with a fork. Place them on a baking sheet and place on the center rack. Bake until the yams are tender, about 1 hour. Remove from the oven and cool slightly.

4. Meanwhile, remove the plastic wrap and line the pastry shell with aluminum foil, then fill with pie weights, dried beans, or raw rice. Bake on the hot baking sheet until the pastry seems set, about 12 minutes. Remove the foil and weights. Leave the oven on.

5. Peel the yams and transfer to a medium bowl. Add the butter and mash with a handheld electric mixer set at low speed until smooth. Beat in the orange marmalade, brown sugar, cinnamon, and salt, then beat in the eggs-yolk mixture and the half-and-half. Pour into the pie shell and smooth the top. Arrange pecan halves around the edge of the pie.

6. Bake for 10 minutes, then reduce the oven temperature to 350°F. Continue baking until a knife inserted into the center of the filling comes out clean, about 45 minutes more. Transfer to a wire cake rack and cool completely. (The pie can be baked up to 2 days ahead, covered in plastic wrap, and refrigerated.) Serve at room temperature with the whipped cream.

Dark Chocolate Cream Pie

Everyone knows that pumpkin, apple, and mincemeat pies are Thanksgiving favorites. I was surprised to hear how many of my friends included chocolate cream pie in their lineup. In my family, Mom's chocolate cream is the most beloved of all her pies. The chocolate flavor, of course, will be impacted by the brand of chocolate used. I prefer chocolate with a cacao content of about 60 percent, an amount that is often listed on the label. The higher the cacao

content, the more bitter the chocolate, but that's the way some folks like it.

Makes 8 servings

Make Ahead: The pie, without the whipped cream topping, can be baked up to 1 day ahead.

Perfect Piecrust 101 for a single-crust pie (page 135)
3 cups half-and-half
2⁄3 cup granulated sugar
1⁄8 teaspoon salt
3 tablespoons cornstarch
4 large egg yolks
4 ounces high-quality bittersweet or semisweet chocolate, finely chopped
2 tablespoons unsalted butter
1 teaspoon vanilla extract
1 cup heavy cream
2 tablespoons confectioners' sugar

1. Following the instructions on page 138, line a 9-inch pie pan with the pie dough and flute the edges. Cover loosely with plastic wrap. Freeze for 20 minutes.

2. Position a rack in the lower third of the oven and place a baking sheet on the rack. Preheat the oven to 400°F.

3. Remove the plastic wrap and line the pastry shell with aluminum foil, then fill with pie weights, dried beans, or raw rice. Bake on the hot baking sheet until the pastry seems set, about 12 minutes. Lift up and remove the foil and weights. Continue baking until the pie shell is golden brown, 10 to 12 minutes longer. Transfer to a wire cake rack and cool completely.

4. When the pie shell has cooled, in a medium saucepan over medium heat, heat 2½ cups half-and-half, the granulated sugar, and the salt, stirring often, to dissolve the sugar, until tiny bubbles appear around the edges. Remove from the heat.

5. In a small bowl, sprinkle the cornstarch over the remaining ½ cup half-and-half and whisk until dissolved. Whisk the yolks in a medium bowl, and gradually whisk in the cornstarch mixture. Gradually whisk in the hot half-and-half mixture, and return to the rinsed-out saucepan. Cook over medium heat, stirring constantly with a flat wooden spatula (to keep the custard from scorching on the bottom of the saucepan), until the custard comes to a boil. Reduce the heat to medium-low and simmer, stirring constantly, for 1 minute. Remove from the heat, add the chocolate, butter, and ½ teaspoon of the vanilla, and stir until the chocolate melts completely.

6. Pour into the baked pie shell and smooth the top. Butter a piece of wax paper and place, buttered side down, directly on the surface of the filling. Pierce a few slits in the wax paper with the tip of a sharp knife (this keeps a skin from forming on the filling). Cool completely. Refrigerate until chilled, at least 4 hours or overnight.

7. Just before serving, in a chilled medium bowl, using a handheld electric mixer set at high speed, beat the heavy cream with the confectioners' sugar and the remaining ½ teaspoon vanilla just until stiff. Spread the whipped cream over the filling. Serve chilled.

Chocolate Banana Cream Pie: Thinly slice 2 ripe bananas and place in the baked pie shell before adding the chocolate filling.

Apple Pie 101

For American bakers, apple pie is the holy grail of desserts. A perfect apple pie has a sweet-tart, chunky, mildly spiced apple filling that doesn't collapse when baked. A number of my friends suggested precooking the apples for the filling—and the trick worked like a charm, as the apples shrink in the skillet, not in the crust. Also, the released apple juices reduce and thicken in the skillet, so the apple flavor intensifies. Allow an hour or so for the apple filling to cool completely before going into the crust.

- **A good pie apple isn't too sweet and has a texture that doesn't break up when cooked. Some apples, like Jonathan and McIntosh, are best for eating out of hand or cooking into applesauce. Unfortunately, a raw apple won't reveal what it is like when it's cooked, even if it tastes delicious. I usually take the advice of the apple stands at my farmers' market—they often have some wonderful dark-horse, heirloom varieties that I would otherwise pass over. As far as supermarket apples go, Golden Delicious is my favorite. A lot of bakers like Granny Smiths, but they tend to shrink a lot and look gray when cooked. My friend Carole Walter, author of *Great Pies*, is partial to Mutsu and Cortlandt apples, separately or together. You can mix two or three varieties—winey Rome and sweet Golden Delicious are another good combination.**

- **For an outstanding apple pie with a crisp, rich, old-fashioned crust, substitute lard for the shortening and butter in the dough.**

- **The filled, unbaked pie can be prepared, without its cream and sugar glaze, covered tightly in plastic wrap and an overwrap of aluminum foil, and frozen for up to 1 month. Glaze, then bake the frozen pie at 375°F until golden brown, about 1 hour and 15 minutes.**

- **The baked pie can be made upto 1 day ahead, covered with plastic wrap, and refrigerated. Serve at room temperature.**

Makes one 10-inch pie, 8 to 10 servings

Make Ahead: See the suggestions above.

5 pounds Golden Delicious apples
2 tablespoons fresh lemon juice
6 tablespoons (¾ stick) unsalted butter
⅔ cup plus 1 teaspoon sugar
3 tablespoons all-purpose flour
1 teaspoon ground cinnamon
Perfect Piecrust 101 for a double-crust pie (page 135)
2 teaspoons heavy cream or milk, for glazing

1. Peel and quarter the apples, cutting out the core from each quarter. Cut each quarter into thirds and place in a large bowl. As they fill the bowl, occasionally sprinkle and toss the apples with the lemon juice. (Don't wait until all the apples are cut, or they may already be turning brown.)
2. In a large (12-inch) nonstick skillet, melt 3 tablespoons of the butter over medium-high heat. Add half of the apples and ⅓ cup sugar. Cook, stirring often, until the apples are barely tender when pierced with the tip of a sharp knife, about 7 minutes. Transfer to a large roasting pan or rimmed baking sheet. Repeat with the remaining butter, apples, and ½ cup sugar. (If your nonstick skillet is smaller than 12 inches, cook the apples in three batches.) Cool completely, stirring occasionally.
3. Position a rack in the center of the oven and place a baking sheet on the rack. Preheat the oven to 375°F.
4. Sprinkle the flour and cinnamon over the cooled filling, and toss well. Following the

directions for a double-crust pie on page 138, line a 10-inch pie pan with the bottom crust. Fill with the apple mixture. Cover the filling with the top crust and flute the edges. Cut a small hole in the center of the top piecrust. (The unbaked pie can be prepared up to 1 month ahead, covered tightly in plastic wrap and an overwrap of aluminum foil, and frozen.) Brush the top of the pie lightly with the heavy cream. If desired, cut out decorative shapes from the dough scraps, place them on the top crust, and brush lightly with heavy cream. Sprinkle with 1 teaspoon sugar.

5. Place the pie on the baking sheet and bake until the top is golden brown and the juices are bubbling through the hole in the crust, about 50 minutes. Cool on a wire cake rack for 30 minutes. Serve warm or at room temperature.

New-fashioned Mincemeat Pie

A simmering pot of mincemeat announces the holiday season with its heady, spicy aroma. As dried fruits were served at the first Thanksgiving, this fruit-packed pie is an appropriate dessert for today's feast. It's an updated mincemeat that breaks with tradition, but in ways that most people would approve. The suet and beef from the old recipes are gone, and the fruit flavor has been increased with apple juice concentrate, which also acts as a sweetener. Supermarket candied citrus peels are usually tasteless, so look for high-quality imported ones. Some mincemeat is aged for months, but this one is ready to go the day after making. The result is a multicolored and deeply flavored mélange that tastes different with every bite.

Makes 8 to 10 servings

Make Ahead: The mincemeat can be made up to 1 week ahead; the pie can be baked up to 1 day ahead.

2 Golden Delicious apples, peeled and grated (use the large holes on a box grater)
One 12-ounce container (1½ cups) frozen apple juice concentrate, thawed
3 ounces chopped dried apples (1 packed cup)
¾ cup (3 ounces) raisins
¾ cup (3 ounces) golden raisins
¾ cup (3 ounces) dried currants
¾ cup dried cranberries (3 ounces)
⅔ cup (about 3 ounces) high-quality candied orange peel or glacé oranges
⅓ cup (about 1½ ounces) high-quality candied lemon peel
½ cup packed dark brown sugar
½ cup dark rum
½ cup Cognac or brandy
4 tablespoons unsalted butter
½ teaspoon ground cinnamon
½ teaspoon ground allspice
½ teaspoon ground nutmeg
½ teaspoon ground cloves
Perfect Piecrust 101 for a double-crust pie (page 135)

1. At least 1 day before baking the pie, in a large, heavy-bottomed Dutch oven, bring all of the ingredients except the piecrust to a boil over medium heat, stirring often. Reduce the heat to medium-low and simmer, stirring often, until the liquid is almost completely evaporated, about 25 minutes. Transfer to a bowl and cool completely. Cover tightly with plastic wrap and refrigerate at least overnight or up to 1 week.

2. Position a rack in the bottom third of the oven and place a baking sheet on the rack. Preheat the oven to 375°F.

3. Following the directions for a double-crust pie on page 138, line a 10-inch pie pan

with the bottom crust. Fill with the mincemeat. Cover the filling with the top crust and flute the edges. Cut a small hole in the center of the top piecrust.

4. Place the pie on the baking sheet and bake until the top is golden brown and you can see the mincemeat bubbling through the center hole, about 50 minutes. Cool on a wire cake rack for 30 minutes. Serve warm or at room temperature.

Cranberry-Ginger Tart with Chocolate Drizzle

This is an elegant combination of ingredients that grown-ups will love: tart cranberries, zesty ginger, and bittersweet chocolate. (You may want to have another, less sophisticated dessert for the kids.) And it's easy to make, thanks to a sweet pastry dough that doesn't need to be rolled out before baking. Just press it into the buttered tart pan, and you're in business. In Perfect Piecrust 101 (page 135), I warn against mixing pie dough in the food processor. But this dough uses more sugar, which tenderizes the crust and keeps the flour's gluten from toughening in the processor. Still, take care not to overprocess the dough.

Makes 8 servings

Make Ahead: The tart can be baked up to 1 day ahead.

SWEET TART DOUGH

1 cup all-purpose flour
3 tablespoons sugar
1/4 teaspoon salt
6 tablespoons (3/4 stick) unsalted butter, chilled and cut into 1/2-inch cubes
1 large egg yolk

CRANBERRY FILLING

One 12-ounce bag cranberries
1 cup sugar
1/4 cup finely chopped crystallized ginger
1 tablespoon cornstarch
1 ounce high-quality bittersweet chocolate, finely chopped
Sweetened Whipped Cream (page 160)

1. Position a rack in the center of the oven and place a baking sheet on the rack. Preheat the oven to 400°F. Lightly butter a 9-inch round tart pan with a removable bottom.

2. To make the tart dough, in a food processor, pulse the flour, sugar, and salt to combine. Add the butter and pulse 10 to 15 times until the mixture resembles coarse crumbs. In a small bowl, mix the yolk with 2 tablespoons water. With the machine running, add the yolk mixture and process just until the dough is moistened. It will look crumbly, but should hold together when pressed between your thumb and forefinger. If necessary, sprinkle with 1 teaspoon water, pulse briefly, and check again. Do not overprocess the dough.

3. Press the dough evenly into the bottom and up the sides of the prepared tart pan. Using a fork, prick the dough all over. Line the dough with aluminum foil and weigh with pie weights, dried beans, or raw rice. Cover loosely with plastic wrap and freeze for 20 minutes.

4. Place the pan on the hot baking sheet. Bake on the hot baking sheet until the pastry seems set, about 10 minutes. Lift up and remove the foil and weights. Continue baking until the pie shell is golden brown, about 15 minutes more. Transfer to a wire cake rack and cool completely.

5. To make the filling, in a large saucepan, bring the cranberries, 1 cup water, sugar, and ginger to a boil over high heat, stirring to dissolve the sugar. Reduce the heat to medium.

Cook, stirring often to avoid scorching, until the mixture is thick and reduced to about 2¼ cups. In a small bowl, sprinkle the cornstarch over 2 tablespoons water and stir to dissolve. Stir into the cranberry mixture and boil briefly until very thick. Spread evenly in the cooled tart shell and cool completely.

6. Place the chopped chocolate in a small bowl, and fit over a small saucepan with very hot, but not simmering, water over very low heat. Melt the chocolate, stirring occasionally. Transfer to a small plastic sandwich bag. Force the chocolate into a corner of the bag. Using scissors, snip off the corner to make a small opening. Squeeze the chocolate in a cross-hatch pattern over the top of the tart. Refrigerate for at least 1 hour until the chocolate is set and the tart is chilled. Remove the sides of the pan, then serve the tart chilled, with the whipped cream.

Caramel Cashew Tart

Talk about a crowd-pleaser! There is something about the combination of caramel and cashews that everyone loves—it must remind us of a candy bar. I sent this tart to a friend's office to get opinions, and it got such unanimous raves, I had to send a second one to placate the disappointed people who missed the first one. Good news traveled fast that day. A few tips: When making the caramel, be careful when adding the cream (it can bubble over if you're not alert), and allow time for the caramel to cool before adding the egg or the filling will curdle. As good as this buttery tart is, it *is* candy-bar sweet and should be served in thin slices.

Makes 8 to 12 servings

Make Ahead: The tart can be baked 1 day ahead.

Sweet Tart Dough (page 148)
¾ cup heavy cream
1 cup sugar
3 tablespoons unsalted butter, melted
1 large egg, beaten
1 teaspoon vanilla extract
8 ounces unsalted roasted cashews (2 heaping cups)
Sweetened Whipped Cream (page 160)

1. Position a rack in the center of the oven and place a baking sheet on the rack. Preheat the oven to 400°F. Lightly butter a 9-inch round tart pan with a removable bottom.

2. Press the dough evenly into the bottom and up the sides of the prepared tart pan. Using a fork, prick the dough all over. Line the dough with aluminum foil and weigh with pie weights, dried beans, or raw rice. Cover loosely with plastic wrap and freeze for 20 minutes.

3. Place the pan on the hot baking sheet. Bake on the hot baking sheet until the pastry seems set, about 10 minutes. Lift up and remove the foil and weights. Continue baking until the pie shell is lightly browned, about 8 more minutes. Cool the tart shell on a wire cake rack while making the filling. Remove the baking sheet from the oven. Keep the oven on.

4. Meanwhile, in a small saucepan, heat the heavy cream over medium heat until small bubbles appear around the edges. (Or heat the cream in a microwave oven, being careful that it doesn't boil over.) Set the hot cream aside.

5. In a tall, medium saucepan over high heat, bring the sugar and ¼ water to a boil, stirring constantly to dissolve the sugar. As soon as the sugar comes to a boil, stop stirring. (Don't stir the boiling syrup or it will crystallize into a thick glop.) Boil the syrup until it turns deep amber, 3 to 5 minutes. While the syrup is boiling, occasionally swirl the pan by the handle to mix it. Wash down any sugar crystals that form on the sides of the pan by dipping a

large pastry brush in cold water and rubbing the wet brush against the crystals. When the syrup is dark amber, reduce the heat to low. Being very careful, slowly stir in the hot cream. The mixture will bubble dramatically, but eventually subside. Simmer, stirring often, slightly thickened, about 3 minutes. Pour into a medium heatproof bowl and place in a larger bowl of ice water. Let stand, stirring often, until the caramel is tepid.

6. Whisk in the melted butter, egg, and vanilla. Using the side of a large knife, coarsely crush about 1 cup of the cashews and spread in the tart shell. Top with the remaining whole cashews. Pour the caramel mixture over the cashews.

7. Place the tart on a cool baking sheet. Bake for 15 minutes. Reduce the heat to 350°F and continue baking until the filling is bubbling in the center, about 15 minutes more. Cool the tart completely on a wire cake rack. (The tart can be baked 1 day ahead. Cover the cooled tart with plastic wrap and store at room temperature.) Remove the sides of the pan, then serve the tart with the whipped cream.

Drambuie Gingerbread

Using Drambuie, a heady Scotch-based liqueur, is an excellent way to add interest to a spicy gingerbread. In fact, one friend, a notoriously picky cookbook editor, told me that this was the best gingerbread she ever had. Was it the liquor talking, or the cake's deliciously moist texture and wonderfully fragrant aroma? If possible, let the cake age for a day before serving.

Makes 10 to 12 servings

Make Ahead: The cake can be baked up to 3 days ahead.

1 cup (2 sticks) unsalted butter, at room temperature
1 cup packed light brown sugar
2 large eggs, at room temperature
½ cup Drambuie
1 cup unsulfured molasses
2¼ cups all-purpose flour
2 teaspoons ground ginger
2 teaspoons ground cinnamon
1 teaspoon baking powder
½ teaspoon baking soda
½ teaspoon ground cloves
½ teaspoon salt

GLAZE
4 tablespoons (½ stick) unsalted butter
⅓ cup Drambuie

1. To make the cake, position a rack in the center of the oven and preheat the oven to 350°F. Lightly butter the inside of a 12-cup *nonstick* fluted tube pan, such as a Bundt pan. Dust the pan with flour and tap out the excess.

2. In a large bowl, beat the butter and brown sugar until light in color and texture, about 1 minute. Do not overbeat. Beat in the eggs, then the Drambuie and molasses.

3. Sift the flour, ginger, cinnamon, baking powder, baking soda, cloves, and salt together. Gradually mix into the wet ingredients, just until combined. Stir in ¾ cup hot water. Scrape into the prepared pan and smooth the top.

4. Bake until a toothpick inserted in the center of the cake comes out clean, about 1 hour. Cool for 10 minutes on a wire cake rack.

5. For the glaze, melt the butter over low heat. Remove from the heat and stir in the Drambuie. Brush the top of the cake with about 2 tablespoons of the mixture and let stand for 5 minutes. Invert onto the cake rack and unmold. Brush the cake with the remaining glaze. Cool completely. If possible, wrap the cake in plastic wrap and let stand at room temperature overnight before serving. (The cake can be baked up to 3 days before serving.)

Pumpkin-Currant Cake

For a pumpkin dessert when pie isn't in the picture, here's an easy spice cake packed with holiday flavors. Substitute dried cranberries for the currants, if you wish. I always hope that there are leftovers of this cake for my Day-After-Thanksgiving breakfast.

Makes 8 to 12 servings

Make Ahead: The cake can be baked up to 2 days ahead.

2½ cups all-purpose flour
1½ teaspoons baking soda
½ teaspoon baking powder
¾ teaspoon ground cinnamon
¾ teaspoon ground cloves
¾ teaspoon salt
12 tablespoons (1½ sticks) unsalted butter, at room temperature
1 cup granulated sugar
1 cup light brown sugar
3 large eggs
One 15-ounce can solid-pack pumpkin (1¾ cups)
¾ cup dried currants
¾ cup toasted, coarsely chopped pecans
Confectioners' sugar, for sifting

1. Position a rack in the center of the oven and preheat the oven to 350°F. Lightly butter a 12-cup fluted tube cake pan (preferably nonstick). Dust the pan with flour and tap out the excess.

2. Sift the flour, baking soda, baking powder, cinnamon, cloves, and salt together. In a medium bowl, using a handheld electric mixer at high speed, beat the butter until creamy, about 1 minute. Add the granulated sugar and brown sugar, and beat until light in color and texture, about 2 minutes. Scrape down the bowl, and, one at a time, beat in the eggs. Beat in the pumpkin. Reduce the mixer speed to low. In three additions, beat in the flour mixture. Stir in the currants and pecans. Scrape into the prepared pan and smooth the top.

3. Bake until a long wooden skewer inserted in the cake comes out clean, about 1 hour. Cool for 10 minutes on a wire cake rack. Invert the cake onto the rack, unmold, and cool completely. (The cake can be baked up to 2 days ahead, covered tightly with plastic wrap, and stored at room temperature.) Sift confectioners' sugar over the top and serve.

Pumpkin-Walnut Roulade with Spiked Cream

A number of my cooking students report that this spicy pumpkin roll has replaced pumpkin pie at their house. Don't be nervous about rolling up the cake—it is very flexible, and if for some reason it does crack, the whipped cream garnish will cover any blemishes. Be sure the walnuts are very finely chopped (the best way is to pulse them in a food processor, being careful that they don't turn into walnut butter) so they can be rolled up with the roulade.

Makes 8 to 10 servings

Make Ahead: The roulade can be made up to 2 days ahead.

ROULADE CAKE

¾ cup all-purpose flour
2 teaspoons ground cinnamon
1 teaspoon ground ginger
1 teaspoon baking soda
½ teaspoon freshly grated nutmeg
⅛ teaspoon ground cloves
½ teaspoon salt
1 cup granulated sugar
3 large eggs, at room temperature
⅔ cup canned solid-pack pumpkin
1 teaspoon fresh lemon juice
¾ cup (3 ounces) finely chopped walnuts
Confectioners' sugar, for sifting

FILLING

Two 3-ounce packages cream cheese, at room temperature
4 tablespoons (½ stick) unsalted butter, at room temperature
½ teaspoon vanilla extract
1 cup confectioners' sugar
2 tablespoons minced crystallized ginger

SPIKED CREAM

½ cup heavy cream
1 tablespoon confectioners' sugar
2 teaspoons dark rum or brandy, optional
¼ teaspoon vanilla extract

3 tablespoons finely chopped walnuts
2 tablespoons finely chopped crystallized ginger

1. To make the cake, position a rack in the top third of the oven and preheat the oven to 375°F. Lightly butter a 10 × 15-inch jelly-roll pan. To line the bottom and sides of the pan, cut a 12 × 16-inch piece of parchment or wax paper. At each of the four corners, cut a diagonal slash about 2 inches long. Fit the paper into the pan, folding the cut ends over each other at the slashes to form neat corners. Lightly butter and flour the paper, tapping out the excess flour.

2. Sift the flour, cinnamon, ginger, baking soda, nutmeg, cloves, and salt together. In a large bowl, using a handheld electric mixer at high speed, beat the sugar and eggs until the mixture triples in volume and is light in color and texture, about 3 minutes. The mixture should form a thick ribbon that falls back on itself when the beaters are lifted about 2 inches from the bowl. Do not underbeat. Mix in the pumpkin and lemon juice.

3. With the mixer on low, gradually beat in the flour mixture, scraping the sides of the bowl as needed. Spread the batter evenly into the prepared pan, being sure to reach into the corners. Sprinkle the batter with the walnuts.

4. Bake until the center of the cake springs back when lightly pressed with a finger, about 15 minutes. Sift confectioners' sugar over the top of the cake. Place a clean kitchen towel over the cake, then top with a baking sheet. Holding

the baking sheet over the cake, turn the cake upside down and invert it onto the towel on the baking sheet. Carefully peel off the paper, then place it back on the cake. Using the towel as an aid, roll up the cake and cool completely.

5. To make the filling, in a medium bowl, using a handheld electric mixer at medium speed, beat the cream cheese, butter, and vanilla until combined. Gradually beat in the confectioners' sugar until smooth.

What Do You Mean Pumpkin Doesn't Grow in Cans?

Finicky cooks like to make their pumpkin desserts from freshly prepared pumpkin puree. It sounds like a good idea, but there are issues to be aware of.

The texture and flavor of canned pumpkin is the same from can to can. With fresh pumpkin, the amount of liquid varies and the puree must always be strained to achieve the same thickness as the canned variety, as most recipes assume that the cook will use canned pumpkin. Using a watery puree in a recipe that was tested with firm canned pumpkin will wreak disaster.

It is very important to choose the right kind of fresh pumpkin. Jack-o'-lantern–type pumpkins are too large, watery, and bland to use in baking. Sugar or cheese pumpkins, available at many farmers' markets and produce markets, are the best for cooking. They are smaller (averaging 2 to 3 pounds) and denser than the familiar huge pumpkins. Ask the produce manager at your market—it's a good bet that the smaller pumpkins on display are eating pumpkins. Or use Hubbard squash. A very close relative of "real" pumpkin, it is an excellent choice. You will need about 2½ pounds of pumpkin to yield about 1¾ cups of puree, the equivalent of a 15-ounce can. If you have any doubts, err on the side of buying too much fresh pumpkin.

Roasting is the preferred method for cooking fresh pumpkin that will be pureed, as it incorporates less water than steaming or boiling. Preheat the oven to 350°F. Using a large knife, remove the stem and cut the pumpkin into quarters. Scoop out and discard the stringy fibers and seeds. Cut the quarters into 2- to 3-inch pieces. Place in a large, lightly oiled roasting pan, skin side down. Add ⅓ cup water, and cover tightly with aluminum foil. Bake until very tender, about 1¼ hours. Uncover, cool, and remove the skin. Puree the cooked pumpkin in a food processor or rub through a wire sieve. Place the pumpkin puree in a cheesecloth-lined wire sieve set over a bowl. Fold up the edges of the cheesecloth to cover the puree. Place a saucer on the puree and weigh with a 1-pound can to force out the excess liquid. Let stand until the puree is the consistency of canned pumpkin, about 1 hour. The pumpkin puree can be frozen in an airtight container for up to 1 month.

6. Unroll the cake and discard the paper. Spread the filling evenly over the cake and sprinkle with the crystallized ginger. Reroll the cake (you won't need to use the kitchen towel) and wrap in plastic wrap. Refrigerate until the filing is firm, at least 1 hour. (The cake can be refrigerated for up to 2 days.)

7. To make the spiked cream, in a chilled medium bowl, using a handheld electric mixer at high speed, beat the heavy cream, confectioners' sugar, optional rum, and vanilla until stiff. Transfer to a pastry bag fitted with a ½-inch-wide open star tip.

8. Transfer the roll to a long serving platter, seam side down. Garnish the cake with swirls of the whipped cream, and sprinkle with the walnuts and crystallized ginger. To serve, cut the cake diagonally into thick slices.

Puckering Up: Persimmons

Persimmons are just beginning to come into season around Thanksgiving. Some varieties are not edible until they have been "kissed" with frost. There are two basic persimmon varieties, and they have totally different qualities. One is best for baking, and the other for salads.

Hachiya persimmons are shaped like large, deep orange acorns. These are the persimmons I grew up with, and many of our neighbors in northern California grew them in their gardens. Unripe, they are extremely tannic and will make you pucker up quicker than a lemon can. They must be ripened until *very* soft and translucent, at which point they take on a honeyed flavor. Hachiya persimmons are rarely ripe at the market when you need them. Buy them about 1 week before using, and let them ripen at room temperature in a paper bag. Once soft, they can be refrigerated for a few days. Because my persimmon timing is often off, I usually cook with thawed persimmon pulp that I have frozen at my convenience. Persimmon pulp can be frozen for up to 3 months, stored in an airtight container. Use Hachiya persimmons in desserts like Grandma's Steamed Persimmon Pudding (page 155).

Fuyu persimmons look like squat, pale orange tomatoes. They do not have to be ripened, and can be enjoyed when crisp-tender, thinly sliced into wedges. I serve them in salads (see Baby Spinach and Fuyu Persimmon Salad with Ginger Vinaigrette on page 36) and on cheese boards. Some cooks ripen Fuyu persimmons until they are soft to use in baked goods, but they take much longer than Hachiyas and their flavor isn't as full.

Grandma's Steamed Persimmon Pudding

This recipe always makes new fans for the underappreciated persimmon. My grandmother made this pudding every Thanksgiving. Of all my holiday dessert recipes, this is one that friends ask me to be sure and include on the menu, and I am happy to oblige, as I get a nice dose of nostalgia every time I make it. The pudding looks humble, but it has a spicy flavor and moist texture that will win you over. Steamed-pudding molds are available at kitchenware stores.

Makes 8 servings

2 well-ripened, medium Hachiya persimmons
1 cup sugar
½ cup milk
2 tablespoons unsalted butter, melted
1 large egg
1 cup all-purpose flour
2 teaspoons baking soda
½ teaspoon salt
½ teaspoon ground cinnamon
Sweetened Whipped Cream (page 160)

1. Generously butter the inside of a 1½- to 2-quart fluted tube pudding mold. Dust the inside of the mold lightly with flour, and tap out the excess.

2. Cut the stems from the persimmons, and remove any large seeds in the pulp. Coarsely chop the unpeeled persimmons. In a food processor or blender, puree the chopped persimmons. You should have 1 cup puree. Pour into a medium bowl and whisk in the sugar, milk, butter, and egg.

3. Sift together the flour, baking soda, salt, and cinnamon. Add to the persimmon mixture and whisk until smooth. Scrape the mixture into the prepared pudding mold and smooth the top. Cover the mold with its lid or a double thickness of aluminum foil.

4. Place a collapsible vegetable steamer in a pot large enough to hold the mold, and put the mold on the steamer. Pour enough boiling water into the pot to almost, but not quite, touch the bottom of the steamer. Bring to a boil over high heat, cover the pot, and reduce the heat to medium-low. Steam the pudding, adding more boiling water as needed, until the pudding is dark brown and a toothpick inserted in the center comes out clean, about 2 hours.

5. Let the pudding stand for 10 minutes. (The pudding can stay in its mold for up to 45 minutes.) Run a sharp knife around the inside of the mold, and invert the pudding onto a platter. Slice and serve warm with whipped cream.

Note: The recipe can be doubled and steamed in a buttered and floured 10- to 12-cup fluted tube cake pan. Cover the pan tightly with aluminum foil. To lift the pan in and out of the pot, tie the cake pan with kitchen string, like a package. The double-batch recipe can also be cooked in the oven. Place the pan in a roasting pan, add enough hot water to come 1 inch up the sides, and bake at 300°F until a toothpick inserted in the pudding comes out clean, about 2½ hours.

Pumpkin Marble Cheesecake

This pumpkin-swirled dessert was inspired by the flavors of Italy, where ricotta cheese and baking the cake in a water bath creates an especially light-textured cheesecake. You'll get a lot of servings (and compliments) from this great-looking finale.

Makes 12 to 16 servings

Make Ahead: The cheesecake must be chilled overnight; it can then be refrigerated for 2 more days.

1½ cups finely crushed amaretti (see Note) or gingersnap cookies (about 7 ounces)
4 tablespoons (½ stick) unsalted butter, melted
½ cup packed light brown sugar
One 32-ounce container whole milk ricotta cheese
One 8-ounce package cream cheese, at room temperature
1 cup granulated sugar
¼ cup cornstarch
5 large eggs plus 1 large egg yolk
⅓ cup heavy cream
1 teaspoon vanilla extract
Grated zest of 1 lemon
One 15-ounce can solid-pack pumpkin (1¾ cups)
1 teaspoon ground cinnamon
1 teaspoon ground ginger
½ teaspoon ground cloves

1. Position a rack in the center of the oven and preheat the oven to 325°F. Lightly butter a 9½-inch round springform pan. Wrap the outside bottom of the pan tightly with aluminum foil.

2. In a small bowl, toss the amaretti crumbs with the melted butter. Press evenly into the bottom and about 1 inch up the sides of the prepared pan. Bake for 10 minutes. Set aside on a wire cake rack.

3. Rub the brown sugar through a wire sieve to remove the lumps, and set aside. Rub the ricotta cheese through the sieve to lighten the texture, and set aside.

4. In a large bowl, using a handheld electric mixer at high speed, beat the cream cheese and granulated sugar just until smooth. Beat in the cornstarch. Reduce the speed to low. One at a time, beat in the whole eggs (but not the yolk). Beat in the heavy cream, vanilla, and lemon zest. Add the ricotta and beat just until smooth.

5. Pour 1½ cups of the cheese mixture into a medium bowl. Add the pumpkin, brown sugar, egg yolk, cinnamon, ginger, and cloves. Beat on low speed until smooth.

6. Pour the plain cheesecake into the prepared pan. Top with large spoonfuls of the pumpkin mixture. Using a table knife, swirl the two mixtures together to get a marbleized look.

7. Place the pan in a large roasting pan and put in the oven. Add enough nearly boiling water to come ½ inch up the sides of the pan. Bake until a sharp knife inserted 1 inch from the edge of the cake comes out clean, about 1¾ hours. The center may seem slightly unset, but will firm upon chilling. Remove the cheesecake from the roasting pan and place on a wire cake rack. Run a sharp knife around the inside of the pan to release the cake from the sides. Cool completely.

8. Remove the foil. Cover the cheesecake with plastic wrap and refrigerate for at least 4 hours or overnight. (The cheesecake can be baked up to 2 days ahead.)

9. Remove the sides of the pan. Serve chilled, dipping a thin, sharp knife into a tall glass of hot water before cutting each slice.

Note: Amaretti are crisp almond cookies, often wrapped in pairs with colorful tissue paper and sold in pricey tins. There are also brands that come in boxes, and they are a less expensive option for making crumb crusts. Amaretti can be found in Italian delicatessens, specialty food stores, and many supermarkets.

Cranberry Cheesecake

Cranberries give this cheesecake an attractive pink tint and a tartness that cuts through the rich, thick, New York–style cream cheese filling. Like any cheesecake, part of its appeal is that it must be made well ahead of serving, so there is little last-minute fussing at serving time.

Makes 10 to 14 servings

Make Ahead: The cheesecake must be chilled overnight. It can then be refrigerated for 2 more days.

1½ cups crushed graham crackers (about 7 ounces)
1¼ cups plus 2 tablespoons sugar
5 tablespoons (½ stick plus 1 tablespoon) unsalted butter, melted
One 12-ounce bag fresh cranberries
Three 8-ounce packages cream cheese, at room temperature
3 large eggs, at room temperature
1¼ cups sour cream
1 tablespoon cornstarch

1. Position a rack in the center of the oven and preheat the oven to 350°F. Lightly butter a 9½-inch springform pan. Wrap the bottom outside of the pan tightly with aluminum foil.

2. In a small bowl, mix the cracker crumbs, sugar, and melted butter until well combined. Press evenly into the bottom and about 1 inch up the sides of the prepared pan. Bake for 10 minutes. Set aside on a wire cake rack.

3. In a large saucepan, combine the cranberries, 2 cups water, and ½ cup sugar. Bring to a boil over medium-high heat, stirring to dissolve the sugar. Reduce the heat to medium-low and cook, stirring often to avoid scorching, until very thick and reduced to about 2 cups. Transfer to a bowl and cool completely, stirring often.

4. In a large bowl, using a handheld mixer at medium speed, beat the cream cheese until smooth, about 1 minute. Add the remaining ¾ cup plus 2 tablespoons sugar and beat for 1 more minute, scraping down the sides of the bowl as needed. One at a time, beat in the eggs. Beat in 1½ cups of the cranberry mixture, the sour cream, and the cornstarch. Pour into the prepared crust, and dot the surface with heaping tablespoons of the remaining ½ cup cranberry mixture.

5. Bake for 15 minutes. Reduce the heat to 325°F and continue baking until the edges are puffed and lightly browned, 50 to 60 minutes longer. Remove from the oven and run a thin knife around the inside of the pan to release the cheesecake from the sides. Cool completely on a wire cake rack. Remove the foil and the sides of the pan. Cover the cheesecake tightly with plastic wrap and refrigerate for at least 4 hours or overnight. (The cheesecake can be baked up to 2 days ahead.)

6. Serve chilled, dipping a thin, sharp knife into a tall glass of hot water before cutting each slice.

Cheesecake Savvy

Cheesecakes are perfect holiday desserts because they are ready and waiting in the refrigerator at serving time. Everyone loves them, even if they are as rich as a dessert can get. Cheesecakes are especially popular on the East Coast, where a Jewish version of the recipe surfaced with the influx of immigrants around the turn of the century. Many recipes call for Philadelphia cream cheese. Cream cheese itself was invented in upstate New York in the 1870s. In 1880, A. L. Reynolds began selling foil-wrapped blocks of cream cheese under the name "Philadelphia." At the time, Philadelphia was the culinary capital of the nation, and consumers associated top-quality foods with the city. Eventually, Philadelphia cream cheese was acquired by the Kraft Cheese Company, where it remains today.

The most common problem with cheesecakes is a cracked top. Cheesecakes usually crack for two reasons. First, too much air is often beaten into the cheese, so the filling rises during baking like a soufflé, then deflates during cooling. The changes in volume and texture make the filling crack. The solution is to beat the cheese just until smooth, no longer. The second cause comes from the batter baking onto the sides of the springform pan. During cooling, the cake cools and contracts, and the tension creates the fissures. Running a knife around the inside of the pan releases the cake, and the tension. A bit of cornstarch also helps to stabilize the batter and make it less delicate and prone to cracking. Gentle baking in a water bath also helps some recipes from cracking. Even if you think your springform pan has a tight fit, wrap the outside of the pan with aluminum foil so it doesn't get a wet crust. The foil prevents the butter from leaking out of the crust.

Pumpkin Crème Brûlée

Crème brûlée remains a favorite restaurant dessert, and every kitchenware store has a hand-held butane or propane torch to help the home cook make the requisite caramelized topping in their own kitchen. It can also be accomplished in a broiler. The real secret to crème brûlée topping is using turbinado sugar, whose beige, coarse crystals are actually easier to control during melting than any other types.

Makes 8 servings

Make Ahead: The pumpkin custards must be chilled for at least 4 hours before serving; they can be baked up to 2 days ahead.

2 cups heavy cream
⅔ cup packed light brown sugar
One 15-ounce can solid-pack pumpkin (1¾ cups)
5 large egg yolks
1 teaspoon ground cinnamon
½ teaspoon ground ginger

1/8 teaspoon ground cloves
About 1/4 cup turbinado sugar

SPECIAL EQUIPMENT

Handheld butane or propane torch, for caramelizing the custards

1. Position a rack in the center of the oven and preheat the oven to 325°F.

2. In a medium saucepan, heat the heavy cream over medium heat, stirring often, until tiny bubbles appear around the edges. Remove from the heat and stir in the brown sugar until it has dissolved.

3. In a medium bowl, whisk the pumpkin, egg yolks, cinnamon, ginger, and cloves. Gradually whisk in the hot cream mixture. Pour equal amounts (about 1/2 cup) of the pumpkin custard into eight 6-ounce custard cups. Transfer the cups to a large roasting pan, and place the pan in the oven. Pour enough boiling water around the cups to come 1/2 inch up the sides. Bake until a knife inserted in the center of the custard comes out almost clean (the custards will continue to cook when removed from the oven), about 1 1/4 hours. Remove the custards from the water and cool completely on a wire cake rack.

4. Cover each custard with plastic wrap and refrigerate until chilled, at least 4 hours or, preferably, overnight. (The custards can be baked up to 2 days ahead.)

5. Just before serving, sprinkle about 1 1/2 teaspoons of the turbinado sugar over each custard. Ignite the torch and wave the flame in a circular pattern about 2 inches above each custard to melt the sugar. Serve immediately.

Cranberry Granita

To most of us, the more sinful the Thanksgiving dessert selection, the better. But I admit that sometimes a lighter finale is in order. Even dessert hedonists will love this granita for its refreshing flavor and bright pink color. When serving a very formal, large meal with many courses, you can serve small portions of this granita as a palate cleanser. Note that the recipe makes only 6 healthy or 8 moderate servings, so this is not a dessert for a crowd. If you want to double the recipe, freeze the granita in two separate pans, as a double recipe takes too long to freeze in one pan. (Or use the biggest shallow metal pan that fits into your freezer.) Serve the granita in well-chilled stemmed glasses—I freeze martini glasses for 30 minutes to get them good and cold.

Makes 6 to 8 servings

Make Ahead: Granita is best the day it is made, but it can be made up to 1 day ahead, covered tightly with plastic wrap, and kept in the freezer.

One 12-ounce bag cranberries
1 cup plus 2 tablespoons sugar
1 tablespoon fresh lemon juice
Mint sprigs, for garnish

1. In a large pot, bring 4 cups water, the cranberries, and sugar to a boil over high heat, stirring often, to dissolve the sugar. Reduce the heat to medium and simmer for 10 minutes until all of the cranberries have burst. Pour into a wire sieve placed over a heatproof bowl and drain well. Press gently on the cranberries to extract as much juice as possible, but don't force the solids through the sieve. Stir the lemon juice into the cranberry liquid. Place the bowl in a larger bowl of ice water and let stand, stirring often, until the liquid is chilled, about 30 minutes.

2. Meanwhile, place a metal 9 × 13-inch baking pan in the freezer to chill.

3. Pour the cranberry liquid into the chilled pan. Freeze until the mixture freezes around the edges, about 1 hour, depending on your freezer's temperature. Using a large metal spoon, mix the frozen edges into the center (leave the spoon in the pan).

4. Freeze again, repeating the stirring procedure about every 30 minutes until the mixture has a slushy consistency, 2 to 3 hours total freezing time. Serve immediately in well-chilled glasses, garnished with mint sprigs, or keep frozen until ready to serve. (If the granita freezes solid, allow it to soften slightly in the refrigerator for about 10 minutes, and try again. Or break it into large chunks and process in a food processor until slushy.)

Sweetened Whipped Cream

Experienced cooks may think it's silly to give a recipe for whipped cream, but a lot of novice cooks are scared of this simple, important ingredient. When Thanksgiving comes around, whipped dessert toppings go on a lot of shopping lists. I hope this recipe convinces those cooks to scratch the artificial stuff and just buy a carton of good old heavy cream. Have we become so lazy in our culture that we can't take a couple of minutes to whip a bowl of delicious, thick, *real* cream? Here's how to do it right, and in record time. Of course, this recipe can be multiplied as needed.

- **For the very best whipped cream, use pasteurized (not ultrapasteurized) heavy cream, available at most dairies and natural food stores. This cream has been less processed than ultrapasteurized, and you can really taste the difference.**
- **Don't serve *un*sweetened whipped cream—it does nothing for your dessert. It tastes almost like butter.**
- **The heavy cream must be well chilled. To keep it cold during whipping, which helps it whip more quickly and hold its shape longer, chill the mixing bowl and beaters in the freezer for at least 10 minutes.**
- **It doesn't matter if you use granulated sugar or confectioners' sugar. Granulated sugar must be added to the cream at the beginning so it dissolves by the time the cream is stiff. However, I prefer confectioners' sugar because it dissolves rapidly and can be mixed in any time. Also, the small amount of cornstarch in confectioners' sugar helps stabilize the whipped cream.**
- **Use a handheld electric mixer to whip the cream quickly. A large balloon whisk with many thin wires to beat lots of air into the cream is a good second choice. A whisk with thick wires won't work as well. Use large standing mixers only for large amounts (over 2 cups) of cream.**
- **If you wish, beat in up to 2 tablespoons brandy, Cognac, dark rum, or bourbon to every cup of cream toward the end of the whipping.**
- **If whipped cream stands for a few hours, liquid sometimes separates from the cream. Just beat the cream again until the liquid reincorporates itself.**

Makes 1½ cups

Make Ahead: Whipped cream can be made up to 1 day ahead.

1 cup heavy cream, preferably not ultrapasteurized
2 tablespoons confectioners' sugar
½ teaspoon vanilla extract

Pour the heavy cream into a chilled, medium bowl, and add the sugar and vanilla. Using a handheld electric mixer set at medium speed, beat just until stiff peaks form. Do not overbeat or the cream will become grainy. (The cream can be whipped up to 1 day ahead, covered, and refrigerated.) Whisk briskly to incorporate any liquid that may have separated out of the cream.

Leftovers

There's Got to Be a Morning After . . .

Friday's leftover turkey sandwich is anticipated just as much as Thursday's big-deal dinner. Sandwiches are great, but that's just the tip of the leftover iceberg. When asked about their favorite leftover uses, Americans gave sandwiches top honors, with soup, casseroles, salads, and stir-fries following behind.

There are so many ways to enjoy turkey leftovers, it could take up a whole book. I have included recipes for the more involved dishes, and a detailed method for making the best turkey soup around. Recipes for using leftovers should never be difficult—after all, you probably feel that you have cooked sufficiently the day before. The cook's creativity and what's on hand are the main elements that turn leftovers into meals. Mexican dishes are especially delicious made with leftover turkey. When faced with a mountain of turkey meat, there is usually a burrito, taco, or enchilada casserole in my future. And sandwiches can be just as inspired. Here are a few ideas using about 4 cups (1 pound) of leftover turkey.

- **Turkey Soft Tacos:** Roll strips of turkey into warm corn tortillas with salsa, guacamole, and shredded iceberg lettuce.

- **Turkey and Black Bean Burritos:** In a medium saucepan, sauté a small onion and a minced garlic clove in olive oil. Add one 15- to 19-ounce can black beans, drained and rinsed, and turkey strips and heat through. Roll up in warm flour tortillas with salsa, shredded cheese, and sour cream.

- **Turkey and Pepper Fajitas:** In a large skillet, sauté sliced red onion, green and red bell pepper strips, and garlic until very soft.

Add turkey strips and cook until heated through. Stir in chili powder to taste. Roll in warm flour tortillas with salsa and sour cream.

- **Turkey Salad Niçoise:** Arrange turkey strips on a bed of red leaf lettuce with tomato wedges, cooked crisp-tender green beans, cooked sliced new potato, and hard-boiled-egg wedges. Serve with your favorite vinaigrette.

- **Curried Turkey Salad:** Mix chopped turkey, mayonnaise, a little yogurt, chopped apples, raisins, and curry powder. Serve on a bed of green leaf lettuce, or use as a sandwich or pita bread filling.

- **Hot Turkey, Cheddar, and Apple Sandwich:** Place sliced turkey on lightly toasted bread and top with thinly sliced Cheddar cheese. Broil until the cheese melts. Add some thin slices of Granny Smith apples and top with another slice of toasted bread.

- **New Club Sandwich:** Mix cranberry sauce with Dijon mustard to make a sweet-sour sandwich spread. Make a triple-decker sandwich with turkey slices, crisp bacon, lettuce, and the cranberry-mustard sauce.

Leftovers Aren't Forever

On Thanksgiving, store your leftovers safely. Get any leftover turkey and stuffing into the refrigerator within 2 hours of serving. Never leave leftovers out overnight.

Slice all of the turkey meat from the carcass and place in shallow plastic containers or self-sealing plastic bags, or wrap tightly in plastic wrap. Scrape all of the stuffing from the carcass, and refrigerate it separately from the turkey meat. If you plan to use the carcass for soup, chop or break it into manageable pieces and store in plastic bags. Refrigerate at 40°F or below, and serve within 2 or 3 days. Frozen leftovers should be used within 3 months.

Friday Turkey Vegetable Soup 101

The most common way of making leftover turkey soup is to toss the carcass and vegetables into a pot and simmer with water until the broth is flavorful. That's a good beginning, but the flavor is also cooked out of the turkey meat and the vegetables, and you have to look out for little pieces of bone in your soup. It's a better idea to treat this broth as the first step in the soup-making process, using it to create a perfect pot of soup that will keep everyone in the house well fed at lunchtime for quite a few days to come. Freeze the soup in 1-pint containers for those winter days when homemade turkey soup is just what the doctor ordered.

- Even if you don't want to turn the turkey carcass into a soup, make the soup base anyway and freeze to substitute for chicken broth in everyday recipes.
- Trim all edible meat from the turkey carcass. Cooked turkey should be added to the finished soup just before serving to heat through. If overcooked, it will be flavorless and tough.
- If there are bits of stuffing in the carcass crevices, leave them alone—the bread will dissolve into the broth and thicken it slightly. If the stuffing includes flavors that would not complement the broth (such as fruit or nuts), rinse the stuffing off the carcass under cold running water.
- The carcass should be chopped into large pieces (3 inches square or so), which helps the bones release more flavor into the broth. Also, it takes too much water to cover a whole carcass, resulting in a weak, watery broth. A heavy cleaver works best, but if you don't have one, use your hands to break up the carcass into manageable pieces. Of course, add any extraneous (drumstick or thigh) bones and skin to the pot, too.
- Sautéing the vegetables gives them more flavor. Don't overdo the vegetables for the soup base, and let the turkey flavor come through.
- Use cold water to make your broth. It will take longer to come to a simmer, but it will draw more flavor from the ingredients as well. If you have any leftover turkey stock from the Thanksgiving turkey, use it in place of some of the water.
- Allow the broth to come to a simmer and skim off the foam before adding the seasonings. If you add the seasonings at the beginning, they'll float to the top and be skimmed off with the foam.
- While a stock is unsalted because it is going to be used in sauces that may be reduced, a soup broth base should be salted. Don't be afraid to add enough salt—it makes the difference between a well-flavored soup and a bland one.
- If your turkey soup base tastes weak, even after seasoning, it is perfectly fine to bolster it with canned chicken broth or bouillon cubes. I won't tell anyone.
- The carcass from a brined turkey could make salty soup. Take great care when seasoning the soup.
- Leftover gravy will thicken and enhance the color and flavor of any soup. Stir cold gravy into the soup (not the soup base) to taste during the last 10 minutes of simmering.

Makes 8 to 12 servings

Make Ahead: The soup base can frozen for up to 3 months, as can the soup.

FRIDAY TURKEY SOUP BASE

2 tablespoons vegetable oil
1 medium onion, chopped
1 medium carrot, chopped
1 medium celery rib with leaves, chopped
1 turkey carcass, chopped into large pieces
4 parsley sprigs
½ teaspoon dried thyme
1 bay leaf
1 teaspoon salt, plus more to taste
¼ teaspoon crushed black peppercorns

TURKEY VEGETABLE SOUP

2 tablespoons unsalted butter
1 large onion, chopped
2 medium carrots, chopped
2 medium celery ribs with leaves, chopped
1 medium turnip, peeled and chopped
2 garlic cloves, minced
2 quarts Friday Turkey Soup Base
2 tablespoons chopped fresh parsley
4 cups cooked turkey, cut into bite-sized pieces (about 1 pound)
Salt
Freshly ground black pepper

1. To make the soup base, in a large soup pot, heat the oil over medium heat. Add the onion, carrot, and celery, and cover. Cook, stirring occasionally, until softened, about 5 minutes. Add the turkey carcass. Pour in enough cold water (about 3 quarts) to cover the carcass by at least 1 inch. Bring to a boil over high heat, skimming off any foam that rises to the surface. Add the parsley, thyme, bay leaf, salt, and pepper.

2. Reduce the heat to low. Simmer, uncovered, adding more water as needed to keep the carcass covered, until the broth is well flavored, at least 2 hours and up to 4 hours.

3. Place a colander over a large bowl or pot. Pour the soup base through the colander, and discard the solids. Let stand for 5 minutes, then skim any clear fat from the surface. (The soup base can be frozen for up to 3 months. Cool completely, then store in airtight containers.) Add enough water to make 2 quarts soup base. Or return to the pot and boil over high heat until reduced to 2 quarts.

4. To make the soup, in a large soup pot, melt the butter over medium heat. Add the onion, carrots, celery, turnip, and garlic, and cover. Cook, stirring occasionally, until the onion is golden, about 6 minutes. Add the soup base and parsley, and bring to a boil. Reduce the heat to low and simmer until the vegetables are tender, about 1 hour. During the last 5 minutes, stir in the turkey. Season the soup with salt and pepper. Serve hot. (The soup can be frozen for up to 3 months. Cool completely and store in airtight containers.)

Amish Turkey Vegetable Soup: This soup is very thick and hearty, thanks to the noodles. Substitute 2 boiling potatoes, peeled and cut into 1-inch cubes, for the turnip, and add during the last 30 minutes of simmering. During the last 10 minutes, add 8 ounces dried wide egg noodles and cook until tender. Season the soup with ¼ teaspoon crumbled saffron threads, or more to taste.

Italian Egg Drop Soup: Mix 2 large eggs and 3 tablespoons freshly grated Parmesan. Season with salt, pepper, and freshly grated nutmeg. After adding the turkey, stirring constantly, add the egg mixture. Simmer until the egg mixture forms tiny flakes.

Tuscan Turkey Ribollita

Here's an Italian rendition on the Friday Turkey Soup theme. In Tuscany, minestrone is often layered with slices of day-old bread and cheese to make a hearty baked dish called *ribollita* (literally, "reboiled"). Turkey is a natural addition to this hearty meal-in-a-dish. It is always served with a cruet of extra virgin olive oil for seasoning the soup. Make the soup in an flameproof casserole that can also bake in the oven.

Makes 6 to 8 servings

¼ cup extra virgin olive oil, plus more for serving
1 large onion, chopped
1 medium carrot, cut into ½-inch cubes
2 medium celery ribs with leaves, cut into ¼-inch slices
1 large zucchini, cut into ½-inch cubes
2 garlic cloves, minced
4 cups packed finely shredded kale (about 10 ounces)
One 28-ounce can tomatoes in juice, drained and chopped
1 teaspoon dried basil
1 teaspoon dried oregano
½ teaspoon salt
¼ teaspoon crushed hot red pepper flakes
5 cups Friday Turkey Soup Base (page 165)
1 cup hearty red wine, such as Zinfandel
4 cups cooked turkey, cut into bite-sized pieces (about 1 pound)
One 15- to 19-ounce can cannellini (white kidney) beans, drained and rinsed
8 large slices crusty Italian or French bread
½ cup freshly grated Parmesan cheese

1. In a Dutch oven or flameproof casserole, heat 2 tablespoons oil over medium heat. Add the onion, carrot, celery, zucchini, and garlic. Cook, stirring occasionally, until softened, about 5 minutes. Add the kale and cover. Cook until the kale wilts, about 5 minutes. Stir in the tomatoes, basil, oregano, salt, and hot red pepper flakes.

2. Add the turkey soup base and wine and bring to a boil. Reduce the heat to medium-low and partially cover. Simmer for 30 minutes. During the last 5 minutes, stir in the turkey and beans.

3. Meanwhile, position a rack in the center of the oven and preheat the oven to 400°F. Arrange the bread on a baking sheet and lightly brush with the remaining 2 tablespoons oil. Bake until the bread is lightly toasted around the edges, about 10 minutes. Set the toasted bread aside. Reduce the oven temperature to 350°F.

4. Add 4 of the bread slices to the soup, pressing them down with a large spoon or a ladle until completely submerged. Place the remaining bread on the top of the soup and sprinkle with the cheese. Bake until the cheese is golden brown, about 20 minutes. Serve in deep soup bowls, including a piece of the crusty bread topping. Pass a cruet of additional olive oil for drizzling.

Turkey Tetrazzini Gratin

Turkey Tetrazzini is an old-fashioned spaghetti casserole named for an opera star of the early 1900s. This is an easy-to-make spin-off of the traditional version. The golden-brown top, with ends of the pasta baked to a crusty turn, is irresistible.

Makes 6 to 8 servings

Make Ahead: The pasta gratin should be prepared just before serving.

3 tablespoons unsalted butter
10 ounces cremini or button mushrooms, sliced

One 10-ounce package frozen artichoke hearts, thawed
½ cup chopped shallots
4 cups bite-sized pieces cooked turkey (about 1 pound)
½ cup dry sherry, such as Manzanilla
1 pound penne
One 15-ounce container part-skim ricotta cheese
1 cup (4 ounces) freshly grated Parmesan cheese
1 cup heavy cream or milk
¾ teaspoon salt
¼ teaspoon freshly ground black pepper

1. Position a rack in the top third of the oven and preheat the oven to 400°F. Lightly butter a 10 × 15-inch baking dish.

2. In a large skillet, melt 2 tablespoons of the butter over medium-high heat. Add the mushrooms and cook, stirring occasionally, until they give up their juice, it evaporates, and the mushrooms begin to brown, about 6 minutes. Stir in the artichokes and shallots and cook, stirring often, until the shallots soften, about 2 minutes. Add the turkey and sherry, and cook until the sherry is almost completely evaporated, about 5 minutes.

3. Meanwhile, bring a large pot of lightly salted water to a boil over high heat. Stir in the penne and cook, stirring occasionally, until the pasta is barely tender, about 8 minutes. Do not overcook the pasta, as it will cook further in the oven. Drain well.

4. Return the drained pasta to the still-warm cooking pot. Add the turkey mixture, ricotta, ¾ cup of the Parmesan, heavy cream, salt, and pepper, and mix well.

5. Transfer to the prepared baking dish. Sprinkle with the remaining ¼ cup Parmesan and dot with the remaining 1 tablespoon butter. Bake until the top is golden brown, 10 to 15 minutes. Serve hot.

Tomatillo Enchilada Casserole

A warm, comforting casserole is a delicious way to take the chill off a cool November evening. This innocent-looking dish can be quite spicy, depending on the heat level of the salsa you use. If you don't have green tomatillo salsa, use green taco sauce or your favorite red tomato salsa.

Makes 6 servings

Make Ahead: The casserole should be prepared just before serving.

12 corn tortillas
One 15-ounce container sour cream
¾ cup milk
1 cup green tomatillo salsa, green taco sauce, or thick-and-chunky-style tomato salsa
2½ cups cooked turkey, cut into bite-sized pieces (about 12 ounces)
1 cup thawed frozen corn kernels
3 scallions, white and green parts, chopped
2 cups (8 ounces) shredded sharp Cheddar cheese

1. Position a rack in the center of the oven and preheat the oven to 375°F. Lightly butter a 9 × 13-inch baking dish.

2. *If you have a gas stove,* turn a burner to medium heat. Place each tortilla directly on the burner grid and cook, turning once, until the tortilla is warm and softened, about 20 seconds total. *If you have an electric stove,* heat an empty skillet over medium heat. Place each tortilla in the skillet and cook, turning once, until softened, about 45 seconds total. Stack the warmed tortillas on a plate and set aside.

3. In a medium bowl, whisk the sour cream and milk until smooth. Spread a thin layer of the sour-cream sauce in the bottom of the prepared dish. Place 4 tortillas in the bottom of

the dish, tearing them to fit. Scatter half of the turkey over the tortillas, then top with ½ cup of the corn and half of the scallions. Top with ¾ cup of the cheese, ½ cup of the salsa, and about one-third of the sour-cream mixture. Top with 4 more tortillas, then the remaining turkey, corn, scallions, and salsa. Drizzle with half of the sour-cream mixture and sprinkle with ¾ cup of the cheese. Top with the remaining 4 tortillas, spread with the remaining sour-cream mixture, and sprinkle with the remaining ½ cup cheese.

4. Bake until the casserole is heated through and the cheese is melted, about 30 minutes. Let stand for 5 minutes before serving.

Mongolian Turkey and Broccoli Stir-fry

Sichuan peppercorns and crushed red pepper give authority to this zesty stir-fry. Scotch may seem like an odd ingredient, but it actually resembles Chinese rice liquor. Sichuan peppercorns can be found at Asian grocers and many supermarkets, but look at them closely. They should be wrinkled and rust-colored—white peppercorns are sometimes mislabeled as Sichuan.

Makes 4 to 6 servings

Make Ahead: Make the stir-fry just before serving.

3 cups broccoli florets
1 tablespoon vegetable oil
2 scallions, green and white parts, chopped
1 medium red bell pepper, seeded and cut into ½-inch wide strips
2 tablespoons shredded fresh ginger (use the large holes of a box grater)
2 garlic cloves, minced
1 pound cooked turkey, cut into ½ × 2-inch strips
1½ cups turkey or chicken broth, preferably homemade, or canned reduced-sodium broth
⅓ cup soy sauce
¼ cup Scotch whiskey or dry sherry
2 tablespoons dark Asian sesame oil
¾ teaspoon crushed Sichuan peppercorns (use a mortar and pestle or crush under a heavy saucepan)
½ teaspoon crushed hot red pepper flakes
1 tablespoon plus 1 teaspoon cornstarch
Hot cooked rice, for serving

1. In a large (12-inch) nonstick skillet, bring the broccoli and 1 cup water to a boil over high heat. Cover tightly and cook until the broccoli is crisp-tender, 2 to 3 minutes. Drain the broccoli and set aside. Dry the skillet and return to the stove.

2. Add the oil to the skillet and heat until very hot. Add the scallions, red bell pepper, ginger, and garlic. Stir until the mixture is fragrant, about 30 seconds. Add the turkey strips and ½ cup of the stock. Cover and cook until the turkey is heated through, about 2 minutes.

3. In a medium bowl, mix the remaining 1 cup stock with the soy sauce, Scotch, sesame oil, peppercorns, and hot red pepper flakes. Add the cornstarch and whisk to dissolve. Stir into the skillet and cook until boiling and thickened. Stir in the reserved broccoli. Serve immediately, spooned over bowls of rice.

Turkey and Black Bean Tamale Pie

My mom is the tamale pie queen, and to many of us children of the fifties, tamale pies represent the best of comfort food. Here's an updated version of this classic, which you can vary according to mood and what you have on hand. Try substituting hominy for the black beans, or adding a chopped green bell pepper to the saucepan with the onion.

Makes 6 to 8 servings

2 tablespoons olive oil
1 medium onion, chopped
1 jalapeño, seeded and minced
2 garlic cloves, minced
3 tablespoons all-purpose flour
2 tablespoons chili powder, or more to taste
2 cups Homemade Turkey Stock 101 (page 34) or canned reduced-sodium broth
One 8-ounce can tomato sauce
1 teaspoon salt
3 cups cooked turkey, cut into bite-sized pieces (about 12 ounces)
One 15.5-ounce can black beans, drained and rinsed
1 cup thawed frozen corn kernels
1½ cups yellow cornmeal, preferably stone-ground
1 cup shredded extra-sharp Cheddar cheese (4 ounces)

1. Position a rack in the center of the oven and preheat the oven to 350°F. Lightly oil a 9 × 13-inch baking dish.

2. In a medium saucepan, heat the oil over medium heat. Add the onion and jalapeño, and cook, stirring often, until the onion is golden, about 4 minutes. Add the garlic and stir until fragrant, about 1 minute. Sprinkle with the flour and chili powder, and stir until vegetables are coated.

3. Gradually stir in the broth, then the tomato sauce and ¼ teaspoon salt. Bring to a simmer, then reduce the heat to medium-low. Simmer, stirring often to avoid scorching, until the sauce thickens, about 5 minutes. Stir in the turkey, black beans, and corn. Pour into the prepared dish.

4. In another medium saucepan, bring 1½ cups water and the remaining ¾ teaspoon salt to a boil over high heat. In a small bowl, whisk the cornmeal with 1½ cups cold water. Whisk into the boiling water and cook, whisking constantly, until the mixture is thick and boiling, about 1 minute. Spread over the turkey mixture as smoothly as possible. Sprinkle with the cheese.

5. Bake until the turkey mixture is bubbling, about 30 minutes. Let stand for 5 minutes before serving.

Thanksgiving Menu Planner

Here are complete menus to fit a variety of Thanksgiving possibilities, from an elegant sit-down dinner to a large buffet that feeds a crowd. Also included are timetables to help you plan and prepare the meal from start to finish. It's a good idea to photocopy the timetable, tape it in a visible place, like on the refrigerator door, and mark off the items as you finish them.

Be sure to read every recipe thoroughly. If you don't have a lot of counter space to hold the cookbook, photocopy the recipe and tape it at eye level on a kitchen cabinet door. This will also keep your cookbook clean of spills and splatters.

Of course, the timing of the meal hinges on when the turkey is done. It is always difficult to estimate the exact roasting time, so allow yourself a certain amount of leeway. Remember that the turkey needs to stand for at least twenty minutes before carving anyway, and you can use that window of opportunity to serve the first course and make or reheat the side dishes in the now empty oven. I actually allow forty-five minutes from when the turkey comes out of the oven until carving, because the cook needs as much time as he or she can get for the other dishes, and the turkey will stay perfectly hot. In all of the menus, I use the time it takes to serve the first course as a grace period. By the time the guests have finished this course, the side dishes will be heated through, and you can move on to the rest of the meal.

Most of the recipes in the book are for eight servings. With the exception of desserts, the recipes can be easily multiplied or divided to fit your guest count. (For desserts, make two different recipes and enjoy the leftovers, rather than trying to make half a pie.) If you are reheating chilled dishes in the oven, add ten to fifteen minutes to the suggested cooking times. Detailed make-ahead instructions are given with each recipe.

Traditional Thanksgiving Feast

This lengthy menu has all of the dishes that most people feel they just must have on the Thanksgiving table. The feast is easiest to prepare with two ovens, but can be prepared in one large oven, if the baking dishes are carefully arranged to fit. There is a flurry of activity as soon as the turkey comes out of the oven, but most of it involves reheating side dishes. Once the gravy is made, turn the heat down to the barest simmer to keep it warm. Then make the oyster stew, which takes only a few minutes, and serve the stew. For beverages, serve a lightly chilled Beaujolais and have sparkling apple cider on hand for nondrinkers.

Savory Cheddar and Jalapeño Jelly Cookies (page 18)

Buttered Cajun Pecans (page 14)

New England Oyster Stew (page 25)

Perfect Roast Turkey with Best-Ever Gravy (page 56)

Bread Stuffing 101 (page 78)

Old-fashioned Mashed Potatoes 101 (page 99)

Candied Yam and Marshmallow Casserole 101 (page 102)

Green Bean Bake (page 94)

Fluffy Angel Biscuits (page 124)

Spiced Cranberry–Orange Mold (page 109)

Famous Pumpkin Pie (page 139)

Apple Pie 101 (page 146)

Hot Coffee and Tea

Timetable

Up to 1 month ahead:

Make turkey stock; freeze

Make piecrusts for pumpkin and apple pies; freeze one for pumpkin pie

Make apple pie; freeze

3 days ahead:

Make cranberry mold; refrigerate

2 days ahead:

Make pecans; store airtight at room temperature

Make biscuit dough; refrigerate

The night before:

Defrost piecrust in refrigerator

If using fresh bread for stuffing, cut into cubes and let stand overnight to dry

Make pumpkin pie; refrigerate

Bake cookies; store airtight at room temperature

8 hours before serving turkey:

Bake apple pie; cool and store at room temperature

6½ hours before serving turkey:

Bake biscuits; cool and wrap in two foil packets

Make green bean bake; refrigerate

Make yam casserole (without marshmallows); refrigerate

Make stuffing

6½ hours before serving turkey:

Stuff turkey (place remaining stuffing in casserole, cover, and refrigerate)

Roast turkey

4 hours before serving turkey:

Peel potatoes; store in cold water at room temperature

Whip cream for pies; refrigerate

Shuck oysters; refrigerate

When guests arrive:

Serve pecans and cookies

When turkey is done (about 45 minutes before serving):

Remove turkey from oven; increase oven temperature to 350°F

Pour turkey drippings into glass bowl and let stand until ready to make gravy

Reheat half of rolls to serve with stew

Cook potatoes for mashed potatoes

Bake remaining stuffing

Cook green bean bake

Bake yam casserole

Place potatoes on stove, bring to a boil, and cook

Make gravy; keep warm

Make oyster stew; serve

Just before serving turkey:

Reheat remaining rolls

Unmold cranberry mold

Top yams with marshmallows; bake until browned

Drain and mash potatoes

After serving turkey:

Make coffee and tea

Serve pumpkin pie and apple pie with whipped cream

A Sophisticated Thanksgiving Dinner

Here's an elegant dinner for grown-ups. It touches all the bases, but doesn't serve overwhelming amounts of food. Keep in mind that wild turkeys are delicious, but they don't have as much meat on them as regular turkeys. Serve a California or Oregon Pinot Noir throughout the meal.

Glittering Spiced Walnuts (page 13)

Roasted Beet, Endive, and Blue Cheese Salad with Walnuts (page 37)

Wild Turkey with Wild Rice and Cherry Stuffing (page 69)

Broccoli with Roasted Garlic Butter (page 89)

Scalloped Yams with Praline Topping (page 104)

Cranberry, Ginger, and Lemon Chutney (page 111)

Pumpkin Crème Brûlée (page 158)

Hot Coffee and Tea

Timetable

Up to 1 month ahead:
Make turkey stock; freeze

Up to 1 week ahead:
Make cranberry chutney; refrigerate

Up to 5 days ahead:
Make spiced walnuts; store airtight at room temperature

Up to 3 days ahead:
Make roast garlic butter; refrigerate

Up to 2 days ahead:
Toast walnuts for salad; refrigerate

The night before:
Roast beets for salad, peel and refrigerate
Make wild turkey stock; cool and refrigerate
Make wild rice stuffing; refrigerate
Make pumpkin custards for crème brûlée (without topping); refrigerate
Cut broccoli into florets; refrigerate

Up to 8 hours before serving turkey:
Prepare yams for scalloped yams; place in baking dish, cover, and refrigerate
Make praline topping for yams

3½ hours before serving turkey:
Reheat stuffing and stuff turkey (place remaining stuffing in casserole, cover, and refrigerate)
Roast turkey

When guests arrive:
Serve walnuts
Remove garlic butter from refrigerator

When turkey is done (about 45 minutes before serving):
Remove turkey from oven; transfer to serving platter
Pour turkey drippings into glass bowl; let stand until ready to make sauce
Finish scalloped yams; bake
Bring water to boil for broccoli
Slice endives and finish salad; serve

Just before serving turkey:
Make sauce for roast turkey
Cook broccoli, drain, and finish with garlic butter

After serving turkey:
Make coffee and tea
Add sugar topping to pumpkin crème brûlée and caramelize

A Chile Lover's Thanksgiving

Spicy flavors season this menu with regional favorites from the Cajun country and the Southwest. I usually serve smoke-grilled turkey with salsa, but you may prefer to offer gravy. If so, make the Head Start Gravy, because the drippings from the turkey may not be usable. Chilled hard cider or a semidry Gewürztraminer would be perfect with these dishes.

Hot Crab Salsa Dip (page 17)

Sweet Potato and Peanut Soup (page 32)

Smoked, Cider-Basted Turkey (page 61)

Head Start Gravy, optional (page 120)

"Tamale" Stuffing with Pork, Chiles, and Raisins (page 82)

Maque-Choux (page 92)

Maple-Glazed Baby Carrots with Pecans (page 91)

Cranberry-Pineapple Salsa (page 114)

Rosemary and Cracked Pepper Corn Sticks (page 129)

Florida Sweet Potato Pie (page 144)

Hot Coffee and Tea

Timetable

Up to 1 month ahead:

Make turkey stock for gravy and soup; freeze

Up to 2 days ahead:

Make sweet potato soup; refrigerate
Toast pecans for carrots; refrigerate
Make piecrust; refrigerate

The night before:

Make polenta cubes for stuffing; refrigerate
Cube bread for stuffing, let stand at room temperature
Make maque-choux; refrigerate
Make sweet potato pie; refrigerate
Make gravy, if using

Up to 8 hours before serving turkey:

Make stuffing; refrigerate
Make crab dip; refrigerate
Bake corn sticks; cool and wrap in foil

5½ hours before serving turkey:

Make basting mixture for turkey; cool
Stuff turkey with seasoning mixture; let stand

4½ hours before serving turkey:

Light charcoal in charcoal grill or preheat gas grill

4 hours before serving turkey:

Grill turkey
Whip cream for pie; refrigerate

30 minutes before guests arrive:

Bake crab dip; keep warm

2 hours before serving turkey:

Make glazed carrots (without pecans)
Make cranberry-pineapple salsa

When turkey is done (about 45 minutes before serving):

Transfer turkey to serving platter; let stand
If making gravy, discard drippings in aluminum pan, leaving browned bits in pan
Place corn sticks in oven; reheat for 10 to 15 minutes to serve with soup
Bake stuffing
Reheat soup; serve

Just before serving turkey:

Reheat carrots; add pecans
Reheat maque-choux
Reheat gravy; stir into turkey pan, scraping up browned bits in pan

After serving turkey:

Make coffee and tea
Serve pie with whipped cream

Thanksgiving for a Crowd

When cooking for a crowd, think *big*. Regular-sized pots and pans are not very much help with this many mouths to feed—have at least one 12- to 14-inch skillet (two is better), and a ten-quart stockpot.

This buffet is geared for twenty-four guests without a plated first course. You will need two ovens to reheat the side dishes. A twenty-four-pound turkey will make enough servings for dinner, but if you want leftovers, roast extra turkey parts, too. For instructions, see page 45.

The turkey is roasted unstuffed—if you want to stuff the bird, add about an hour to the roasting time. If you have to bake and serve the side dishes from large disposable aluminum foil pans, allow at least one hour at 375°F for reheating to compensate for the added bulk.

Because it doesn't need refrigeration and keeps for a couple of days, Pumpkin-Currant Cake is a good dessert choice. Order pies and rolls from a bakery. Use a large-quantity coffeemaker, allowing about one hour for the coffee to brew.

The Famous Disappearing Spinach Dip, with crudités (page 15)

Spicy Cheddar and Pecan Balls (page 14)

Perfect Roast Turkey with Best-Ever Gravy (page 56)

Pan Gravy 101 (3 batches, page 117)

Roasted Turkey Breast (see above), optional

Mason-Dixon Corn Bread Dressing 101 (2½ batches, page 83)

Not-Your-Grandmother's Succotash (3 batches, page 93)

Make-Ahead Mashed Potato Casserole (3 batches, page 101)

Rum-Baked Yams and Apples (2 batches, page 102)

Homemade Cranberry Sauce (2 batches, page 113)

Pumpkin–Currant Cake (2 cakes, page 151)

Hot Coffee and Tea

Timetable

Up to 1 month ahead:
Make turkey stock for gravy; freeze

Up to 1 week ahead:
Make cranberry sauce; refrigerate

Up to 3 days ahead:
Make Cheddar cheese balls; refrigerate

Up to 2 days ahead:
Bake pumpkin cakes; store at room temperature
Make spinach dip; refrigerate

The night before:
Bake corn bread for stuffing; let stand at room temperature to stale
Prepare crudités; refrigerate
Chop ingredients for stuffing; refrigerate
Make succotash (without the tomatoes); refrigerate

7 hours before serving turkey:
Make stuffing; refrigerate
Make mashed potatoes; refrigerate

About 6½ hours before serving turkey:
Roast turkey
Prepare yams; let stand at cool room temperature

When guests arrive:
Serve spinach dip, shrimp dip, and Cheddar cheese balls

When turkey is done (about 1 hour before serving):
Transfer turkey to serving dish
Pour drippings into glass bowl; let stand until ready to make gravy
Bake stuffing
Bake mashed potatoes
Bake sweet potatoes
Make gravy; keep warm

1 hour before serving dessert:
Brew coffee

15 minutes before serving turkey:
Reheat succotash in skillet

After serving turkey:
Boil water for tea
Serve pumpkin cakes
Serve coffee

Index